D0626715

Soft Weapons

Soft Weapons

Autobiography in Transit

GILLIAN WHITLOCK

The University of Chicago Press   Chicago and London

GILLIAN WHITLOCK is professor of English in the School
of English, Media Studies, and Art History at the University of
Queensland, Australia. Her most recent book is *The Intimate Empire:
Reading Women's Autobiography* (2000).

The University of Chicago Press, Chicago 60637
The University of Chicago Press, Ltd., London
© 2007 by The University of Chicago
All rights reserved. Published 2007
Printed in the United States of America

16 15 14 13 12 11 10 09 08 07   1 2 3 4 5
ISBN-13: 978-0-226-89525-3 (cloth)
ISBN-13: 978-0-226-89526-0 (paper)
ISBN-10: 0-226-89525-4 (cloth)
ISBN-10: 0-226-89526-2 (paper)

Library of Congress Cataloging-in-Publication Data

Whitlock, Gillian, 1953–
    Soft weapons : autobiography in transit / Gillian Whitlock.
      p. cm.
    Includes bibliographical references and index.
    ISBN-13: 978-0-226-89525-3 (cloth : alk. paper)
    ISBN-13: 978-0-226-89526-0 (pbk. : alk. paper)
    ISBN-10: 0-226-89525-4 (cloth : alk. paper)
    ISBN-10: 0-226-89526-2 (pbk. : alk. paper)
      1. Middle East—Biography—History and criticism. 2. Iraq
    War, 2003—Biography—History and criticism. 3. Afghanistan—
    Biography—History and criticism. 4. Exiles—Iran—Biography—
    History and criticism. 5. Autobiography. I. Title.

CT1866 .W47 2007
920.056—dc22

                                          2006016447

♾ The paper used in this publication meets the minimum requirements
of the American National Standard for Information Sciences—
Permanence of Paper for Printed Library Materials, ANSI Z39.48–1992.

The focus of this book is . . . not on the reality of the Other but on the circumstances of its construction and the "we" who play and are played by this language game.   JOHN FROW, *CULTURAL STUDIES AND CULTURAL VALUE*

Contents

Acknowledgments

This project was supported in part by a Discovery grant from the Australian Research Council and study leave from the University of Queensland.

Earlier versions of two chapters have appeared elsewhere: chapter 2 in *Biography* 28, no. 1 (2005) and chapter 4 in *Australian Literary Studies* 21, no. 4 (2004b). Successive versions of arguments were presented to audiences at the University of Queensland, the University of Tasmania, Stirling University, the Modern Language Association of America (MLA), and the Chinese University of Hong Kong. I am grateful for all the comments on those occasions, most memorably the opportunity to discuss first thoughts with the late Gabi Helms in Hong Kong.

I acknowledge the gifts of testimony received here, and those who have shared their research generously for this project: Leigh Gilmore, especially, and also Helen Buss, Susanna Egan, Richard Freadman, John Frow, Ken Gelder, Craig Howe, Margaretta Jolly, Suvendrini Perera, Joseph Pugliese, Kay Schaffer, Sidonie Smith, Therese Taylor, Andrew van der Vlies, Penny van Toorn, and Julia Watson. I am indebted to David Parker, whose invitation to give a keynote in Hong Kong encouraged the burka paper, and to English at the University of Tasmania, which took me to Melbourne in November 2003 where it all began. The obligation to write about asylum seekers in particular began with Simon During's Antipodean testimony at the MLA, New York.

Robert Dixon and Michael Gorra were the first readers for all of this, and they rapidly became its Ideal Readers;

their suggestions are woven throughout. My colleagues at the University of Queensland supported this project in many ways, most particularly Leigh Dale, Martin Duwell, Amanda Lohrey, Lisa O'Connell, Tom O'Regan, Jude Seaboyer, and Graeme Turner. Special thanks also to Ros Gresshoff and to Angela Tuohy. I have worked with some outstanding postgraduate students in the recent past who helped me formulate ideas, in particular: Kylie Cardell, Kate Douglas, Leili Golafshani, Joan Holloway, Victoria Kuttainen, and especially Robert Clarke, who has been a superb research assistant and now colleague, and Margaret McDonell, who edited the original manuscript. To the Griffith diaspora—Tony Bennett, Pat Buckridge, David Carter, Mark Finnane, Ian Hunter, and David Saunders—my thanks and affection as always.

Last—and most—my family has lived with this book and its preoccupations with generosity and patience to the end, and it is dedicated to them with love: this is for Gerry, Annika, and Sam and in memory of Joan and Bob Whitlock.

Brisbane, May 2006

Introduction:
Word Made Flesh

To what extent does our theorizing itself need to be remade by contemporary practice at these "rumpled" sites of the experimental, so that we may take account of changing autobiographer-audience relations, shifting limits of personal disclosure, and the changing technologies of self that revise how we understand the autobiographical?

SIDONIE SMITH AND JULIA WATSON, "THE RUMPLED BED OF AUTOBIOGRAPHY"

In late September 2002 a new autobiographical subject was born. Called Salam Pax, he was from the start an ambiguous and virtual creature, a hyperactive kid with a pseudonym. He was conceived online, and he grew in stature, fed on demand by unprecedented and ongoing interactivity: an intimate exchange between an author and his readership. This was made possible by a new genre of autobiography produced by changes in communications technology: the weblog, or "blog." Salam Pax is the Baghdad Blogger, a "cyberlebrity" who is being transformed into more traditional and "proper" forms. Within a year his first weblog *Where Is Raed?* was hard copy and published as *The Baghdad Blog* (a pale imitation of its online precursor).

It is now a given in autobiography criticism that the "I" of autobiography and memoir has never been anything but virtual.[1] Even so, Salam Pax creates some new horizons for thinking about autobiographical agency, and *Where Is Raed?* is one of those "rumpled sites" where changes in autobiographical practice come into view. Here is a reminder that, although virtual, the "I" of autobiography can pack a

1

punch in the material world, and life narratives have a distinctive role to play in the struggle to shape dialogues across cultures. Salam Pax is of course not the first blogger. Blogging (or weblogging) sites were introduced in 1998 and, with the introduction of Blogger software in 1999, starting an online diary has become a simple procedure. There are currently tens of thousands of diaries being kept on the web. But, of all the cyberlebrities spawned by blogging, Pax is special. For as long as he could, Salam Pax used his weblog to record in real time the experience of being in Baghdad during the bombing raids that initiated the Coalition invasion of 2003. For example, at 3:13 PM on March 21, 2003:"The most disturbing news today has come from al-Jazeera. They said that nine B52 bombers have left the airfield in Britain and are flying 'presumably' towards Iraq. As if they would be doing a spin around the block! Anyway, they have six hours to get here." And, at 6:05 PM:

Please stop sending e-mails asking if I am for real. Don't believe it? Then don't read it. I am not anybody's propaganda ploy—well, except my own.
  Two more hours until the B52s get to Iraq. (*Where Is Raed?*)

Within the week, Salam Pax is on antacids as soon as the air-raid sirens start: "my brother starts humming Nirvana's 'Pennyroyal Tea': 'I'm on warm milk and laxatives/Cherry-flavored antacids.' But these Iraqi antacids have no flavour—it feels like you are chewing plaster of Paris" (1/4/03). Pax is a stunning example of synchronic connections between the virtual and material worlds that can be wired through online life writing. Pax's tastes, desires, and disorders, his belly and his bowels, are signs of a human presence and local habitation in Baghdad that was erased in pro-invasion propaganda at the time. In speaking out of crisis, synesthesia occurs: "You can hear the sound of the planes. Look this is what you hear!" (March 25, 2003).

For all kinds of reasons, Pax engaged with a cynical readership, as this exchange above. Was he real? Not surprisingly, many readers thought he was an agent of the Baathist regime, the CIA, or Mossad, and they told him so. As we read *Where Is Raed?* as critics of autobiography, our current tools of trade and debates about technologies of the self call his presence into question. And yet Salam Pax is a virtual "I" that assumes flesh in that space of excess between language and experience, and we must decipher and attend to his body in time. Using the pseudonym Salam Pax, a twenty-nine-year-old Iraqi blogger is able to represent himself with an eloquence and force so that, against all the odds, those of us who read the blog in places where the B52 bombers come from can feel "he is just like us" (Katz 2003, ix). This feeling, this humane engagement with an autobiographical avatar, creates a space for dialogue, and this is what makes the contemporary forms of autobiography that I discuss in this book such potent yet flawed weapons for cross-cultural engagement and the pursuit of human rights. The sense of affinity that Ian Katz expresses in his introduction to *The Baghdad Blog*—the euphoria that Iraqis, too, listen to Nirvana and talk about eBay—is a reminder of the metropolitan networks of power and patronage that must be negotiated by autobiographers on the peripheries. For example, why is Pax the ideal chat-show guest and celebrity author of one of the first blogs to cross the line between virtual and material worlds? What if his narrative resisted that desire of consumers of autobiography in the West to pierce the skin of cultural difference and recognize someone comfortably familiar? Add narcissism to cynicism as characteristics of the fickle readership, and globalization as one of the issues that critics of autobiography must handle with care.

Any snapshot of the transits of life narrative must engage with the work of contemporary autobiography as it moves across cultures in conflict. Autobiography circulates as a "soft weapon." It can personalize and humanize categories of people whose experiences are frequently unseen and unheard. To attend to a nauseated body at risk in Baghdad, or to hear a militant feminist body beneath a burka, to attach a face and recognize a refugee is to make powerful interventions in debates about social justice, sovereignty, and human rights. Life narrative can do these things. But it is a "soft" weapon because it is easily co-opted into propaganda. In modern democratic societies propaganda is frequently not the violent and coercive imposition of ideas but a careful manipulation of opinion and emotion in the public sphere and a management of information in the engineering of consent. Life narrative can be complicit in these processes. The chapters that follow include the testimony of men and women who identify as Muslims and/or speak from Afghanistan, Iraq, and Iran (as in chapters 1 and 2); testimony and memoirs from the diasporic and exilic communities of the Middle East and Central Asia (the subjects of chapters 3 and 7); memoirs by those who write from the war zones of Afghanistan and Iraq (for example, the journalist memoir in chapter 6); and the "fanciful longing" of American best-sellers (in chapters 4 and 5). These are life narratives in English that trigger conversations and interactions across cultures in conflict, and in the chapters that follow these exchanges are tracked to map the changing routes of autobiography in the "war on terror."

Soft Weapons begins with Pax, an uncharted subject of life narrative, to emphasize transformation and experiments in ways that selves are imagined and constructed now. Life narrative circulates as an exotic commodity in a world of mobile texts, multinational publishing enterprises, mass media, and migrant audiences. These are recurrent issues in this book. As an autobiographical subject of almost unprecedented global mobility, Pax brilliantly challenges established ideas about cultures, tastes, and subjectivities in terms of the homogenous, the temporal, or the teleological. New technologies have altered the fabric of autobiographical expression. Pax requires new mythographies, new imaginaries, and different ways of thinking about the volatile networks of consumption, pleasure, and agency that carry life narrative here and now. This is autobiography *in transit:* on the move in unpredictable passages across cultures, vital to the imaginative work of modern subjectivity and struggles for a place to speak in the public sphere. Pax watches al-Jazeera and *Dharma and Greg* (with a queer eye on Greg), he reads the *Economist,* listens to Bjork, is as familiar with downtown Vienna as Baghdad, and he reads the *Tao Te Ching* with more interest than the Koran. It is no surprise that when Pax emerges with a new weblog in 2004 he is passionate about his iPod and the possibilities of podcasting from Baghdad.

At the same time, Pax is a reminder of some of the contradictions of contemporary life narrative, for he is learning to regrow his roots in Iraq and nurtures traditional and authentic ways of being and belonging in his home city. There is a deliberate process of transculturation at work here, for Pax points out the similarities between Saddam Hussein and George W. Bush; he comments ironically on Western democracy and the New World Order; and he talks back to those who misread his "Arablish" as "cryptic personal notes" rather than a collective resistance to the standard English of the Internet.[2] Pax uses new media to remind us of his specific time and place, the fickle desires of his audience, and his local signature: "Sorry to blow your bubble but all I can do is tell you what is going on in the streets and if you think journalists are doing a better job of it then maybe you should go read them. One day, like in Afghanistan, those journalists will get bored and go write about Syria or Iran; Iraq will be off your media radar. Out of sight, out of mind. Lucky you, you have that option. I have to live it"(30/5/03). When the bombing ceases, Salam and his friend Raed Jarrar go out and count the bodies of the civilian dead, using digital cameras to bring "collateral damage" in view online. This is a situation where cultural and social dynamics that may seem to be very different coalesce. On the one hand we can read *Where Is Raed?* in terms of a cosmopolitan and postmodern culture shaped by globalization, transgression, and hybridity. And yet, on the other hand, Salam Pax is under siege, his life is at risk, and his grave situation is a reminder of the persistence of other narratives and histories: the resurgence of fundamentalist forms of cultural identification based on religion or nationalism that are renewed in the armed conflicts of the war on terror; the horror masked by the euphemism "collateral damage"; and the prerogatives and power of "Lucky you," looking on from another world.

Globalization

Pax is a sign of a world that is "massively globalized" in the recent past as a result of two revolutionary and interconnected processes that shape modern subjectivity: mass media and mass migration (Appadurai 1996, 9). He uses technology to offer unprecedented access to his everyday life and to the ebb and flow of his emotions, thoughts, and desires. Yet Pax is also a reminder that neo-imperialism travels on routes embedded in earlier colonialisms: the B52 bombers fly east on familiar flight paths. In *Where Is Raed?* Pax's irony, cynicism, wit, and resistance draw on a dizzying array of multimedia resources and references to describe the invasion of Iraq by a U.S.-led coalition in March 2003. This can only be understood in terms of long-established and intransigent antagonisms that, since 9/11 in particular, are often represented as a war between worlds: East and West, Muslim and Christian, traditional and modern. But Pax gives lie to the war between worlds theory, for he himself inhabits both and pulls his readers into mobile spaces of interaction and debate. Pax is paradoxical: he suggests how new technologies facilitate distinctively contemporary experiments in self-projection and new resources and disciplines are in place for the construction of imagined selves and imagined worlds. Yet these selves and worlds are deeply rooted in past antagonisms and struggles for power and legitimacy, and Pax is pinned down in place and time.

Life narrative is often invoked in discussions of what globalization might mean, although it can be difficult to grasp the contradictions and connections that occur in self-representation. For example, in his *Globalization: A Very Short Introduction,* Manfred B. Steger almost immediately turns to a "breathing shape," Osama Bin Laden, to ground this vague concept in the present, and he unerringly introduces as well the implications of the war on terror in thinking about what globalization means:

In the autumn of 2001, I was teaching an undergraduate class on modern social and political theory. Still traumatized by the recent terrorist attacks on the World Trade Centre and the Pentagon, most of my students couldn't quite grasp the connection between the violent forces of religious fundamentalism and the more secular picture of a technologically sophisticated, rapidly globalizing world. . . . "I understand that 'globalization' is a contested concept that refers to sometimes contradictory social processes," a bright history major at the back of the room quipped, "but how can you say that the TV image of a religious fanatic who denounces modernity and secularism from a mountain cave in Afghanistan perfectly captures the complex dynamics of globalization?"

Struck by the sense of intellectual urgency that fuelled my student's question, I realized the story of globalization would remain elusive without real-life examples capable of breathing shape, color and sound into a vague concept that had become the buzzword of our time. (Steger 2004, 1)

The class (probably located at the University of Hawaii where Steger teaches) is looking at the videotaped statement condemning the activities of "international infidels" that was broadcast worldwide on October 7, 2001—within a month of the bombings in New York and Washington. Steger reads Osama bin Laden's image as an example of the dynamics of globalization at work. In a remote region of Afghanistan, al-Qaeda possesses hi-tech equipment and immediate access to sophisticated telecommunications that keep them informed of international events in real time. The Cable News Network (CNN) broadcast a copy of the tape within hours of its arrival at the al-Jazeera office in Kabul; bin Laden's speech was available to a global audience almost instantly. His dress— military fatigues over traditional Arab robes—signals "the contemporary processes of fragmentation and cross-fertilization that globalization scholars call 'hybridity'": "The mixing of different cultural forms and styles facilitated by global economic and cultural exchanges" (5). He has a Russian assault rifle at his side; on his wrist is a Timex watch. The watch, like Pax's taste for *Dharma and Greg*, is the small detail that signifies the reach of mass-market commodities that is one characteristic feature of globalization. In this way the intricate, contradictory, and anachronistic interdependencies between what are often interpreted as very different "worlds" (North and South, West and non-West, developed and underdeveloped, first and third, metropolitan and peripheral, Muslim and Christian) permeate bin Laden's image and the speed of its transmission. Steger's definition of globalization—a set of social processes that create, multiply, stretch, and intensify worldwide interdependencies and exchanges while at the same time fostering in people a growing awareness of connections between the local and the distant (13)—emphasizes the acceleration of social and cultural exchanges and world-wide connections in the very recent past. Interdependency operates in some distinctive and unexpected ways. But what needs further emphasis here is power, and the effects of this in mapping the location of this undergraduate classroom in the autumn of 2001.

How images are used to locate and constitute audiences and readerships as "Western" is important. For example, Steger's interpretation indicates some recurrent features in the self-presentation of audiences engaged by Pax and bin Laden. American students are traumatized, innocents in the face of fanaticism, and caught unawares by "a technologically sophisticated, rapidly globalizing world" (1) that empowers a terrorist organization deep in Afghanistan. This small sketch alerts us to an issue that recurs time and again in the chapters that follow: life narratives are constantly caught up in circuits of self-construction, where Islam is objectified as the obverse of Euro-American societies that self-identify as "the West," driving a constant creation and re-creation of imaginary boundaries between "we" and "others." "The West" can only be defined relationally. It is not a geographic location but a locus of symbolic and grounded power relations emanating from the United States and Europe; there is no ground for identifying an essential "Western" subject, and, as Seyla Benhabib (2002, 8) reminds us, the "other" can only be relational, always also within us and one of us (a lesson of Abu Ghraib). We can understand this, too, from the transactions of life narrative. Since 2002, a proliferation of life narratives from Iraq, Afghanistan, and Iran is produced for the mass market readerships in the West—the United States most specifically—and most of its readers occupy a place of relative privilege that is succinctly grasped by Pax: "Lucky you." The epigraph to *Soft Weapons,* from John Frow, marks my concern precisely: "the focus of this book is . . . not on the reality of the Other but on the circumstances of its construction and the 'we' who play and are played by this language game" (1996, 4).

Of course, life narrative can also be used to mask privilege and to reify dominant social relations and naturalize the *doxa* of globalization: the neoliberal discourse of the free circulation of ideas, goods, and peoples in global networks of exchange. Steger's thumbnail sketch of Osama bin Laden indicates some of the rhetorical uses of life narrative. Here a U.S. audience feels left behind in a rapidly changing world. How can this be? The global spread of Anglo-American lifestyles and commodities surrounds bin Laden and Salam Pax, and it is American B52s flying from British bases that will bomb Afghanistan and Iraq around and about them. A Timex watch is a sign of the global flows of commodities; it is not a sign of a fundamental redistribution of power and authority to men in caves. Tony Schirato and Jen Webb argue that diagnoses, definitions, and (probably) self-dramatizations of global subjects are almost inevitably rendered docile. Globalization and the neoliberal ideology most strongly associated with it—the idea of freedom as the unfettered circulation of capital and goods—have "a kind of life of their own," creating subjects in their own image and getting them to do their bidding (2003, 201). Life narrative can be co-opted to reproduce the neoliberal endorsement of globalization at the same time as it appears to circulate disinterestedly. To this extent, the effects of globalization have been "dropped over" the aftereffects of colonialism as cross-cultural exchanges and interdependencies become a means for the imposition of Western values and interests.[3] The point here is to emphasize the co-presence of what are sometimes seen to be mutually exclusive phases in the cultural politics of modernity and postmodernity or different strata in lineal histories of imperialism and postcoloniality.

Globalization is a flawed concept, to be used with caution; nevertheless it reaches toward the transnational circuitries of images and narratives that are a feature of contemporary culture. By talking about autobiography *in transit* I mean to focus on the work of life narrative as a commodity that moves across cultures in ways that are distinctly contemporary. Globalization is often characterized in terms of flow: a movement of capital, images, people, commodities, and ideas that transforms identities, institutions, and cultures. This in itself is not new; the Euro-colonial empires of the eighteenth and nineteenth centuries established intricate global networks that were constantly galvanized by new technologies and new ways of thinking about the self. Before this, within the Islamic world global interactions and exchanges of goods, ideas, and people occurred from Dakar to Jakarta, and these have continued from the seventh century to the twenty first: "from Hajj to hip hop" (Cooke and Lawrence 2005). Nevertheless, contemporary life narrative is uniquely shaped by the extensive and unprecedented speed and power of cultural exchanges in the present. Reading across various life narratives and genres synchronically captures its presence, dynamism, ubiquity, and its agency. Recent technological developments shape new routes for autobiographical acts. For example, *Where Is Raed?* transforms time and space and, in turn, the ways that the autobiographer and his readership interact. This "real time" dialogue between a blogger in Baghdad and his online correspondents evaporates locations into e-mail addresses. Is this a sign of the transcendence of space and time promised by a utopian technoculture? Probably not. Like bin Laden's Timex, *Where Is Raed?* is a marker not of transcendence but of trafficking in commodities, conversations, beliefs, and identities across local, regional, national, and supranational communities. Life narratives from Afghanistan, Iran, and Iraq are compelling and urgent, and autobiographical acts are enmeshed and active in conflicts where lives are at risk here and now. Pax takes every opportunity to remind us of this.

We need to ask old questions about these autobiographical acts, which are implicated variously in contemporary culture wars, liberation movements, and armed conflict. Which bodies are breathed into life, and which lives are being brought into view by autobiography? Do life narratives circulating via new technologies facilitate social justice and thinking about sovereignty, community, and subjectivity across cultures? If life narratives exert transformative agency—as they have on behalf of subordinated peoples in the past—in whose interests, and to which ends, at the present time? The stage for contemporary life narratives is framed by the war on terror that dramatically shapes their jurisdiction. This includes events such as the attacks on New York and Washington in September 2001, the subsequent campaigns of armed intervention and insurgency in Afghanistan and Iraq, terrorist attacks in Europe, Africa, the Middle East, and southeast Asia, and the creation of a carceral archipelago, the deterritorialized spaces of detainment that stretch from Guantánamo across to Abu Ghraib and down to isolated detention centers in the Pacific. It also includes the renewal of fundamentalisms, the ideological shifts to patriotism and homelands, the renewed vigor of Orientalism and Occidentalism in the constructions of self and the other, and a pervasive strengthening of modes of state power that operate diffusely to regulate populations and reproduce subjects in relation to strategic policy. I take Timothy Brennan's point that trends in book markets are not equitable with decisions made in corporate boardrooms or with speeches by the American president on the New World Order (1997, 3). Life narratives are "soft weapons," but what follows is a series of essays on how the war on terror ripples in and through life narrative, a sign of contraction in the public sphere that is mediated in the private domain to political effect and emotional affect.[4]

Two arguments are particularly important here. One is Derek Gregory's characterization of "the colonial present": the reinscription and rehabilitation of colonialism through the distinctive "architectures of enmity" that have been energized by fundamentalism and the war on terror. The other is Judith Butler's discussion of how these events produce a newly precarious sense of life and responsibility to others. Life narrative has always been implicated in producing what will and will not count as viable speaking subjects and reasonable opinion in the public domain, and Butler's reminder that the reality of certain lives and deaths falls from this suggests that we do need to think carefully about how book markets are connected to boardrooms and centers of command.

Narrativity and the Self

Where Is Raed? raises questions about relations between readers and narrators, and how autobiographical narrative is marketed, consumed, and taken up into debates about the politics of identity in times of crisis. In *Soft Weapons* I respond to this challenge by making some large claims about the cultural, social, and political work of autobiography. There are particular risks in working with contemporary texts and contexts. This is not the world of Renaissance self-fashioning, to be reassembled by careful archival operations on shards and remnants of another age; this is the world we inhabit, and where we engage in our own most intimate work of self-invention.

This contemporaneity establishes beyond doubt that autobiography is fundamental to the struggle for recognition among individuals and groups, to the constant creation of what it means to be human and the rights that fall from that, and to the ongoing negotiation of imaginary boundaries between ourselves and others. Life narrative plays a vital role in the public sphere as it deals in and through private lives. It renegotiates and redefines how we imagine and rehearse cross-cultural encounters and how we know and identify ourselves in relation to others. Because this is work going on in and around and through us (as readers, critics, consumers, teachers, citizens) we can grasp how contradictory, complicated, and historical the transits of life stories can be, and just how variously we can be drawn into quite different and perhaps contradictory affinities, identifications, and ways of imagining the self. This is not particular to the present, but it is perhaps only by looking to the contemporary that we can grasp subjectively and intuitively the dialogic and narrative constitution of the self. Contemporary life narrative touches the secret life of us; indeed, it is part of how we come to imagine "us."

Both the nature of our times (characterized by cultural conflict and violent contestation) and the fact of its "presence" to us make especially compelling theories that stress intersubjectivity and the dialogic constitution of the self. We encounter each other and ourselves in narrative, and Seyla Benhabib's notion of the constant creation and re-creation of identity and difference is useful for thinking about this as a dynamic process: "I can become aware of the *otherness of others,* those aspects of their identity that make them concrete others to me, only through their own narratives" (2002, 14). We are born into webs of narrative: micronarratives of familial life and macronarratives of collective identity, codes of established narratives that define our capacities to weave individual life stories. From this point of view, autobiographical narrative emerges as a risky dialogic act and as essential to the shaping of an individuality understood as the "fragile achievement of selves in weaving together conflicting narratives and allegiances into a unique life history" (16). The "unofficial" public sphere of literary, cultural, religious, and artistic movements are vital to political contestation and opinion formation; from this it follows that autobiographical narrative is an agent in complex global dialogues and encounters and a way of thinking through the interdependencies of conceptions of the self and other. And so, for example, we see Pax weaving a self through narrative in a series of "languages": the Arablish in which he seeks to reconnect to his Iraqi heritage, the "new Englishes" of information technologies and pop culture, and the codes of the gay subculture are all part of his positioning. Notions of cultures as unified, seamless and whole can seem archaic and fundamentalist in the face of the increasing hybridization of cultures, peoples, and languages. However, across contemporary life narrative, the hybrid and the syncretic always coincide with identifications that pursue authentic, continuous, and homogenous self-identities through, for example, tradition, heritage, locality, region, nation, ethnicity, or the sacred. Furthermore, present conditions demand that we recognize how Benhabib's "unofficial" public sphere contracts and congeals to privilege some identities and allegiances over others.

We consume life narratives voraciously from pages and screens because they tap into dreams and desires; into newly imagined possibilities of life for ourselves and for others, both individually and collectively; and into our own autobiographical narrative in the process of everyday life. But life narratives are not innocent. Despite all that we know of the virtual "I," the fragility of the autobiographical pact, and the ambiguous location of life narrative somewhere between fiction and history, life narrative retains a powerful role in our thinking about the "social imaginary" (Taylor 2004, 23).[5] Autobiography is a cultural space where relations between the individual and society are thought out intensely and experienced intersubjectively; here the social, political, and cultural underpinnings of thinking about the self come to the surface and are affirmed in images, stories, and legends. This personal and highly engaged way of grasping relations between the self and others is intrinsic to the transits of life narrative and the narrative imagination it engenders.

Life narrative touches the world in distinctive ways, then: it refers to lived experience; it professes subjective truths; and above all it signals to the reader an intended fidelity to history and memory. It engages the reader powerfully, imaginatively, intimately, to the point that it becomes part of our own self-creation.[6] Philippe Lejeune's notion of the autobiographical pact is helpful here (1989). This may seem contradictory, for testimony and autobiography rarely feature that individual signature and proper name that anchors Lejeune's pact; "Latifa," "Zoya," "Souad" are among the most recent in a string of pseudonyms and devices used to give a personal account of atrocity and loss. Nevertheless, the pact grasps the gestures of sincerity, authenticity, and trust that we might deconstruct as language effects, but not dismiss as characteristics of life narrative that shape our expectations and engagements with it, and that produce its political effectiveness and rhetorical power. The particular empathic investments of readers in life narrative come to the surface when this sincerity is confected. For example, when Norma Khouri's best-seller *Honor Lost,* published elsewhere as *Forbidden Love,* an apparently autobiographical account of love and death in Jordan, was revealed as fiction in 2004 the power of life narrative to limit perceptions of Islam became a matter of public debate. Despite the painfulness of betrayed trust, literary hoaxes are useful: they bring to light the investments elicited by life narrative, and they also remind us of the risks of emotional engagement for readers, publishers, and critics.

Muslim life narratives have been taken up variously in the recent past, in a time of crisis when recognition of viable speaking subjects in the public sphere has become an urgent issue. The chapters that follow map some of the routes of these life stories. Life narrative is of course fundamental to the process of opening spaces for "the speaking person" (Butler 2004, xx) and for attending to the recounting of experiences that have previously been silently excluded—as Afghan feminist activists are quick to point out when given the opportunity: "There was a time that no pen moved to write a poem or article that reflected the realities of Afghanistan . . . and the image of the Afghan women, silent under the burqa, does not tell the truth of our lives nor our resistance" (Brodsky 2003, ix). The issue of how life narratives appear and gain legitimacy is critical, and this will return us time and again to the ways that readers in the mass markets for life narrative take up autobiographical stories empathically, identifying in and through trauma and in terms of human rights campaigns for social justice that play to Western traditions of benevolence. This is the transit lane that allows life narratives to move from East to West rapidly and to become highly valued commodities for a "primed" readership. Discourses of human rights offer a universal and seemingly uncontested ethics of cross-cultural relations, an inevitable and natural moral grammar, which is part of the *doxa* of globalization.

In thinking these issues through otherwise, I frequently turn to recent work on communicative ethics as a mode of questioning how life narratives are used to mediate relations across cultures in the public sphere. Iris Marion Young's approach to these issues is pragmatic rather than programmatic, and each of the chapters that follow explores a series of texts-in-context with a quite specific and practical orientation in mind. Thinking about cultural difference in a precise and contemporary frame consistently suggests that autobiographical writing is a force to be reckoned with in the politics of consent and critique, and it understands life narrative as deeply engaged in the social and discursive production of identities, but it deploys various strategies to grasp what I understand to be a dynamic synchronic field of narrative. Life narrative is instrumental in debates about social justice, and narrative can inspire readers' imaginations to rethink communicative ethics in ways that engage with difference without resorting to either identification (which produces the empathic response) or othering (which looks to the antithesis of the self across cultures). Young (1997) is inclined to downplay the usefulness of symmetry—putting oneself in the place of others—in favor of working toward moral respect through asymmetrical relations, which recognize differences of history, social position, and experience that cannot be transcended. This is very useful to begin a critical discussion of how Muslim life narratives are marketed into the West as valuable commodities, and how they are caught up in fantasies that the West likes to tell about itself. Equally well, it suggests how life narratives can be used strategically to grasp an opportunity to talk back, to reflect on the rhetorical construction of autobiographical acts, and to bring into view processes of othering and self-fashioning. In the chapters that follow, I argue that what readers do with texts, and how texts circulate as commodities, must become vital components of autobiography criticism. We need not consume life narratives to self-aggrandize; we can also read them for a piercing reminder of our own tenuous grasp on a self and its place to speak humanely. They can produce an openness to narrative that decenters us and allows us to think beyond ourselves, implicated in lives that are not our own. This is the urgent work of criticism now: to interrogate the emergence and vanishing of the human at the limits of what we can know, what we can hear, what we can see . . . (Butler 2004, 151).

Shelf Life

To engage with the dynamics of self-fashioning in our own presence, I track how life narratives circulate by reading texts and paratexts. Paratexts are the liminal features that surround and cover the text and, following Gerard Genette, I distinguish two elements. The first, "peritext," includes everything between and on the covers, and reading the covers of life narrative is particularly important here. The second, "epitext," are the elements outside of the bound volume: interviews, correspondence, reviews, commentaries, and so on. By introducing these thresholds into interpretation, we can track the textual cultures of autobiography, and these are a vital component of any enquiry into the cross-cultural routes of contemporary life narrative. Textual critique needs to be immersed in a thoroughgoing sense of the material processes and ideological formations surrounding the production, transmission, and reception of autobiographical texts: these are the components of textual cultures.

This criticism has a practical and materialist emphasis, and it attends to synchronicities and intertextuality by taking the pulse of autobiography. For example: walk into a bookstore in the affluent West, look at the shelves and assess the passages of life narrative in block displays for special promotion, in seasonal and topical arrangements, or just in the alphabetical order of "nonfiction." Attend to the glossy materiality of each text, how they present on the jacket and on the shelf; how they "look" and feel. Peel away the layers of peritext: the covers, introductions, acknowledgments, dedications, blurbs. Add to this your ongoing immersion in epitexts: reviews and criticism across various mass media, the carefully synchronized marketing and trade of life narratives; the movements of the celebrity circuit; the book prizes and the calendar of literary festivals. The questions to ask here are simple: Who is getting to speak autobiographically, how and why? To what effect? What becomes a best-seller, and what is remaindered or republished? How do these elicit our attention? What kinds of engagement come into play? How do these appeal to readers, and what kind of consumers are we asked to become? Log onto Amazon.com and cruise around a cybermarket, one that includes all kinds of qualitative and quantitative information about how life narratives are being consumed and cataloged now. This virtual bookstore obliterates the local and regional and (for some of us) national emphases that are taken up in the local domains of autobiography, but to order from the U.S.-based Amazon.com website and to receive books shipped from Hamburg via Sydney is to begin to grasp some of the curious and global transits of books in the material world.

The interpretation of contemporary autobiography must learn from the dynamism of these things that (like Pax) call into question the isomorphism of place, space, and culture. Bookshops—real and virtual—are a reminder that critics of the contemporary must hold things together: books on the shelf, production and consumption, addressee and addressor, and our own imaginative work of self-identification. The notion that we might call for fair trade in our dealings with life narratives is one argument that follows from thinking about the textual cultures of life narrative in this way. Affluent consumers know to ask questions about imported commodities such as coffee, sneakers, and clothes: What does this product do to the community of origin? In what follows, I ask that same question time and again of life narratives as they move westward from the Middle and Far East.

Of course, business is risky in this economy. The recent global commodification of cultural difference—"the alterity industry"—offers both opportunities and constraints for writers, publishers, readers, and critics. Local and oppositional discourses and cultural products from the periphery circulate and are contained by metropolitan and capitalist systems of production and consumption. Life narrative is part of a culture industry that is oriented toward large metropolitan readerships. It is also a commodity that is marketed and surrounded by paratext to authenticate and legitimate the narrative and secure its reception by the powerful reading communities that range from the metropolitan intelligentsia and the suburban book clubs, to the fans of the best-seller. Postcolonial criticism and its rhetoric of resistance as well as culturally "othered" goods (such as subaltern life narratives) have themselves become popular consumer products in the recent past, as Graham Huggan points out. Ethnic autobiography is highly valued for its exotic appeal and educational value, for the status it confers on the consumer as an enlightened, sympathetic, and politically correct individual, and for that comforting narcissistic recognition that denies difference across cultures. Ironically, the power of autobiography to induce empathy across cultures is also its risk for minority narrators. As we can see from the reception of Pax, his blog is able to produce that spark of identification with the exotic: "He is just like us."[7] Yet Pax is also able to remind some of their relative privilege, looking on, as many of us do, "from a high orbit."

The risk here is that the urge to identify and empathize, evident in

15

patterns of consumption of exotic life narrative, can come at the expense of knowledge of other cultures beyond the comfort zone of many readers. As Pax's blog unfolds online he is forced to engage with the turbulent passages between himself and his readership. Characteristically the production and circulation of these texts remains complex and unpredictable as they maneuver in the global ebb and flow of social change and conflict. Readerships of life narrative are fickle and on the move. Prices, remainder bins, and Amazon.com's sales rank measure the marketability of lived experience, on a daily basis. There is no single reading public or metropolitan readership, for life narratives in English circulate through a complex of diverse cultures and communities, and critical work needs to chart their reception with care and precision. For this reason Appadurai's suggestion that we need to examine commodities in motion and that they can profitably be regarded as having "life histories" is a useful one (1996, 17). This distinction draws attention to possibilities for thinking about the unique operations of certain styles or genres within the larger class of life narrative. The approach to textual cultures in the following chapters unpacks life narrative into its various genres and specific modalities. In *Soft Weapons*, testimony, memoir, popular best-sellers, and autoethnography will be read with a view to their distinctive life cycles as commodities in a boom market. For example, Azar Nafisi's *Reading "Lolita" in Tehran* is a best-selling memoir fueled by the acceleration of the war on terror, and yet so too are the very different veiled best-sellers by Jean Sasson and Norma Khouri. Conversations about life narrative need to work across high, middlebrow, and mass cultures of autobiography and grasp relations between "literature" and "Literature," which are discussed in chapters 4 and 7.

Synchronicity: The Work of Genre

This synchronic and materialist study of autobiographical cultures and the conditions of their production is always concerned with the realities of certain lives and deaths. It carves a track through what might seem to be quite different contemporary narratives and locations to examine the intertextual relations among them, and their relevance for the passages of bodies in place and time. Genres of life narrative and various ways of imagining the self autobiographically become emergent, dominant and recessive. At any one time, there are various genres of autobiography copresent in the marketplace. The shifting relations among various genres—testimony, autoethnography, and memoir, for example—signifies a dynamic flow of life story that signals who gets to speak autobiographically, and how they sustain their authority and power. These shifting relations shape the chapters that follow, that begin with "minority" genres, the testimonies of those who struggle for cultural authority, and conclude with the memoirs of those public intellectuals who possess cultural capital to speak autobiographically.

Pax launches the first four chapters of this book into a series of readings across contemporary testimony and autoethnography with a view to mapping the life cycle of these "minority" genres in the recent past.[8] Minority narratives are synthetic and dynamic and subject to ongoing change and various affiliations. They need to be read in terms of politicized and strategic locations and in ways that are "worldly": attentive to the mediations of editors and collaborators and to the market operations of international publishing networks.[9] So, for example, Pax and his blog are a "hot" narrative in these times, a valuable commodity alive on the celebrity circuit. Who else is empowered to testify? The appearance of multiple autoethnographies about Afghan women in 2003 is—like *Where Is Raed?*—a sign of how history and politics elicit and shape the marketing of subaltern narratives and how opportunism and agency emerge through life narrative. These Afghan narratives are almost entirely collective and pseudonymous. Characteristically they are jacketed with images of the burka-clad Afghan woman, and in this way they invite curiosity and announce directly and polemically their entry into debates about Muslim women, fundamentalism, and modernity. These too are "hot" commodities, but their embodiment, technology, and address to the reader is quite different to *Where Is Raed?*

The discussion of these autoethnographies in chapter 2, "The Skin of the Burka," examines how they circulate in the West and empower feminist activism in Afghanistan at the same time as they appeal to Western fantasies about one of the most intractable signs of cultural difference: the veil. There are extraordinary opportunities for unauthorized narrators to attract attention and engage with readers at the present time, but this engagement is open to co-option and containment. Afghan life narratives are put to different uses by various interest groups within the Western intelligentsia and by organizations of Afghan activists, most notably the Revolutionary Association of the Women of Afghanistan (RAWA). Testimonies are co-opted as propaganda, for example, and we can discern a struggle for control over representations of Afghan women in the intelligentsia as the handling of these narratives circles out to include the U.S. celebrity Oprah Winfrey, the author of *The Vagina Monologues* Eve Ensler, as well as the various research agendas of scholars in psychology, sociology, women's studies (and life narrative!). Yet like *Where Is Raed?* the cultural biographies of recent Afghan life narratives also suggest that new media technologies offer opportunities for complex circuitries of transmission and reception in the public domain. The commodification of life narratives in various textual forms can further the aspirations of subaltern peoples in ways that they themselves authorize and control. Every chapter of this book returns to this contradiction one way or another, for it is at the heart of the contemporary transits of life narratives: these texts travel on very different and perhaps even divergent routes in various public spheres at one and the same time, and they can be put to very different uses.

In chapter 3, "Testimony Incarnate: Read My Lips," I examine the conditions where life narratives about trauma in Afghanistan, Iraq, and Iran are excluded and suppressed, unable to break through into the mass market to exert political influence. Refugee narratives are carefully controlled and contained, like the bodies of refugees and asylum seekers themselves. We may be inclined to be dismissive of the power of life narrative as a political act; however, the extraordinary lengths that are taken to deny a face and history (that it to say, an autobiographical presence) to individual refugees indicate that attaching an autobiography to an individual can be a powerful act of resistance. Refugee narratives rarely reach the threshold that allows testimony to spill into the public domain. What we find instead are fragments and glimpses, autoethnographies that are carefully managed in both hard copy and webdiary by benevolent activists who struggle to authorize and legitimate these testimonies. In the life cycle of testimony, this is a story of containment and failure to escape the circuits of control and exclusion. This is the other side of the Pax phenomenon: in times of crisis, testimony is carefully managed. The soft edges of propaganda swerve toward the hard lines of censorship and we must learn to read silences and scars. Under these circumstances, testimony is written on the page, on the screen, and on the body and it strikes the reader with visceral force.

Reading the textual culture of minority narratives synchronically in this way emphasizes their political and ethical force. For those who lack social, cultural, and political power, the technologies of the self made available through life narrative allows agency and carefully defined authority. In these minority genres, shelf life is limited—although of course there can be other lives as autobiographies from the past are recycled in the present. This suggests again the life cycles of genres: minority narratives are hostages to fashion, but there and again they can be revived and recirculated. Testimony, both individual and collective, can surface from the depths of the past and it brings with it burdens that can profoundly disturb the present and demand response.

Harem literature, "the veiled best-seller," is the subject of chapter 4. Critics rarely look at best-selling life narratives, although of course many readers do. Jean Sasson's *Princess* trilogy, recently republished and constantly in print since its original publication last decade, set the style for the veiled best-seller in the wake of the first Gulf War. Sasson is an important broker in the processing of popular life narrative about Muslim women, and her celebrity reflects the particular dynamics of this genre of nonfiction in the marketplace. Sasson herself published a new book in 2003, *Mayada: Daughter of Iraq.* This romantic auto/biography is associated with the occupation of Iraq in 2003. Fantasy allows Sasson to enter into Iraq, but the story of this chapter is also about the risky business of going to war. The epitexts to *Mayada* suggest it, too, is ultimately caught in hubris and controversy. By paying attention to the role of the Sasson Corporation in marketing the exotic, a different dimension of the cultural field of life narratives by and about Muslim women comes into view, and the chapter sets out to establish a methodology for reading the textual cultures of popular life narrative.

At a time when Muslim life narratives become a valuable commodity, it is almost inevitable that a pretender will enter and trade on the valence of an authoritative life story with a "faddish fib." Chapter 5, "Tainted Testimony," examines what happens when a "hot" life narrative is outed as a hoax text, and a potent moral and political force turns cold, with its potency diminishing in a painful aftermath. Value—moral, ethical, and economic—dissipates, and the authority and veracity of the testimony is challenged in courts, legislatures, and the classroom. Norma Khouri's *Honor Lost* (published as *Forbidden Love* elsewhere), ostensibly a testimonial narrative about honor killing in Jordan, is the hoax we had to have. This dark side of autobiography is extraordinarily useful for criticism, and in this chapter I use the hoax to return to the "transit lane" that is produced by the connections between the marketing of testimony and campaigns for human rights on behalf of Muslim women. This is a particularly modern set of associations that places life narratives as carriers of rights discourse. A hoax offers an opportunity to examine the politics of reading and the formations of reading communities for subaltern life narratives. The confection of trauma raises issues about the communicative ethics of testimony, and how testimony can be used as propaganda: speaking untruth in the interests of power.

The chapter on the veiled best-seller marks a turning point, for with Jean Sasson and Norma Khouri we clearly move away from the domain of testimony. The remaining chapters of *Soft Weapons* turn to a different style of autobiography in transit. The autobiographical narrator in minority genres speaks on behalf of a collective, a subordinate speaking truth to power, with the rhetoric of truth, and witnessing trauma in person. For this reason, minority life narratives are surrounded by "peritexts": endorsements and authorizations in the form of introductions, prefaces, appendixes, and blurbs that guide the reception of the text. These narrators are not left to speak for themselves. Activists, celebrities, psychologists, sociologists, lawyers, and academics surround autoethnographies by refugees, indigenes, and subalterns with benevolent affirmations. These public intellectuals confer authority on the narrator; they both encourage and instruct the reader to read the text properly. Recall, for example, Salam Pax's concern that he will be read as a propaganda ploy or as something less than human, and it is the work of Ian Katz's introduction to counter this in the published version of the blog. The publishers of Norma Khouri's *Honor Lost* needed the authority and reputation of a "gatekeeper" such as Jean Sasson in their cover blurb to authorize Khouri's entry into the specific market of the veiled best-seller. Peritexts can be read to signal anxiety about autobiographical authority in minority texts, and they are an almost inevitable accompaniment to subaltern autobiographical expression.

However, to invoke the bookshop metaphor again: we know from the most cursory examination of the shelves that very different kinds of autobiographical writing coexist, and these take up the personal effects of social crisis differently. Minority writing secures its place through struggle, and it is hostage to circumstance and shifts in cultural authority and influence. Elsewhere, narrators can locate themselves differently in history and through crisis. The memoir is a genre for those who are authorized and who have acquired cultural legitimacy and influence. Like testimony, memoir can personalize history and historicize the personal, place the self in relation to public history and culture, and draw on the discourses of history and literature. It tends to focus on the times in which the life is lived and is clearly closely related to testimony (Buss 2001, 595). "Memoir" in this book is understood as a specific genre of life narrative, more specific than its current common usage as a synonym for autobiography at large.[10] It is a form of self-reflective writing that is personal, often conversational, and a meditation about the place of the self in history. Buss suggests that "the first question we should ask of a memoir is not "why is this person's life an important or distinguished one?" but "what is the place of this writer in the culture . . . ?'" (595). In contemporary autobiography, memoir is the prerogative of those who possess cultural capital, and it follows that the place of the memoirist in culture is quite "other" to that of those who testify. For this reason, the arrangement of chapters in *Soft Weapons* places testimony and memoir in dialectical relation, circulating together in an uneasy coexistence.

So, for example, the extensive peritexts that surround life narratives in the minority genres is replaced by a brief cover blurb when we turn to memoirs, as cultural authority falls from professional status for writers authorized by their institutional location. In chapter 6, "Embedded: Memoir and Correspondents," I turn again to what Leigh Gilmore calls the "limits" of autobiography: its trading in trauma—and war, in this case. Although the dealing in trauma through life narrative predated the war on terror, the sense of crisis in the present has shaped a different set of conditions for speaking about trauma. Journalism is often the first stage of writing to witness traumatic experience for the public record. By reading together three journalist's life narratives about the Iraq war, this chapter places memoir as a vehicle for haunted and fragmented accounts of the professional self in a specific historical context. Journalists' memoirs have been underestimated as a meaningful writing of history, subjectivity, and culture, and yet they have plenty to say about the grounds and ethics of speaking, writing, and mourning after September 11.

The final chapter of *Soft Weapons* considers a memoir of power and influence. Alongside *Where Is Raed?* as an autobiography for these times, and Salam Pax as a new kind of subject, is Azar Nafisi's *Reading "Lolita" in Tehran: A Memoir in Books,* and her extraordinary autobiographical performance of professorial authority in defiance of Islamic fundamentalism in Iran. Nafisi's memoir refurbishes an ethical place for literary criticism and the role of the literary critic as a public intellectual. Random House scheduled a first print run of 12,000 copies for Nafisi's memoir when it purchased the option in 1999. Following the events of 9/11 this first print run became 50,000 copies. In the build up to the war in Iraq Azar Nafisi became a popular commentator in the West, and the book sold 95,000 copies in hardcover. It made its paperback debut on the *New York Times* best-seller list in January 2004 and has sold 484,000 copies: "Pushed by world events that have made Muslim women interesting to American book club readers" (Salamon 2004), the book is well-established on the paperback best-seller list of the *New York Times*. Along with David Bowie, Freddy Adu, and William H. Macy, Azar Nafisi has been part of a marketing campaign to sell Audi cars in North America, and so her ideas find a brand. In May 2004 a picture of Nafisi suspended in air, afloat and free in front of a shelf of books, appeared in Condé Nast publications such as *Vanity Fair, Vogue,* and the *New Yorker.* "We wanted people who weren't just famous or rich but who are doing something really cool," the manager of this campaign says. "Azar is to literature what Audi is to cars." Ironically, the tagline of the Audi campaign is "never follow."

"Ironic" because *Reading "Lolita" in Tehran: A Memoir in Books* is all about tradition and reaffirming a well-established disciplinary practice of literary criticism. This is a memoir that grafts into itself intertextually the great modernist books of the Western canon. By authorizing herself autobiographically as a professor in a didactic and humanist tradition, Nafisi re-presents the West back to itself via Tehran in a congenial and immediately familiar guise. Like David Denby's memoir *Great Books* (1997), *Reading "Lolita" in Tehran* reasserts the universality and greatness of the Western canon but, unlike Denby, Nafisi's memoir imports this humanism in terms of a clash of civilizations, which is resolved with the civilizing effects of English Literature. This needs no paratextual endorsement other than Geraldine Brooks's remark on the front cover: "Anyone who has ever belonged to a book group must read this book." And so Nafisi's book is launched into the circuits of a powerful location for shaping middle-class taste in the West: the book club. Nafisi herself becomes a commodity, which can be employed to signal why people of taste and distinction should buy Audi. That the author of an autobiography can become a celebrity translated into capital alongside Bowie, Adu, and Macy is a reminder, if we need one, that life writing is a powerful conduit in contemporary culture. This is the double agency of life narrative—it can work in very different interests and constituencies at one and the same time. It can promote dialogues between cultures, and it can obscure the various power relations that come into play.

Like Pax, Nafisi is one of the figures who "breathes shape" into how we might read the condition of autobiography, and yet these two can hardly be more different one from the other. They are equally open to question as propaganda ploys and as interventions in how we might invent more inclusive and democratic social imaginaries. The point remains: how life narratives from and about Muslim societies are used to constitute audiences and identities as "Western" is important. We need to read Nafisi alongside the autoethnographies by feminist activists from Afghanistan too, for one of the preoccupations that recurs here is the debate about the veil. The barefaced Nafisi of the Audi promotion is liberated from the chador, the contrast is quite literally figured in black and white, and this appeals to powerful ideas of how Muslim women might be freed by Western secular culture. Not surprisingly, *Reading "Lolita" in Tehran* has struck a chord in the American marketplace.

The question of how theorizing is being remade at the "rumpled sites" of autobiography posed in the epigraph to this chapter sends this book on its way, and so too does the autobiographical avatar Salam Pax. In a brief "Book End" to *Soft Weapons,* he has the last word too, and I follow his passionate endorsement of not just another autobiographical avatar but a very different technology of life narrative as well: comics, most specifically Marjane Satrapi's *Persepolis* and *Persepolis 2.* In her discussion of representations of terrorism and the war on terror, Marianne Hirsch argues that as "biocular" texts comics have a special role to play in times of trauma and censorship, and here I read the two volumes of *Persepolis* to explore the possibility that newness does come into the world through the frames and gutters of graphic autobiography (2004). Ultimately this leads to a final frame rather than a last word by way of an ending. By following autobiography in transit I am, finally, less interested in its ends and its traditions than its capacity to perform small acts of cultural translation in a time of precarious life.

ONE

Arablish:
The Baghdad Blogger

The question of culture in relation to the Internet involves a risk, a step into the unfamiliar precisely with respect to the figure of the self.

MARK POSTER, *WHAT'S THE MATTER WITH THE INTERNET?*

During the invasion of Baghdad in the (northern) spring of 2003, there were 20,000 hits daily at a weblog called *Where Is Raed?* an online diary maintained by an unknown and allegedly Iraqi blogger called Salam Pax. Visiting this site became the thing to do, and as the intensity of the war on terror increased, the sheer volume of traffic to the site caused problems. What do we make of Salam Pax? A new species? A new autobiographical genre? What happens to Pax and his weblog when they are pulled offline, extracted from the hot links of cyberspace, and shelved in cold copy: a book version of Pax's weblog edited and published as *The Baghdad Blog?* What do we make of the slowly dying remains of *Where Is Raed?* online now: an archive at http://dear_raed .blogspot.com, threaded with links that no longer respond to the mouse, its rich "Arablish" language fading away? And why is it almost impossible to resist talking metaphorically about Pax and his webdiary as organic, living things in this way?

Here is the inevitable place to begin reading, thinking, writing about the transits of life narrative from Iraq, because Pax fundamentally alters ideas about how these passages might take place, and to what effect. As Mark Poster suggests (tentatively): new media does not merely reinforce existing cultural figures of the self; rather, it is a space that encourages practices that construct some new possibilities for political action. These subjects are not outside of history, or transcending difference: "[New] media . . . are not themselves born innocent but arise from existing patterns of hierarchy in relation to class, race and gender. But they enable practices that fit badly with earlier complexes of domination, putting them into question and thereby opening the field . . . to new spaces of politics" (2001b, 11). Pax and his blog "fit badly" with what we know; they are elusive when translated into familiar ways of thinking about how autobiography touches the world, and what kinds of political interventions can be made in and through autobiographical acts. Pax is a sign of what happens when testimony—the act of bearing witness to an event, of providing or establishing evidence before an actual or projected audience—moves into cyberspace and goes to war; both of these things produce transformations.[1] From his home in Baghdad, Pax offers an Iraqi eyewitness account of the invasion and its aftermath, the occupation. A critical question here is not how existing identities are empowered by the possibilities opened up by the blog; it is, rather, how these identities and cross-cultural relations are reconfigured and reformulated as the work of testimony is engaged in a new medium and in a time and place of crisis.[2]

Transcendence

The origins of Salam Pax are uncertain, in part because his mastery of blogging software was gained at the expense of his early postings. The signs that remain are in the archived first volume of his online blog *Where Is Raed?* From the very beginning (in August 2002) the technological and discursive devices Pax uses to such good effect in "writing" a distinctive weblog are there: the hyperlinks to coverage of the impending war in major publications and commentaries in the West and elsewhere; and the personal and slightly cryptic conversational address to his erratic good friend Raed Jarrar, who is in Jordan as this first blog is posted, but omnipresent as the ostensible addressee, and the coauthor in theory at least, for as we are reminded at the start of every cache: "Raed started writing on this Blog. Salam Pax kindly asks you to always check who is posting. Raed's brain derails sometimes. My ramblings are in orange, his in white." There is also the struggle to sustain an online presence amid power shortages and state censorship of online access; and the selective glimpse of the embodiment—tastes, desires and daily preferences—of Salam, a twenty-nine-year-old gay architect, a gossip, and a geek who lives with his family in Baghdad before and during the invasion of Iraq in 2003. Also there from the start is the quotation from Samuel P. Huntingdon: "The West won the world not by the superiority of its ideas or values or religion but rather by its superiority in applying organized violence. Westerners often forget this fact, non-Westerners never do." The archive of *Where Is Raed?* has three caches in volume 1— August–November 2002—and then a series of seventeen caches that begin in January 1, 2002, and end as cryptically as they begin at 2:16 AM on April 10, 2004: "I think Hiatus is the word. Thank you very much ladies and gentleman." By the time Pax makes that last rather grand posting that ends *Where Is Raed?* he is an international cyberlebrity. In August 2004, after a premature retirement, Salam Pax returned with a new blog, *Shut Up You Fat Whiner;* he is "still fat, fuzzy and as bent as a dog's tail" in this new incarnation. The latest version of Salam Pax is, as we might expect, passionate about iTunes and podcasting and using Google Earth to map the transformation of Baghdad as an occupied territory. The new blog includes a photograph of Pax and, in October 2005, he chose to identify himself: he is Salam al-Janabi.[3]

By invoking "Hiatus" to close his first blog, Pax deliberately creates a break in the records and incidentally gestures one last time to the cultural literacy of his creator and his expectations that a significant proportion of his readership enjoys language play of all kinds. Subsequently, encouraged by Pax's success, Iraq is now a rich site for weblogs, and the margins of the *Where Is Raed?* archive feature a series of live links in real time to contemporary weblogs that are local successors: *Baghdad Burning* (Riverbend's blog, published in hard copy in 2005), *Healing Iraq, A Family in Baghdad* (which includes Raed Jarrar's blog), *The Mesopotamian, Hammorabi.* Finally, after a late start, the Iraqis are catching up to the Persians on the web; Pax will be pleased: "I am really jealous. First Persian Top Weblogs Competition. . . . when are we arabs going to have something like that? and why have persians taken to blogging so easily than arabs? why isn't there a single arabic weblog? why?why?why? Raed dear you should start one today, i promise i will always raed it" (December 18, 2002).

Like Raed, Pax, too, is elusive. Concepts derived from criticism of print-based autobiography are helpful in reaching out for him to a degree. So, for example, we can take John Zuern's point that the "I" of autobiography and memoir has never been anything but virtual (2003, xi). In their *Guide* to reading life narrative Julia Watson and Sidonie Smith carefully separate the various "I" of life narrative (2001a, 59). There is

the "real" or historical "I" (an Iraqi architect called Salam), the narrating "I" and the narrated "I" (both called Salam Pax, a symbolic gesture
to peace and democracy), and the ideological "I" (the subjectivity made
available to the narrator through, for example, new technologies, his
situation as a civilian in a city under siege, and queer identity politics).
This elaborate schema is useful in the case of the Baghdad Blogger because it is a reminder of the separation between the historical "I," who
lives in the world and goes about his business in everyday life and whose
surname was not revealed in public until October 2005, and the "I" who
tells the autobiographical narrative, the elaborate narration of an autobiographical self by Salam Pax, a tactical invention that is deliberately
crafted and symbolically named for a precise time and place in history:
Baghdad in the momentous months before, during, and after the invasion of March 2003: "There is a lot that I have not told you about, and
I don't see an obligation to do so. You hide behind your blog names
and keep certain bits of your life private" (May 30, 2003). Fundamental
to the extraordinary power and authority of Salam Pax is the ideological "I." This dimension of the autobiographical subject, understood by
Smith and Watson as "the concept of personhood culturally available to
the narrator when he tells his story," is the ideological work of invent-
ing a self in *Where Is Raed?* which sets out to engender a new space of
politics from a war zone.

The creation of the weblog and Pax, so slyly subversive and sharply
critical of the Hussein regime during its last days, was a brave act of resistance, and readers in the West constantly feared for his safety at the
hands of Hussein's intelligence agency, the Mukhabarat. When Western
journalists finally succeeded in making a link between Salam Pax, the
blogger and virtual subject, and a friendly and highly effective guide
and interpreter called Salam who worked with them in Baghdad after
the invasion, there was a sense of occasion: "Salam—this is his real first
name—was sitting in a chair . . . reading Philip K. Dick's *The Man in
the High Castle*. I knew, at that moment, that I would hire him" (Maass
2003). It is the journalist Peter Maass, in his article "Salam Pax Is Real,"
who first describes Pax as "cherubic."[4] This sense of occasion and rever-
ence recurs in later descriptions of meetings with Salam—he is larger
than life, a presence. For example a former American soldier returned
from Iraq, the blogger Moja (2004) invokes Maass's metaphor again at
his "turningtables" blog:

I sat waiting by the elevator for someone I've never met in person whom I knew I
would know once I saw . . . a man whom I've known for over a year and a half . . .

who shared the difficulties of life with me . . . who helped to open up my eyes to the bigger picture . . . who I once read resembled a cherub stepped out of the elevator directly in front of me and also knew me instantly . . . he opened up more eyes than my own . . . you are amazing . . . be safe Salam.[5]

Salam Pax is an iconic figure then; a winged celestial creature who flies in virtual space and says "thingy" too often. The wings "stick" in what is surely a tribute to the extraordinary power of the intervention he makes through his artful use of the webdiary. It is not unusual to find invocations of the transcendent in discussions of digital text, and this is frequently dismissed as an expression of "cyberenthusiasm," utopian celebrations of transits into a posthistorical and posthuman age of globalization (Zuern 2003, 2). Pax is not a cherub in this transcendent order of things. To the contrary, this avatar (a virtual image of the self) is used to insert locality, flesh, and time into landscapes that have been evacuated of bodies and history by propaganda from all sides of the war on terror. Pax inhabits Baghdad, a city we virtually occupy, fantasize, and play with in his absence all the time. This isn't a skirmish, it is a war.

Returning to Baghdad

In autumn 2003 a new Xbox product Conflict: Desert Storm II—Back to Baghdad was released.[6] At his "intelligent gaming" site Luke Guttridge reviews the game:

Never a company to shirk an opportunity to make a buck or two, Take 2 Interactive today officially announced Conflict: Desert Storm 2—Back to Baghdad for a release on the Xbox and PS2 this autumn. The game will allow players to take to the role of the British SAS or US Delta forces and promises a realistic third-person shooter experience inspired by recent world events.

"Conflict: Desert Storm 2 takes the squad-based realism of the first title and dramatically improves on it at every level of play," commented Jamie Leece, president of Gotham Games (Take 2). "From the sharper graphics to the more intuitive controls and enhanced AI, this title is sure to be a blast for fans of action and combat games."

This is a reminder that, although new media may open new spaces for politics, at one and the same time they offer new scenarios for propaganda and conquest. They are, to return to Poster again, not "born innocent" and they distribute "squad-based realism" widely for profit. The relationship between virtual and real worlds is of course troubling, and one can only observe that elsewhere this game is reviewed as a "half-assed high-school theater production, nothing works as it should and no one seems to be doing the right thing" (Shawn 2003, 202). Either way, Desert Storm 2 sometimes coexists with Pax's blog in my household, and the soundtrack occasionally filters in from another room as I browse Pax's webdiary. My son Sam boards a Humvee to cruise the streets of Baghdad as a member of an elite U.S. Delta squad. The coincidence of our differently mediated occupations of Baghdad in an antipodean household should not surprise, for although few of us may choose to board imaginatively the Humvee and look at a virtual Baghdad through the sights of an assault rifle, the fact is that we frequently occupy this city through an invasive discipline of views. Even though we may not have actually walked its streets, the idea of "returning" to Baghdad is a way of acknowledging just how frequently and freely we have entered its spaces, via one medium or another: "Everybody should recognize this mosque, it is the background to all broadcasts from Iraq. . . . The big silhouette that looks like a ziggurat in the background used to be the ministry of foreign affairs, now it is part of the palace complex, a beautiful building, at sunset with the right light it looks like something fit for [*Blade Runner*]" (February 8, 2003). In his brilliant essay on Iraq in *The Colonial Past,* the geographer Derek Gregory (2004) points out that a legacy of Gulf War I is this highly militarized mapping of Baghdad—Pax calls this "watching from a high orbit" (April 7, 2003). Coverage of the first Gulf War featured a convergence of intelligence-gathering satellites and planetary television networks, which apparently made Iraq fully visible and available and, at the same time, reduced it to a series of accessible targets. Robert Stam's suggestion that "we were encouraged to spy, through a kind of pornographic surveillance, on a whole region, the nooks and crannies of which were exposed to the panoptic view of the military and the spectator" (quoted in Gregory, 163) suggests this objectification of the Iraqi landscape, the creation of a vantage point that privileged the American viewer (or its surrogate) and delivered a war of apparently surgical precision. This "conspiracy" between the eye of the military and the television camera effaced the materiality of places, the presence of the natural world, and the corporeality of bodies; the war was presented to its audience "as live yet distant, instantaneous yet remote, as dramatically real yet reassuringly televisual" (Ó'Tuathail in Gregory, 163). Here we begin to see the origins of both the Xbox landscape and an engaged and militant resistance to it: Salam Pax's use of the weblog to populate Baghdad, to make a tactical insertion of a precocious and visceral body as the city again becomes a war zone subjected to "smart" technology.

The campaign of "shock and awe" launched in March 2003 was again accompanied by a mobilization of imaginative geographies that situated Western viewers to advantage in carefully constructed lines of sight. Here again Iraqi inhabitants were rendered invisible, the collective subject of apparently humanitarian intervention, were rarely individualized or placed in familial situations or seen going about the practices of every-day life: "[Life] goes on—which, by the way, is driving the foreign jour-nalists crazy. They want some action here and seeing people go about their daily lives is just a waste of time and film, it seems" (March 11, 2003). As in Gulf War I, there is no official count or account of Iraqi casualties and a careful management of images of suffering and grief for Western viewers prevails: "Bodies romanticized, viewer anaesthetized" (Gregory 2004, 165). Iraqi people are filmed by Western media, for ex-ample, as they disinter victims of Saddam Hussein's brutality from mass graves; however, with few exceptions, it is only viewers of Arab media such as al-Jazeera who see contrasting images of the suffering and grief among civilians caused by the present war or the devastation of specific inhabited areas in the major cities.[7] Live broadcasts by embedded jour-nalists, another innovation of this war, were inclined to produce more of the same—an elaborately staged and militarized view of Iraq: remote, controlled, and firmly centered in and through a narrative of libera-tion that brings democracy to an oppressed people. Pax includes heavily ironic linkings to some "embedded journalism": "The article is really good; you can feel the reporter running with the soldiers" (January 26, 2003).[8] I will return to take up this issue of the "embedded" view later, in chapter 6. Gregory charts a series of interventions that prepared the American people for the disembodied spectacle of an urban war in Iraq, including the circulation of militarized mappings of Baghdad in the American public sphere. For example, in November 2002 CNN broadcast a program on urban combat that asked students to design a simulated city to be used for war games, with specific reference to a particular city: Baghdad (Gregory 2004, 200). On media websites, interactive graphics offered maps of Baghdad, which reduced the city to a series of military targets, and users could gain closer views of these at a click of the mouse. New media constantly renders Baghdad as transparent and available and, yet, simultaneously a place where deceit and danger threaten at every turn.

It doesn't do to underestimate how propaganda of this sort is taken up, resisted, consumed, contested, and used variously and actively as it travels in the public and private spheres of the West. Sam, for example, points out that the digital landscape of the Back to Baghdad game is obviously contrived, for it features factories producing weapons of mass destruction (WMDs). The accumulating authority of Pax's weblog, in pace with the escalation of the war in Iraq, led to unprecedented activity on the web as users went in search of more independent and alternative representations of Baghdad, and this is a reminder that audiences are volatile. The projection of romanticized bodies and militarized landscapes does not necessarily induce mass anesthesia, although propaganda is of course insidious, invasive, and manipulative in ways that can be hard to recognize, let alone contradict, especially in times of war. Ultimately the extremes of Occidentalism—the self-construction of the West in and through its constructions of the other—reach a point of excess where the oppositions they construct collapse in disarray. For example, the images that emerged from Abu Ghraib prison in the summer of 2004 comprehensively unraveled the Pentagon's war without bodies, and the abstraction of the Iraqi people as "the other" to a civilized, disciplined West. In the month immediately before the bombing campaigns of March 2003 Salam Pax carefully chronicles in pictures and words an inhabited and beloved place with an architect's eye, a "virtual tour" of Baghdad that melds place and people intimately, celebrating the kind of synthesis that Sneja Gunew describes as the lifelong duet between our bodies and their contexts (2004, 53): "Here you can see the Kadhim minaret very clearly. Do you see those wooden boards sticking out of the wall? This tells you that this was built between 1920 and 30, after that the use of steel I-beams became popular; it was brought into the country by the British. Either the producing company or the importer were called Shellman or something close to that because to this day they are not called I-beams but shellmans (being Iraqis we like our vowels long so it is more like sheeeeelmaaaaan)" (February 24, 2003). This directly contests the evacuation of Baghdad in popular representations, and it uses autobiographical expression to engage in a struggle for jurisdiction and to make a claim to an alternative and oppositional authority.[9]

The Virtual Self

The notion that war and crisis drive the development and uses of new technologies and representations of all kinds is familiar. In the case of the war against terror, it rapidly became evident that developments in

new media offered advanced weaponry for ominous projections and identifications of the self. For example, insurgents used webcam and video
to distribute images of the ritualistic killing of hostages; the capacity to
project images of himself globally and at will was intrinsic to the rene-
gade charisma and authority of Osama bin Laden; the shocking images
from Abu Ghraib prison were never just private, they are digital images
designed for coercive interrogation (Ignatieff 2004, np); and corpora-
tions marketed games that allowed players to board Humvees to conquer
Baghdad time and again. As his name suggests, Pax's diary was established to engender accord, to orchestrate dialogue across intractable difference. *Where Is Raed?* is written in the name (and I want to argue here
in the *process and pursuit*) of peace as well as resistance. Those sightings
and identifications, which link the virtual Pax to an unprepossessing
Baghdad architect and likable geek, record an uncanny sense of a body
that is both virtual and magic and, yet, known intimately. As Pax assumes flesh, to return to the Smith and Watson catalog (2001a) briefly,
different "I's" coalesce, but traces of their various embodiments remain.

The brilliance of Pax is that he exploits this new autobiographical
technology, the weblog, in the pursuit of a sophisticated "I" that talks
back from Baghdad. Pax is not only a docile cherub, he is also the very
soul of James Clifford's "disconcertingly hybrid 'native' met at the ends
of the earth": "I'm always running up against a problematic figure, 'the
informant.' A great many of these interlocutors . . . turn out to have
their own 'ethnographic' proclivities and interesting histories of travel.
Insider-outsiders, good translators and explicators, they've been around"
(1997, 19). To understand the cultures of new media, we need to take into
account both the machines and the specific space/time configuration
they engender in representations of the subject. For this reason, Poster
(2001b) turns to the issue of the ways that selves are formed variously
in relation to different media. Features that distinguish the Internet from
print and broadcast media include: the facilitation of many-to-many
communications; the simultaneous reception, alteration, and redistribution of cultural objects; the dislocation of communication from terri-
torialized spatial relations (such as the neighborhood and the nation);
and instantaneous global contact and networking in real time. These
features enable quite different styles of autobiographical performance
and self-constitution: "One invents oneself and one knows that others also invent themselves, while each interpellates the others through
those inventions . . . digital authorship is about the performance of self-
constitution" (Poster 2001b, 75). If this seems too obscure or utopian, we
can turn directly to *Where Is Raed?* to understand how these capacities

of new media allow Pax to engage in an electronically mediated self-authorization that reformulates the genres of testimony. Pax transforms the act of giving witness, seizing the technology of the weblog to insert a dialogic, direct, and intimate process of exchange just as the "split geographies" of "us and them," "civilization and barbarism," "Good and Evil" return so violently in the war on terror, unleashing virulent strains of Orientalism abroad again, ubiquitous, "revivified and hideously emboldened" (Gregory 2004, 11, 18).

If we understand changing communications technologies to be linked directly to changing technologies of the self, the question of how the online diary in particular might facilitate and enable acts of testimony is an important one. Advancing claims to truthfulness in a medium with a facility for role-playing and identity tourism is problematic, and Pax is dogged by readers' suspicions about his veracity and authenticity.[10] However, the online diary has features uniquely designed to facilitate the kind of ideological work of cross-cultural engagement and eyewitnessing that is performed through this weblog. Prior to March 2003, in particular, *Where Is Raed?* fairly bristles with links to other media and text. Narrating a lead up to invasion, measuring the gradual accumulation of evidence, Pax establishes his authority and legitimacy by networking in real time, by making connections of all kinds to other documents circulating in the public domain and independently verifiable. These links can be made in a spirit of irony, humor, or trepidation, but the effect is a consistent and rigorous verification of what Pax sees around and about him in Baghdad and how he interprets what this means. By the time the invasion comes, Pax has form, a reputation, and the links, in volume 2 of the weblog, begin to run the other way. Online cross-references to *Where Is Raed?* become a measure of integrity and engagement among the American intelligentsia; the author William Gibson acknowledges the blog and Pax sucks in the energy: "Do you have any idea what it feels like when GOD says he's a fan. Dear sir: I think I can recite the sprawl trilogy by heart, I am a believer" (July 30, 2003).[11] At this point, *Where Is Raed?* is the epicenter of a vast, dispersed virtual community, and Pax has perfected a space for a Brechtian performance just in time for the main event. Against the odds he has embedded his community of (mainly Western) virtual visitors outside the Humvee and into the domestic space of "Hotel Pax" along with his family, before shock and awe starts.[12] Salam Pax is using new media to imagine, project, and perhaps to preserve a local and domestic occupation of Baghdad even as it falls in chaos to a foreign occupation.

The question inevitably arises as to whether the entry of this new media into postcolonial landscapes is the much-awaited moment when the subaltern speaks.[13] A more appropriate question may be how the language Pax devises for himself, Arablish, is shaped as a register that can penetrate and counter the processes of Occidentalism, that constant invention of the Western subject in and relation to others. How is Arablish designed as a register to be heard by public intellectuals in the West? How can an Iraqi presence penetrate Euro-American public spheres to shape opinion? How can Pax colonize the imagination of others? We need to keep in mind that when Pax is finally outed as "real" by Peter Maass he is in the lobby of the Sheraton Hotel in Baghdad reading a Philip Dick novel; Pax has a knack for becoming memorable and capturing the imagination through his relationship to the West in this way. *Where Is Raed?* is both hypertextual (filled with hot links to other digital text) and intertextual (replete with references to American and European books, music, and sitcoms that Pax consumes with pleasure). As a performance, the role and characterization of Pax are carefully devised, and the self-representation as a voracious consumer of Euro-American cultures, in both popular and elite manifestations, is an important component of the autobiographical characterization. We know just enough about Pax's tastes and preferences for this avatar to be recognizable and feasible as a secular cosmopolitan intellectual. This modern language of cosmopolitanism is the necessary register for any kind of effective insurgent response to the discursive colonization of Baghdad from the West. Pax can speak to us and be heard, because Salman Rushdie, Dharma and Greg, Philip Dick, and Coldplay are in his repertoire. In *Where Is Raed?* "massive attack" means both cruise missiles and a contemporary music band.[14]

Working from Amanda Anderson's definition of cosmopolitanism, Robert Dixon stresses that cosmopolitanism is a "characterological achievement," a form of strategic self-fashioning or self-performance that can be mobilized as a provincial response to the metropolitan, and a way of overcoming the supposed belatedness or supplementarity of provincial cultures (2004, 122–23).[15] In Pax's weblog cosmopolitanism becomes a tactical attempt to alter the lines of sight that target Baghdad, and a device that can be used to suggest that Iraqi people might be just like us: bodies that count! This works—see, for example, Ian Katz's affirmation in his introduction to the print version of Pax's weblog, *The Baghdad Blog:* "[Pax] was just like us. By now we had got used to a portrayal of Iraqis as poor, anti-Western, frequently hysterical and altogether very different from us; here was one who addressed using perfect idiomatic English, was obsessed with David Bowie lyrics and awaited the release of the new Massive Attack album as eagerly as any Glastonbury regular" (ix). Katz misreads Pax; this is not perfect idiomatic English, it is Arablish and it is a language of mimicry. In this register, an obsession with David Bowie becomes tactical, a rhetorical ploy, and one of the ways an Iraqi blogger characterizes himself as "human" for a literate Western readership, thereby making it harder for the addressee to "spy" with comfort and ease. The idea of self-performance is useful for understanding Pax as a virtual creature, and it grasps some of the conditional and precarious qualities of his enterprise, the reaching out for something located between "the claims of the past and the needs of the present" (Bhabha 1994, 219).

Just a month before he signs off, Salam Pax adopts a new screen saver, which says: "Re-examine every thought and concept you have." First among these are hopes for the political entity and civil society that needs to be built in Iraq, and it follows that "what it means to be [Iraqi] has to change" (February 7, 2003). The presence of Raed Jarrar, a Palestinian resident in Iraq, is important in the tentative exploration of what "Iraqi" might mean, for he is Pax's interlocutor on these matters: "I have spent half my life out of this country and had to be taught how to re-grow my roots by someone who isn't even Iraqi by nationality, he just loves the place (thank you Raed)" (October 10, 2002). "Pax" recoils from the notion of identity as it is conventionally understood, as a cultural attribute that can render experience coherent and structure a self-consciousness, and so this avatar is not in a process of "re-growing roots" in any singular or organic way. He is not an Iraqi nationalist, for example, and stands aside from tainted colonial forms of identity politics. As Anderson's definition of "cosmopolitanism" suggests, multiple forms of affiliation, reaffiliation, and disaffiliation coexist, and the medium of the weblog lends itself to this:

I wish there was another Iraqi blogger. I have done a sort of mental exercise on how that weblog would be. . . . To start with it would be in Arabic, and discuss very little politics as possible, if cornered it would be very pro-Palestinian and pro-Saddam. Just to stay on the safe side. It would also be filled with quotations from the Quran and Hadith, or maybe Um-Kalthum songs. What I am trying to say is that most "western" readers wouldn't get it because it would be so far out of their cultural sphere. The mess I am in really bothers me; with all my talk of anti-Americanism. . . . I still reference their culture, their music, and their movies. . . . I feel like the embodiment of cultural betrayal. The total sell-out, and this is making me contradict myself all the time. . . . OK that's enough. This is as confessional as it gets. (December 21, 2002)

The dissociated and unstable incarnation of the subject as an avatar in the online diary is very different to the analogue autobiographical author and to stable and consistent identifications in terms of belief, gender, or sexuality more generally. In that sense Pax is an embodiment of cultural betrayal. How does Pax use this tactically? Clearly the weblog is well-suited to a performance that destabilizes the terms of the oppositions that currently struggle to define the Iraqi subject. Pax may well wish there was an "Iraqi" blogger who performs a stable pro-Islamic Baathist orthodoxy, but he has no desire to *be* that blogger. The copresence of Western and Arabic cultures, tastes, and spaces in Pax's repertoire queers them all, and it means that Pax can generate a language of extraordinary hybridity to engage with interlocutors of all persuasions. His purpose is to generate links, to occupy the space of the infidel and "oh did I mention that I am a pervert as well?" (October 29, 2002).

Linguas polutas

Arablish is the language of this autobiographical avatar, a language devised to effect a careful engineering of the self in the virtual spaces of a webdiary. This specific choreography of time, space, and body is essential to the complex characterization of Salam Pax as an ideological "I." We can begin by characterizing Arablish as a *linguas polutas*—like Spanglish and Franglais it is a language of resistance to English as the unquestioned lingua franca of the Internet. Practitioners of *linguas polutas* on the net set out to use Englishes to "color" virtual space and "infect" its lingua franca with a varied repertoire of mythologies, poetics, beliefs, embodiments, and histories (Gómez-Peña 2002, 282). Arablish momentarily stops the rapid and seamless process of reading that English speakers take for granted on the net. Most obviously this occurs when Pax engages in Arablish language play and openly draws attention to an Iraqi coterie: "It sounds better in Arabic because it rhymes: tamra9* tatwa8af tin3idim. Cheers" (December 17, 2002). Sometimes an Arablish effect is more dramatic: a hypertext link from Pax draws up a screen of Arabic script, which is a sharp reminder that English dominates but does not own the net, and there are places this lingua franca can't penetrate. By and large, Pax is a careful shepherd in devising hypertextual and intertextual links that place his webdiary in relation to other texts, and this is necessarily so. He infects monolingual English readers (his primary addressees in the public sphere) with Iraqi perspectives in a spirit of dialogue, and so the register of Arablish must be carefully managed and gauged for precise rhetorical effect. For all his dissembling, colloquial-isms, and uncertainties, the cherubic Pax flies on carefully targeted and precisely engineered trajectories in virtual space.

But this is too simple. It is not enough to think of the language of this webdiary only in terms of a hybrid of ethnic or national languages, for Pax's Arablish is also a generational language that queers English into Englishes along other lines of fracture. For example, reading *Where Is Raed?* can be a struggle if the transnational cultures and networks of trip-hop music or the geek-speak of programmers is unfamiliar. Part of the cosmopolitanism of Pax is his pleasure in language effects such as palindrome (Dear Raed) and synesthesia, his play with classical terms such as "hubris" and "Pax," his familiarity with popular culture, and his capacity to see some fundamental similarities between Christian and Muslim beliefs. Equally essential to the Arablish of *Where Is Raed?* is its medium: the vicissitudes of servers, the intricacies of blog software, and exchanges between bizarre avatars and domain names: Pandavox, Insta-pundit, and Riverbend, for example. In this way, technology becomes part of rhetorical technique in *Where Is Raed?* A webdiary does not tran-scend the terms and conditions of its production, and in fact it reflects back on them constantly and sometimes obsessively; Pax does not blur the medium of his message, he revels in it: "Bigger, better, faster. So stop harassing me about the font size" (March 5, 2003). I am pushing "Ara-blish" here to reach toward an adequate sense of how the language and rhetorical effect and the transformations of writing in an online diary work in *Where Is Raed?* Pax deploys these effects to shape a particular and spectacular medium for cross-cultural communication and an un-precedented venue for testimony.

Weblogs and more user-friendly blog software mediate access of pri-vate lives to the public sphere differently to print technologies. Although the Internet in general and blog software in particular privileges the flow of online life material generated in English and from the USA, never-theless it does engineer a situation where others—like Pax—can jostle for virtual space. The interactive loops and circuits of weblogs are styled in the absence of some traditional commercial and political gatekeep-ers of testimony: editors and publishers, the benevolent advocates and sponsors of subaltern narrative, although Pax does have to record a debt to "the people at Blogger." At this different interface a direct and some-times bracing interaction and engagement with readers—a key rhetori-cal feature of online life writing—takes on the work of mediation, and the process of testing and questioning authenticity and truth becomes more open and explicit, especially as skeptical and, occasionally, openly hostile readers engage. As Madeleine Sorapure suggests, in online journals "writing" is redefined to include images, navigation choices, and site structure (2003, 8). In fact, the database model of identity with its non-narrative discrete pieces of information coded and stored is remarkably similar to what Rebecca Hogan identifies as the parataxis of the print diary form (1991). And yet the various technologies, print and online, that provide the autobiographical versions of Salam Pax, are a fine example of how online lives do represent a radical ontological departure for testimony. The book version of extracts from *Where Is Raed?* (published in 2003 as *The Baghdad Blog*) is scarcely recognizable as the same text. Although the publishers do their best to use typographic signs to suggest the effects of the online text, the book is at best a cold cut of the original. Of course, blogs by definition cannot be reduced to hard copy, for they are infinite, immersed in endless narrative loops and linkages that come to life in the process of active reading in real time. Without the hot links and images, which are markers of its location in an ocean of virtual text, *The Baghdad Blog* is a flawed translation. Quite simply, it is no longer Arablish.

Critics have begun to speculate that reading digital texts may require new styles of critical practice for, after all, the space/time configurations of online diaries reconfigure the acts of reading and of writing. In what remains the only extended discussion of online diaries to date, the pioneering critic of autobiography Phillipe Lejeune devises a new method to work with these interactive, forking, hybrid texts that reconfigure representations of the self.[16] In his book *Cher écran* (2000), Lejeune emphasizes the transformative possibilities of the almost simultaneous act of diary writing online and the act of reading, which adds a new interactive component to the production and reception of diary. This privileges the moment the material is created and exchanged, and it initiates the extraordinary intimacy that is characteristic of the weblog, as Andreas Kitzmann suggests (2003). Lejeune alters how he works with diary in *Cher écran*, using a daily anthology to map his reading across various blogs, a practice of horizontal reading that is facilitated by this technology. By reading across a series of online journals for a specific period of time, Lejeune's critical practice recognizes the impulse to read this genre synchronically, being faithful not to any single diary in a diachronic and lineal pattern of reading and interpretation but, rather, pursuing the pleasures of browsing across various diaries in real time.

This synchronicity means some extraordinary things for the practice of testimony in particular; for example, it fundamentally alters the relations between the conditions of reception and the authority of the author. The risks are self-evident too: going to an entry in a different diary, or going elsewhere via the links Pax embeds in his own journal, is as easy as going to the next entry in the same diary. As Lejeune recognizes, webdiaries do not invite immersion in the individual life. Rather, they produce a concatenation across various lives captured at a moment in time. Any ideological project generated through online journals necessarily must seize synchronicity as a precondition and an opportunity, it must use the distinctively online reading practices of "surfing" and "browsing." Webdiaries can collectively "shudder" in horror; look, for example, across the series of Iraqi blogs in June 2004 for the ripples set in motion by Abu Ghraib or the killing of hostages in the months that follow. This collective dismay, anger, and horror that percolates through disparate online diaries is a more eloquent response than any single online diary can record, and it is a mark of the extraordinary synchronicity of the genre. *Where Is Raed?* captured this seismic effect that online diaries record so well and orchestrated it into a collective cross-cultural register.

Raeding

Testimony is intimately concerned with personal effects, with "attempts to make lives and deaths matter" (Franklin and Lyons 2004, ix). The synchronicities that are distinctive features of the online diary—real time engagement, the access to a private life captured in the process of writing, the hot links to other sites—offer new horizons for testimonial engagements. In *Where Is Raed?* synchronicity generates the affective force of some memorable entries:

The images we saw on TV last might (not Iraqi, jazeera-BBC-Arabiya) were terrible. The whole city looked as if it were on fire. The only thing I could think of was "why does this have to happen to Baghdad." As one of the buildings I really love went up in a huge explosion I was close to tears. Today my father and brother went out to see what was happening in the city. . . .
   We start counting the hours from the moment one of the news channels report that the B52s have left their airfield. (March 24, 2003)

These examples suggest how online witnessing produces enhanced yet recognizable testimonial effects: Pax is embedding a civilian presence into a war zone and eliciting empathic engagement across the lines of fire. The domesticity and "real time" of this presence is affective, and a deliberate supplement to the "coverage" of Baghdad in the Western media: "Powell speech is around 6pm in Baghdad, the whole family is getting together for tea and dates-pastry to watch the (Powell Rocks the UN) show. Not on Iraqi TV of course, we have decided to put up the satellite dish to watch it. . . . A quick run through what is going on in Baghdad before uncles and aunts flood the house" (February 5, 2003)

Fundamental to the work of *Where Is Raed?* is an intellectual and political project driven by this ideological "I" who uses synchronicity to raid and relocate, appropriate, and resignify digital texts of all kinds. Pax is not vulnerable to the "browser" mode of online reading then, he *uses* it tactically, as a raider (or perhaps a raeder!) himself. So, for example, at a posting in December 2002 he is a skeptical reader of the "Guiding Principles for U.S Post-Conflict Policy in Iraq" report published by the Council on Foreign Relations (CFR). He links to the report, and to the website of the CFR, and, ever mindful of the transient attention span of his online reader, he focuses attention:

If you don't feel like reading the whole report just take a look at the last 3 pages, "the three phased approach" the paper suggests is outlined in a chart. there is another interesting article on that site: ["Reconstruction: A Checklist for Would-be Nation-Builders in Baghdad after the Fall of Saddam"]

It is the gist of that 35 pages paper. Some of it sounds like the list my mother would have given my baby-sitter.

Go slow, but steady, on democracy.

Strengthen Ties that Bind.

Mind the neighbours. (December 28, 2002)

Pax similarly "raeds" the wording of the Iraq resolution in November 2002, splicing together in a single posting links to the *New York Times,* the British *Independent,* local Iraqi media, various other personal blogs, and Reuter with sharply satirical remarks (November 9, 2002). In the course of Pax's blogs readers are linked to Middle East maps online, websites promoting Arab soap operas, advertisements in mail order catalogs, Islamic blogs and information about the Qu'ran, and any newspaper article or official and bureaucratic document that catches his eye, taken there by Pax with satirical, political, or sometimes aesthetic intent (eye candy!). In these ways Salam Pax uses the liquidity of digital text to associate and incorporate resources of all kinds into his performance—a digital circus orchestrated, imported, and edited on his polemical terms. *Where Is Raed?* is not depleted by coexisting online text, it is incorporated by Pax, who is a master trader in an economy of sharing, the currency of exchange in the online community.

This is a reminder that testimony is "foremostly a profoundly political act, rather than primarily one of self-expression and self-making" (Franklin and Lyons 2004, ix), and from this it follows that weblogs are logically a potentially rich resource for the politics of testimony, and one that alters the processes of authorization and recognition that have been established in print media. *Where Is Raed?* can be read diachronically, following the life of entries in the wake of a flickering and mobile presence called Pax. But the momentum of the weblog is synchronic and dialogic—as Lejeune recognizes: a process of engagement in real time. As testimony goes digital, it travels differently and acts differently. It is self-evident that we are not in the presence of a posthistorical or apolitical process or the posthuman subject here. A problem in debates about cultural production, identity, and new media has been the absence of worked examples of how digital text and avatars can be used tactically. Thinking in terms of rigid oppositions between real and virtual domains means that discussions of how political work might get done in and through online life narrative remain limited. Salam Pax is held in high regard and affection as we know; it detracts from this not at all to suggest that his virtual presence is mercurial, quite deliberately and cherubically so, and all the more powerful for this. If we think of Pax instrumentally, as a style of self-fashioning that uses the online diary to engender a politics of accord, we might then begin to understand this as an intervention in a distinctive political process and historical moment.

So what is the nature of this intervention? It is a process, a practice. Characteristically Pax spells out his views in debate with another blogger, the American Al Barger, who supports an invasion and writes an "Open Letter to an Iraqi citizen." Pax replies as a citizen of Iraq:

It's OK really.

I understand your point. But I also have the right to have a different opinion (well at least here on the Internet) and I can't just sit by and say, go on, bomb away. Because no matter what you say to me I will still see what is happening now . . . as the part of the USA's ongoing process to impose its control abroad . . . look at what the American government is doing through non-American eyes and you'll see a different picture. . . . This whole mideast/iraq/islam chaos is not bringing us any closer to peace. . . . I personally, although I am not religious and would not choose islam as a religion if I were forced to choose one, see myself as a person who belongs to a culture that is Islamic and Arabic and who is very happy with his "identity" (shut up

Raed, I mean it), the constant verbal bashing of arabs and muslims does make me uncomfortable. . . . Bush is defiantly not invited to my Chai party. But you can come along, bring a friend and we'll talk about war and peace. I'll even make dates-pastry, I'll surprise you they are better than they sound. (November 15, 2002)

This is one of a number of entries we can take as a manifesto. These are almost always about the process of dialogue and exchange, a practice of Pax's desire for democracy in Iraq: "Do support democracy in Iraq. But don't equate it with war" ("Rant," March 16, 2003). Pax's identity is provisional and shaped by crisis, and his method sets out to rehearse the practice of a democratic, secular Iraqi citizenship in the complete absence of the institutional structures of a democratic state. Given this, in a time of crisis and chaos, Pax uses new media—the only public space available for him to speak freely—to practice his ideological commitment to what might best be described as the process of deliberative democracy: an engaged struggle, an open and ongoing public discussion about justice, freedom, and human rights. In the midst of an invasion designed to "deliver" democracy to Iraq, Pax demonstrates just how illusory this is via, on the one hand, an ongoing critique of the imposition of liberty and equality by force from the West and, on the other, an open engagement with democratic process using new media as a forum that shapes a new and virtual public sphere. Democracy is an engagement and a process that must be homegrown. "We have to do the hard work ourselves, change has to come from within . . . when was the last time the Iraqi 'man-in-the-street' had the right to express an honest and free opinion about the government's policies? Answer: 1962 . . . I can only hope our American friends bring extra copies of 'Democracy for Dummies'" (October 20, 2002)

In this way Pax uses his online journal to engage in a practice of communicative ethics, an expression of moral respect that begins with a willingness to enter into an exchange with others and to take their perspectives openly into account. In her discussion of deliberative democracy Iris Marion Young suggests that this model emphasizes the creation of a public sphere in and through a process of public deliberation and speaking "across differences of culture, social position, and need, which are preserved in the process" (1997, 68). It is in this spirit that Pax orchestrates texts of all kinds, with links that are not only technological but also discursive, addressing (primarily) a literate first world to make an ongoing polemical, tactical intervention into debates about Iraq and the war on terror. The very nature of the Internet makes this intervention unwieldy and unresolved, but communicative ethics is about managing a process of interaction. For example, Pax engages with Pandavox, a New York blogger who supports the invasion—"awww Pandavox how I wish things were as clear cut as you put them in your fairytale" (September 21, 2002)—and the hyperlinks swerve out from *Where Is Raed?* to Pandavox's blog just as it is absorbed with the first anniversary of 9/11 in New York. It captures Pandavox in an extraordinary moment of self-absorption: "Everybody loves their own city, but the whole world hearts New York. And now everybody hearts New York more than ever" (September 11, 2002, www.pandavox.blogspot.com). Pax makes no remark on the consequences of "everybody hearts New York" for Baghdad, and this is a reminder of the asymmetrical and unresolved nature of the exchanges that are conducted through the diary. Because we access the Pandavox blog via *Where Is Raed?* our response to this may of course be infected by Pax's irony.[17] In a similar amicable spirit Salam initiates a "world premier Iraqi blog-fight: Roll up your sleeves Riverbend, let's talk about al-Hakim's death" (July 31, 2003) on their different interpretations of the assassination of Mohammed Baqir al-Hakim. Inclusiveness is important to Pax's method: "The first time I got an email from an American soldier here I wasn't sure how to react. These days I read a couple of US soldier blogs and a couple even send me emails every now and then. I was answering one of them from [Mr. Somewhere-in-the-north-of-Iraq] when I decided later to post it on the blog. So here it is" (February 12, 2004). Pax is a device then, a way of generating an ongoing process of deliberation, introducing his interlocutors and exchanging views in a way, which is, in and of itself, a practice of democratic engagement in the affairs of Iraq. As avatars, Pandavox and Pax alike are situated cyber-selves, they are not outside of history, but their copresence online in a discursive and rhetorical space can alter lines of sight and produce socially transformative effects. In a recent interview Salam Pax remarks that over thirty Iraqi blogs have proliferated since the occupation, and he regrets that many of these make a political statement by labeling at the top "whether you love the Americans or you're a Saddamist." *Where Is Raed?* occupied shades of gray in between, and this was its political statement and methodology: the pursuit of democracy as a process, as a sustained exploration of different positions of speech that remain asymmetrical and incommensurate, yet that can become interactive, given sufficient humor, respect, and compassion.

There's nothing inherently liberating or democratic about weblogs in particular or new media in general. The connections between "cyberdemocracy" and the progress to a civil society in Iraq can only be tenuous. Pax frets that the price of freedom for Iraq will be "Beirut-ification," a long period of chaos will be the price for learning "how we should live as a free country and respect each other" (August 21, 2003). This is the period he now charts in *Shut Up You Fat Whiner!* Salam Pax is a reminder that newness can come into the world in the struggle over representations and the conduct of war, and in the protocols of civil society and the conduct of relations among its subjects.[18] The Internet can be a public sphere where groundbreaking work that might empower individuals in new and more democratic ways can occur. What remains of *Where Is Raed?* is, even now, an amazing autobiographical performance and political intervention, and we must recognize him: "He opened up more eyes than my own . . . you are amazing . . . be safe Salam."

TWO

The Skin of the Burka: Recent Life Narratives from Afghanistan

More than a rational calculation of interests takes us to war. People go to war because of how they *see, perceive, picture, imagine and speak of* others: that is, how they construct the difference of others as well as the sameness of themselves through representation.

JAMES DER DERIAN, QUOTED IN GREGORY, *THE COLONIAL PRESENT*

In Transit

How can we read the image of the burka on the cover of *My Forbidden Face?* In November 2003 in the Newslink bookstore at the Melbourne airport a massed presentation—called a "block display" in the book trade—pushed books of a kind before the customer. In fact there were only three different books on display—*My Forbidden Face* by "Latifa," Jean Sasson's *Mayada: Daughter of Iraq,* and Azar Nafisi's *Reading "Lolita" in Tehran: A Memoir in Books.* Arranged en masse, canny marketing threw into sharp relief the icon that presents these as books "of a kind." Stretched across the back wall of the bookstore were multiple images of veiled Muslim women—the totally effaced woman in the burka on the purple cover of *My Forbidden Face* (fig. 1), the more erotic sexualized gaze over the chador on the glossy black cover of *Mayada: Daughter of Iraq,* and the dark monotone of the young veiled women in chador on the sepia cover of *Reading "Lolita" in*

LATIFA
UN INTERNATIONAL WOMAN OF THE YEAR 2002

MY FORBIDDEN FACE

GROWING UP UNDER THE TALIBAN:
A YOUNG WOMAN'S STORY

1   Front cover design from Latifa's *My Forbidden Face*

Tehran. Different modalities of life narrative are gathered here: the auto-ethnography by Latifa, the veiled bestseller by Sasson, and the academic memoir by Nafisi. That exotic display of dozens of copies of Muslim life narrative together, and all published in 2002–3, is haunting. How can the reader resist interpellation as a liberal Western consumer who desires to liberate and recognize Latifa by lifting the burka and bringing her alongside us, barefaced in the West? Is there a more nuanced language that makes the veil a vehicle for a reflective and ethical practice of cross-cultural engagement? The production and carefully targeted marketing of "veiled" life narratives in the West raise intractable problems about the practice of communicative ethics between women. To reach across cultures in sight of the veil requires a strategy that recognizes and attends to difference and that resists the ethnocentrism that is so powerfully and strategically evoked by the mass marketing of these images of absolute difference in times of resurgent fundamentalisms.

Through Latifa, the pseudonymous autobiographical narrator of *My Forbidden Face,* the reader can vicariously assume the burka:

I look at this garment, its woven cloth flowing all the way down to the ground from a loosely fitting bonnet which completely covers the head. . . . But what really frightens me is the little bit of embroidered latticework around the eyes and the nose. . . .

I can feel the rustle of my own breath inside the garment. I'm hot. My feet get tangled up in the material. I'll never be able to wear this. I now understand the stiff robot-like walk of the "bottle women," their unflinching look directly in front of them. . . . These phantoms that now roam the streets of Kabul have a terrible time avoiding bicycles, buses and carts. It's even worse trying to run away from the Taliban. This is not a garment. It's a moving prison. (40–41)

Afghan women's life narratives rarely offer this kind of subjective and emotional response. For this reason *My Forbidden Face* is one the most popular of these life narratives from Afghanistan.[1] To pull Western eyes under the burka is a powerful rhetorical strategy; it elicits both sympathy and advocacy that can be put to quite different political and strategic uses. Like other narrators—"Zoya," "Sulima," "Hala"—Latifa's life story is shaped by a series of invasions and conquests in Afghanistan since 1973, when the overthrow of the monarchy began a series of coup d'etat, foreign interventions, and civil wars among mujahideen that culminated in the vicious Taliban regime that was displaced by Allied and American military attacks on Afghanistan in October 2001. The effects of all this is translated for Western readers with difficulty, and these women carry the burden of speaking for so many, as Latifa suggests: "I hope [this] will serve as a key for other women, those whose speech has been padlocked and who have buried their testimony in their hearts or their memories" (np). As a sixteen-year-old girl, Latifa has never known a time other than civil war, and *My Forbidden Face* begins graphically with the terrible events in Kabul on September 27, 1996, that initiated a new phase of terror when the Taliban took the city and hanged President Najibullah in full view: "The spectacle is humiliating and so frightening that . . . I'm both disgusted and afraid. So is my sister. But neither of us can stop staring" (11). For the next five years, Latifa is reduced to a "phantom," unable to move freely around the public spaces of Kabul due to what she calls the "stunning sexual racism" of the Sharia Law imposed by the Taliban.

A surge of life writing about women under the repressive fundamentalist regimes in Afghanistan uses this dark and confined space of the burka to suggest the discipline of views imposed by the gender apartheid of the Taliban. From these recesses of the burka we can attend to experiences of loss, grief, and dispossession that until the very recent past were unheard and unseen in the West. The burka becomes an icon that covers this life writing at every turn, a trope that shapes its metaphorical repertoire and that it, in turn, embraces—sometimes unexpectedly. How can feminists in the West understand the veil, catch its meanings, and use it to fabricate more subtle and perceptive cross-cultural communication? No one can read the veil from a neutral space, so how then can we read the stories of these women who speak through the burka? Equally important, can the burka be used to look back at "the West" otherwise, to grasp its implications in the dynamics of Western ethnocentrism here and now?

In her history of the veil (a term she objects to because of its associations with Orientalist imagery) Fadwa El Guindi describes veiling as a rich and nuanced phenomenon, a language that communicates social and cultural messages in Christian and Muslim traditions, for men and for women (1999, xii). However, given that the veil is frequently adopted in the West as the sign of Islamic women's oppression and subordination, this more nuanced language resists translation into cross-cultural dialogues. Can the circulation of these veiled autoethnographies from Afghanistan initiate a process of transculturation? Mary Louise Pratt defines autoethnography with political intent: she uses this term for autobiographical narratives where colonized subjects undertake to represent themselves in ways that engage with the colonizer's own terms. Autoethnographic texts are those testimonies constructed in response to, or in dialogue with, metropolitan representations, and in this way indigenous or oppressed subjects may both collaborate with and appropriate a dominant culture's discursive models (Pratt 1992, 7). This suggests that, despite radically uneven power relations, the production and reception of autoethnography draws attention to interactions between differently located subjects and subjectivities in a way that has the power to unsettle metropolitan expectations.

What do we "buy into" with this kind of cultural exchange through Afghan life narratives? Why is the burka in particular a haunting sight? The deeply embedded interpretive frameworks of Orientalism, exoticism, and neoprimitivism that produce the East for Euro-American consumption have hardened in ideological support of the war on terror: these narratives are marketed in association with campaigns to "liberate" Afghanistan from the Taliban. There can be no mistake, they are deployed as propaganda to represent and justify a military intervention in the name of (among other things) the liberation of women oppressed by Islamic fundamentalism. But this is not the sum total of what these narratives do in their circulation as lucrative commodities. Tracking the various politics of performance and representation that occur in and through autoethnography has never been more important than now. When we enter bookstores and find life narratives cloaked in the burka arranged for our consumption (and pleasure) we need to pay sharp attention to how these are produced, promoted and marketed in the name of benevolent citizens of modern "first" worlds.

Occasions of estrangement and recognition of "Western eyes" in consumer culture, such as that moment in Melbourne, can be critically productive. They raise ethical issues that require imaginative and emotional resolutions. In her classic essay "Under Western Eyes," first published in 1984 and revised in 2003, Chandra Talpade Mohanty talks about the ongoing production of the monolithic, singular subject of the "Third World woman" for Western consumption.[2] Outside history and unchanging, this woman remains a passive and powerless subject, unable to represent herself. The image of the veiled woman in particular is a powerful trope of the passive "third world" subject, and it sustains the discursive self-presentation of Western women as a secular, liberated, and individual agents. In her more recent essay on third world women and the politics of feminism, Mohanty reminds us there is nothing natural or inevitable about the appearance of commodities such as these Afghan life narratives en masse: "The mere proliferation of Third World women's texts, in the West at least, owes as much to the relations of the marketplace as to the conviction to 'testify' or 'bear witness.' . . . The existence of Third World women's narratives in itself is not evidence of decentering hegemonic histories and subjectivities. It is the way in which they are read, understood, located institutionally that is of paramount importance" (Mohanty 2003, 77). Can we read these narratives as autoethnographies that suggest ways to understand the burka otherwise, attending to not only the various cultural meanings the burka carries for the women who wear it but also to the "very idioms of agency that are relevant for such women" (Butler 2004, 47)?

Afghan feminist activists use the burka strategically. Quite literally so—messages, weapons, and banned publications were transported beneath its folds during the Taliban regime. Activists in Afghanistan were quick to adopt the burka as a shroud of anonymity and disguise. For these reasons, the burka is a complex symbol. It is a reminder of an oppressive regime, but it is also an icon of brave and successful resistance. Many Afghan women will choose to sustain the burka as a powerful symbol of nationalist and feminist resistance, and many feminist activists will question the uses to which the figure of the burka-clad woman is put to in the West. Images of Afghanistan during the Taliban years are rare, almost all of them—including the film footage of the shooting of Zarmeena in the Kabul soccer stadium in 1999, which has been shown many times in the West since September 11—were bravely filmed with cameras hidden beneath burkas. They were smuggled out of the country that way too. Copyrights on most of the images of Taliban atrocities belong to the Revolutionary Association of the Women of Afghanistan (RAWA), a feminist collective, which distributes these images to international media organizations. The association also markets mugs and mouse mats, posters, and calendars from the website they established in 1997, www.rawa.org. The power of RAWA to participate in the exchange of images of Afghan women in their interests is an important issue, and the organization has exerted an extraordinary influence on the emergence of recent life narratives by Afghan women, who must speak on behalf of many. This production and circulation of alternative images as commodities funds local strategies of feminist resistance to Islamic fundamentalism, such as literacy programs and RAWA schools and hospitals in Afghanistan and the refugee communities in Pakistan.

Leila Ahmed (1992) suggests we might usefully think in terms of a discourse of the veil to capture its radically different significations in place and time, such as these simultaneous and yet contradictory representations of the burka. The veil is never just an item of clothing; it is, in Ahmed's phrase, a signifier, which is "pregnant with meaning" (166). Debates about the veil are integral to negotiations about sexual, political, economic, and cultural boundaries in Islamic societies. Struggles about the veil involve challenges to thresholds of authority (Mernissi 1987, xvii) within and between Islamic communities and in the larger global confrontations between Islamic and non-Islamic cultures and societies. The veil, then, is a shifting signifier, open to various and strategic uses and frequently invoked as an intractable symbol of cultural difference. It is no surprise that the war on terror is associated both with renewed polemic about veiling and the oppression of women by Islam and with a revival of the veil as a symbol of resistance. Daphne Grace points out that since 9/11 the veil has taken on hitherto undreamed of political and religious significance as a corroboration of the righteousness of the Western alliance campaigns in Afghanistan and Iraq (2004, 19). In 2003, then, the appearance of the burka on the covers of a series of Afghan life narratives is part of a campaign that condenses and simplifies a conflict of extraordinary complexity into a single whole cloth.[3]

The Electronic Marketplace

Amazon.com confirms that there has been a rush of Afghan life narratives onto the market since 2002. Amazon's browser is helpful, threading together a series of texts with consummate soft sell: "Better Together is *My Forbidden Face* and *Price of Honour: Muslim Women Lift the Veil of Silence on the Islamic World,* Buy Both Now"; "Customers who bought titles by Sunita Mehta also bought titles by Sulima and Hala, Anne E. Brodsky and John Follain"; "if you liked *My Forbidden Face* you will want to own *Voices behind the Veil,*" and, with the precision of technology-driven and mindless cataloging: "Customers interested in *Women for Afghan Women* may also be interested in *Perfect Senior Fitness.*"[4] This is a marketplace after all; you stumble across the unexpected—although sometimes these rogue traces prove to be useful. As you mouse around the site more than a dozen titles cohere—some autobiography, some biography, and others hybrid versions of both. Sometimes you mouse over an edge into another domain, or do you? For example there are links from *Zoya's Story* to MuslimMatrimonialsNetwork.com (a photo gallery to meet Muslim singles) and FindMyMilitaryBuddy.com (a site where investigators will help you locate a U.S. military pal). More startling is a browser-induced link to Croutier's book *Harem: The World behind the Veil*. A naked woman is on the cover, and the foreground is all creamy flesh and bare buttocks. This is Ingres's painting *La grande odalisque* (1814), a classic of Orientalist art, which shows a concubine in a Turkish sultan's harem. Reclining amid silk sheets and peacock feathers, the concubine looks over her shoulder into the eyes of the viewer; the pelvis in the foreground is unnaturally elongated, which accentuates her role as a sex object for the sultan's pleasure, and the viewer is positioned as his surrogate. This is an edge, and an image that confirms the paradigm: the promise that the veil can be pierced to reveal the compliant sexualized woman who is waiting, desiring, needing to be unveiled and taken. This is the classic colonial fantasy of the veiled female body becoming available to our gaze. The Orientalist iconography of the harem confirms the promise that shadows every cover where we see a veiled woman and are promised a lifting of the veil.[5]

Another fantasy of unveiling coexists with this erotic fantasy of the harem in the West. Its exoticism takes another form. In *Zoya's Story*, Zoya describes her trip to New York as a representative of RAWA and her appearance at a meeting in Madison Square Garden in February 2001. Here is the obverse of Latifa's description of veiling in *My Forbidden Face:*

When the time came for me to go on stage, after Oprah Winfrey had read [Eve Ensler's poem] "Under the Burqa," all the lights went off save for one that was aimed directly at me. I had been asked to wear my burqa, and the light streamed in through the mesh in front of my face and brought tears to my eyes. A group of singers was singing an American chant, a melody full of grief, and I was to walk as slowly as possible. . . . I had to climb some steps, but because of the burqa and the tears in my eyes, which wet the fabric and made it cling to my skin, I had to be helped up the stairs.

Slowly, very slowly, Oprah lifted the burqa off me and let it fall to the stage. (2002, 211)

Audiences who attend these functions in the West came to set much store by this symbolic unveiling of Muslim women in 2002, in this context understood as an act of liberation and benevolence. With the assistance of RAWA, Eve Ensler was smuggled into Afghanistan to see the condition of women for herself. These performances of stripping capture the burka as a symbol of the fundamentalism of the Taliban, and its brutal containment of Afghan women under a system of gender apartheid. When Allied troops entered Kabul in 2001, journalists gathered with the specific intent of broadcasting images of women abandoning their burkas. Like men shaving off their beards, for the international media these were apocalyptic symbols of the turn from archaic fundamentalism to modernity and a mark of liberation that justified the military intervention. But Afghans were reluctant to participate in these spectacles. Zoya is asked to wear the burka in this carefully staged event in New York, and she then becomes part of the spectacle of a public unveiling through consent.

The resonances of this are troubling, for this almost inevitably affirms the invocation of Mohanty's "Third World woman" *under* Western
eyes; in this scenario, she is awaiting liberation rather than being an
active agent in history. Furthermore, it is almost impossible to separate
this spectacle from other violent episodes of stripping.[6] Recently both
Angela McRobbie (2004) and Judith Butler (2004) have been compelled
to write by the sight of the generic "girl in the blue burka," expressing
their disquiet and ambivalence as Afghan women remove their veils for
the Western media, a sight that captures the impossibility and urgency
of imagining styles of cross-cultural engagement otherwise. Is Zoya one
of the "girls" that haunt McRobbie and Butler? Is this unveiling, with its
intricate implications of Ensler, Winfrey, and Zoya herself, the spectacle
that has initiated their recent discussions on the subject of the burka?
In *Precarious Life: The Power of Mourning and Violence,* the unveiling of
Afghan women as spectacle compels Butler to turn to Levinas to imagine a feminist politics that can address such intractable difference with
a sense of openness, a turning to the face of the other with the intent of
recognizing its humanity. Like Gayatri Spivak (1999), Butler questions
the adequacy of benevolence and empathy for a feminist politics of ethical engagement with Afghan women.

Massed displays of veiled women are a powerful and canny exercise
of book marketing when there is a desire and urgency in the West to
understand more about the Muslim societies, and it brings into view
a distinctive shift in the publishing of life narrative since 2001. Narratives from Afghanistan circulate in the war on terror as commodities
that become part of a debate about the politics of intervention and resistance. What does the flood of life narratives make available to the
metropolitan West: spaces for dialogue and exchange, or a reemergence
of the stereotypical and mythic East? Graham Huggan's discussion of
exoticism is useful here, for he stresses that objects, places, people are
not inherently "exotic" and "strange" but, rather, exoticism is a particular
way of "manufacturing otherness" (2001, 13). In this process objects are
taken as both strange and familiar at one and the same time. A process
of domestication occurs, which renders the object recognizable and familiar, and yet the aura of mystery is also sustained: "exoticism is a kind
of semiotic circuit that oscillates between the opposite poles of strangeness and familiarity" (13). Huggan turns to exoticism to interpret how
contemporary postcolonial texts in particular circulate as objects that
become desired commodities in the West because they offer imagined
access to the other through consumption.

Since 2001, the expanded market for representations of a monolithic, threatening, and spreading Islam shapes the terms and conditions that bring almost a dozen life writings about Afghanistan onto bookshelves in the West. The speed of this is extraordinary. Although we are accustomed to thinking of digital technologies and mass media in terms of speed and mobility, we are less familiar with the fact that the global publishing industry can produce and market hard-copy life narratives for popular consumption so fast in response to current affairs and popular taste. This tells us something about life narrative in its popular forms: it is porous, it is open to fashion, and it maneuvers in networks of power in complex ways. This is particularly true of subaltern testimony when "exotic" cultures are fashionable.

These narratives circulate in networks vulnerable to "soft power," the carefully coordinated management of information across a variety of contemporary media. This is propaganda, a strategic regulation and control of channels of communication and information. This control takes the forms of the dissemination of certain categories of information and produces the engineering of consent through the gentle persuasion of public opinion management (Robins and Webster 2001, 107). "Soft power," for example, allows an Afghan feminist activist access to an audience of thousands at Madison Square Garden where she speaks directly and powerfully about women's experiences and draws attention to the fact that the Taliban was nurtured and armed by the United States and allied governments in the very recent past. But prior to this speech, there is the extraordinary spectacle of the Afghan woman being assisted to the stage to be liberated from the burka, released into eloquence with the benediction of American celebrity Oprah Winfrey, to the tune of "American chants." This ceremony becomes a synecdoche for the liberation of Afghanistan itself, and it explains why at the Amazon.com site there are links from Afghan women's life narratives to FindMyMilitaryBuddy.com. This is surely what Inderpal Grewal (1996) and Arundhati Roy (2004) mean when they point out that feminist libratory narratives of movement from victimhood to freedom are not necessarily anti-imperialist.

Life narrative is of course one of the most seductive forms for the projection and naturalization of the exotic and an offering of authentic others. Those of us who read, teach, and perhaps write in autobiographical forms in the recent past need to be canny about the uses to which it has been put. Life writing has played a major role in the global commodification of cultural difference that has been a boom industry in the recent past. How are life narratives by unauthorized subjects circulated and used in the metropolitan centers of the West? My recoil at the block display of life narratives at the Melbourne Newslink bookstore was produced by a sharp sense of being interpellated as a consumer confronted by culturally othered goods. Alterity has been fashionable for some time in Euro-American commodity culture. If we are what we consume, buying life narratives from Afghanistan is a way of indicating cosmopolitan tastes, openness, sympathy, political commitment, and benevolent interest in cultural difference. The notion of "soft weapons" captures the double-edged nature of these forms of life narrative. They can be harnessed by forces of commercialization and consumerism in terms of the exotic appeal of cultural difference. They can also be used to buttress aggressive Western intervention in so-called primitive or dysfunctional national communities. And yet they can also be used to describe experiences of unbearable oppression and violence across a cultural divide. In the foreword to Brodsky's *With All Our Strength,* for example, RAWA takes the opportunity to say this collaboratively:

There was a time that no pen moved to write a poem or article that reflected the realities of Afghanistan. No filmmaker made a film that showed the true oppression of our people. No country's or government's conscience was awakened enough to do anything to change the situation in Afghanistan. After too many years of knowing about our tragedy, only September 11 forced some governments and institutions to take action, claiming at this late date that they did so because they cared about Afghanistan and the liberation of Afghan women. . . . The tragedy of our country has been reduced to the image of the Taliban and the burka and a narrow 5 year-period of our history. . . . And the image of the Afghan women, silent under their burka, does not tell the truth of our lives nor our resistance. (Brodsky 2003, ix)

These texts are valuable to different interests and concerns, and they both empower the dispossessed and consume them yet again in terms of familiar stereotypes. They also open spaces for Afghan women to contest these representations. The exchange between metropolitan and marginal cultures is always uneven and, as Graham Huggan points out, the West consumes exotic products in an economic climate in which colonialisms of the past are perhaps less significant than imperialisms of the present (2001, 16). This is precisely the point that the Afghan women make when given the space of Brodsky's foreword. However, if we understand processes of the production and reception of autoethnography as intersubjective, as Pratt suggests, then we can entertain the idea that subjects can lure readers into different engagements across cultures. Subaltern subjects, who claim and exercise autobiographical agency in unexpected ways, can draw down this power through autoethnography.

For example, neither Latifa nor Zoya regard the West in the way we might anticipate. While they need the support of Western women, they have no desire to be like them, and what Butler (2004) refers to as their "idioms of agency" are very different. These narratives offer few signs that Afghan women desire to become Westernized (although of course they seek the kind of access to education and health and welfare resources that are available in more affluent democratic communities). Rather, they speak as patriots and as members of an organized resistance dedicated to a dream of an independent and democratic sovereign nation. Zoya is scornful of those who turn away from the deserts and ruins of Afghanistan, and when a distant cousin offers her a new life in Canada she chooses to stay with her homeland: "I did not tell him that I thought his heart was as small as a bird" (108). She visits the metropolis as an activist, and consumer culture in the cities of Italy or the United States holds no allure. For Latifa, too, freedom is not understood in terms of a life in the West when it becomes available to her. She leaves Afghanistan as an ambassador, and gives testimony in France on behalf of other Afghan women, but her story ends in silence when she is unable to return to Kabul: "Azadi means freedom in our language. But who speaks Afghani? I no longer know" (175). These activists defend Afghan traditions and Islamic belief; what they have to say draws on a language of cultural identification in terms of nation, religion, and gender that is very different to the faiths of their liberal and feminist champions in Europe and the United States. Latifa and Zoya do not forget that when the vast majority of Afghan men and women leave home they lose their country and all forms of belonging to enter the limbo of the refugee. This silence is the subject of the next chapter; however, it is worth remarking here that the specter of the refugee haunts those Afghan women who pass into the West as celebrities and champions of freedom. This must be so, for they openly carry the burden of representing others who cannot speak, and the privileges of privacy and individualism are not part of their idioms of agency.

Shelf Life: Peritexts

These memoirs are powerful and contradictory things, then. We know this without taking them off the shelf. In his study of paratexts, Gerard Genette (1997) talks about the work that books do on the shelf, and he makes a useful distinction between the public and the reader as different addressees. The public is not the totality or the sum of readers. Sitting in Borders or Dillons with a skinny latte, watching a PowerPoint display of covers at a conference, or even just walking into the airport bookstore, you absorb these texts, and you participate in their dissemination and "reception." You are then an addressee, even though you may not become a reader. By focusing on texts as product, Genette draws attention to a series of features that become particularly important when we are looking at autoethnography: the cover, the title and subtitle, pseudonyms, the name and status of the author, forewords, dedications, epigraphs, prefaces, maps, endorsements, blurbs, and notes. These are peritexts, and they are consumed in the most casual acquaintance with the book—the glance, the flick through. Genette pauses on the threshold to absorb consciously all the liminal devices that mediate the relations between text and reader. This raises questions about when, how, and why a text has emerged, its mode of existence, the situation of its communication—its sender and addressee—and the functions it aims to fulfill.

The frontiers between the text and the reader of these life narratives from Afghanistan indicate complex mediations between the autobiographical subject, the publisher, the public, and the reader. As Philippe Lejeune suggests, given the way the fringe of the printed text controls its reception, it is a strategic attempt to produce a legitimate reading (quoted in Genette 1997, 2). Autoethnography is a particularly valuable commodity in the market economy, and its circulation in the public domain is always carefully managed. From this we can understand why these life narratives from Afghanistan are embedded in peritext: the endorsement of others. Many of them feature maps, which establish in broadbrush strokes the political geography of the Middle East, Iraq, Iran, and Afghanistan with a special emphasis on their location in relation to the United States. One cannot speak of "authors" of these autoethnographies, for they are stories told to and shepherded by advocates: *Zoya's Story* (the testimony of a RAWA activist written by the journalists John Follain and Rita Cristofari), Latifa's *My Forbidden Face* (written in collaboration with the activist and founder of Afghanistan Libre, Chékéba Hachemi), *Behind the Burqa* (the story of two sisters, "Salima" and "Hala" as told to Batya Swift Yasgur [2002], a freelance writer), and the biography of *Meena* (written by the American social justice activist, Melody Ermachild Chavis). Some of the life narratives are threaded together with institutional and organizational histories of the Revolutionary Association of the Women of Afghanistan in particular (Anne E. Brodsky's *With All Our Strength,* and Cheryl Benard's *Veiled Courage,* for example). *My Forbidden Face* has a particularly complex passage into the American market, as it has a prehistory as a magazine story in *Elle* and is told through a collaborator and then translated from the French by the well-known

Canadian feminist writer, Lisa Appignanesi. The covers of these narratives often feature endorsements: writers and celebrities including Alice Walker, Dan Rather, Katha Pollitt, and Arundhati Roy. Again these are names that have authority in the United States, a primary market. The role of Walker and Roy, like Winfrey's place in the Madison Square Garden event, indicates the particular role of women of color in legitimating these subaltern narratives in the North American market.

Characteristically the titles draw on the burka metonymically: *Veiled Courage, Unveiled, Veiled Threat, Behind the Burqa, Voices behind the Veil.* This indicates how powerfully and variously the veil functions in this market. Subtitles follow to anchor the title to the image on the cover: *Voices of Women in Afghanistan, The Hidden Power of the Women of Afghanistan, Inside the Afghan Women's Resistance, Muslim Women Lift the Veil of Silence on the Islamic World.* These texts are carefully positioned to project the gender apartheid imposed by Islamic fundamentalism toward a receptive market. The veil facilitates the trope of truth and authenticity revealed in life narratives such as these, tapping into a fantasy of the illicit penetration of the hidden and gendered spaces of "the Islamic World." The veil sharply defines the boundaries of public and private, for in fact it secludes the woman within an individualized gendered space in public. Peritexts promise a rupture of these boundaries.

Cover images repeatedly draw on saturated color, indigo and cobalt, to emphasize the burka as an icon. Ironically there is some historical verisimilitude here: book covers are public spaces, and Taliban orthodoxy imposed a gender apartheid that required women to wear the burka in public. On these covers the veiled women become ethnicized subjects. We have no idea who the figure on the cover is, and, besides, these pseudonyms are not birth names. Afghan women who testify are almost always disguised, one way or another. Even when the burka-clad figure is individualized there is no guarantee of authenticity to the individual subject and to a proper name, and this is strategically important. A number of the covers demonstrate how, to Western perspectives, the veil imposes uniformity; the covers of the Armstrong (2002), Goodwin (2003), and Benard (2002) books, for example, feature clusters of veiled women and suggest that when the photographer aims his camera at a veiled woman the visual field necessarily incorporates repetitions of the figure.

The isolation and enlargement of detail comes into play on a number of these book jackets. The camera often seeks the eye in close-up, a glimpse of the individual body part that draws the dehumanizing effect of the garment into sharp relief. In this there is the promise of distinguishing one veiled woman from another, and the suggestion that the woman in the burka can look back at the spectator, mute but eloquent, is a humanizing strategy. All of these covers draw on the genre of documentary photography, which frequently presents the powerless—the subject of the image—to the powerful—the consumer (Rose 2002, 16). Although some have argued that the burka discourages scopic desire—the voyeurism of the photographer—these haunting covers question that.

One cover in particular presents visual images that satisfy this desire to see Afghan women liberated from the burka in 2001: on the cover of Harriet Logan's *Unveiled* (2002) there is a monotone image of a woman's eye through the grill of the burka—the foreground brings into sharp relief the burka as a primitive thing, with its hand-stitched grill and its rough texture (fig. 2). Prior to the Taliban this was the garb associated with poor rural women. Through this mask, there is the glimmer of the eye and a small expanse of skin: the visual sign of a living body that will speak in this text; this is an image of Marina, Logan's interpreter, in 1997. The burka obliterates the expressive body. On the back of *Unveiled*, the image is reversed: the color of the burka now background, and the garment itself out of sight, the living body of a young Afghan girl revealed holding a doll. This is Sanam, photographed by Logan when she returned to Afghanstan immediately after the retreat of the Taliban from Kabul in 2001. We see a face and expression, and we see a figure familiar to the Western eye and without ethnicized markers of difference: she is just like us (although, as we have seen, Latifa, Zoya, and other Afghan activists frequently give testimony that refuses this gender-based sameness and speaks in terms of tradition, faith, and patriotism). Logan herself remarks that on the streets of Kabul women remained cautious and reluctant to shed the burka in public.

These images, the titles, and the subtitles are designed to grab the Western eye with a glimpse of absolute difference, of the exotic. This is a way of positioning them for metropolitan markets. But, as John Berger suggests, we never look just at one thing, we are always looking at the relation between things and ourselves (quoted in Rose 2002, 12). Another photojournalist, Mario Tama (n.d.), captures some of this in his photograph of a girl on the streets of Kabul in the heady days of 2001. This image, reproduced in his online portfolio, presents an elaborate staging that throws the exoticism of the genre of documentary photography into sharp relief. Here conventions are reversed: it is the Western eye of the viewer that is in an enclosed and framed interior space, looking out to the Afghan girl on the bright street. Artifice is signaled dramatically in this composition: by the intense red paper roses, which are magnified by the perspective of the lens, and the spectrum of color from red to

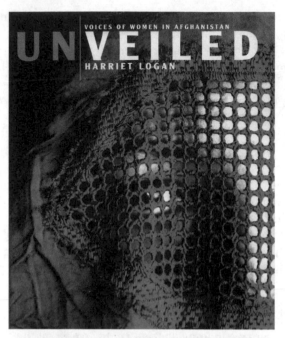

2 Front and back cover design from Harriet Logan, *Unveiled: Voices of Women in Afghanistan*

blue that unfolds serially across the image. This is no spontaneous and naive glimpse of the face of the Afghan girl, and in its carefully staged framework we are invited to see ourselves seeing the faces of Afghan women. This highly aesthetic image contrasts sharply with the remainder of Tama's portfolio of photographs from war-ravaged Kabul, and it draws attention to the scopic regime that organizes representations of Afghan women (a point I will return to in chapter 3):

> The American viewer was ready, as it were, to see the face, and it was to the camera, and for the camera, after all, that the face was finally bared, where it became, in a flash, a symbol of successfully exported American cultural progress. It became bared to us, in that moment, and we were, as it were, in possession of the face; not only did our cameras capture it, but we arranged for the face to capture our triumph, and act as the rationale for our violence, the incursion on sovereignty, the deaths of civilians. Where is loss in that face? And where is the suffering over war? Indeed, the photographed face seemed to conceal or displace the face in the Levinasian sense, since we saw and heard through that face no vocalization of grief or agony, no sense of the precariousness of life. (Butler 2004, 142)

Characteristically the covers of Afghan women's autoethnographies play on similarity and difference and on the threshold of what can be recognized as human, with the burka securely placed as a metonymic sign of the absolute Other, obscuring the promise of a familiar woman's body beneath. These signs work to secure a reading of the life narrative that follows. But how are these life narratives being consumed? Another dimension, which Genette establishes in his discussion of paratextuality, is useful at this point: "epitext." These are the messages located outside of the book that nevertheless signal its presence: media interviews, reviews, articles, readings, and private communications such as letters and diaries.

Epitext: The Eye Opener

We can return to the Amazon.com site for a particularly useful set of epitexts: the reviews posted by customers. This is of course to privilege a particular national, metropolitan, and technologically literate readership. Life narratives from Afghanistan are explicitly directed to U.S. citizens, often women in particular, as the addressee. Peritexts such as maps reinforce this presentation. So, too, do reminders that Jordan is about the size of South Carolina (Goodwin 2003, 250) or comparisons between shopping in the Emirates and Rodeo Drive. At the Amazon.com site the inclusion of publisher's blurbs and reviews, by editors and readers, gives some idea of how these texts are being both marketed and consumed in the United States and elsewhere. Those who choose to submit their responses to the site characteristically stress two things. First, their need for knowledge about Islam, the desire to reach beyond stereotypes by gaining access to the other, and to be able to think critically through independent reading. Second, the tendency of life narrative to produce a humanist and ethical response that stresses shared humanity over and above differences of culture and religion is repeated.[7]

Huggan's remarks (2001) on how the exotic is processed are useful here. It is not unusual for American readers to remark on similarity—between American and Afghan urban life as they perceive it in *My Forbidden Face*—and difference—such as the absence of interiority, which is the mark of the romantic individual subject they desire as readers of life narrative. They observe that, in their terms, they really do not get to know much about the subject of the life narrative here. This is true, and it is a point that allows us to begin to understand how Afghan women use the opportunities to speak on their own terms, which is to say how they negotiate with and against Western expectations of agency. Auto-ethnography is a mode of life narrative that historically situates the subject in a social environment, which incorporates the lives and actions of others and which is inclined to represent an "I" or subjectivity that is externalized and dialogical (Smith and Watson 2001a, 198). This is the kind of subjectivity that leaves readers wanting more—"more" being personal details and desires, a more complex sense of interiority and personal revelation, a continuous and multidimensional life narrative. The promise of hearing voices behind the veil, of piercing the burka, can be deceptive, in the way commercial branding generally is.

We can turn to another epitext at this point. The anthropologist Clifford Geertz (2003) has surveyed what he describes as an avalanche of books about Islam by historians, journalists, students of comparative religion, sociologists, anthropologists, and inspired amateurs. Interestingly there is no life narrative in Geertz's overview, and it follows, perhaps, there is no discussion of gender issues either. However, what Geertz says about this emerging literature is useful for understanding the particular place of life narrative in this context. He identifies four main approaches, or fields of argument and interpretation, in this coverage of Islam:

1. the civilization approach, which opposes "the West" as a whole to "Islam" as a whole and compares their fates;

2. the attempt to place Muslim thought in terms of a culturally familiar grid: bad/real/authentic/tolerant/terrorist varieties of Islam are
distinguished;
3. the conciliatory efforts to place Islam in relation to other major religious traditions in ways that minimize its difference and suggest
convergences;
4. the place or people- or nation-focused studies that conceive of Islam
less as a cohesive entity persisting through time than as a collection of
particular, disparate traditions coming into more and more immediate and difficult contact with one another and with the non-Muslim
world as the vast and entangling forces of globalization and modernity advance.

If we consider these approaches, it is evident that life narrative occupies a particular space. The notion of Islam as a civilization—imagined
as autonomous, continuous, and unchangeable—is not necessarily engendered in life narrative, which takes us into the swirl of particular and
conflicted incidents, places, traditions, neighborhoods, organizations,
lives, and relationships—in fact, exactly where Geertz argues we might
best find a surer path to understanding "Islam," "that resonant name of
so many things at once" (30). Life narrative can offer access to that class
of younger, semisecularized, and cosmopolitan Muslim intellectuals—
teachers, professionals, journalists, students, academics, activists—who
may use life narrative to explore and create new forms of Islamic identity, to argue for social justice and more democratic forms of social organization than are offered by their ruling elites. This thinking dismantles
a historical macro-entity that is erected in opposition to Christianity,
the West, and modernity and puts in its place a "disorderly field of en-
tangled differences" that are at once various and volatile.

To return to peritexts: there are several covers that deliberately present images of Afghan women as volatile subjects, rejecting the established iconography of nationality and the burka. Book jackets can suggest a different set of conventions and an alternative use of the veil as
an icon. These images and narratives emerge from RAWA, the collective
that has played such a vital role in the circulation of images of Taliban
atrocities. Chavis's biography *Meena,* an important book for RAWA and
the first biography of its founder, presents a photo portrait of a face; the
veil accentuates her beauty and expressiveness and signals her faith. This
cover draws on a different palette: no cobalt burka, no accentuated tones
for dramatic effect. Similarly, the cover of Brodsky's *With All Our Strength*
(fig. 3) and Sunita Mehta's edition of feminist essays, *Women for Afghan*

"A ringside view of RAWA, the extraordinary women's movement that is as doggedly committed to democracy as it is to dreaming of another, better world." —Arundhati Roy

WITH ALL OUR
STRENGTH

THE REVOLUTIONARY ASSOCIATION OF THE WOMEN OF AFGHANISTAN

Anne E. Brodsky

3 Front cover design from Anne E. Brodsky's *With All Our Strength: The Revolutionary Association of the Women of Afghanistan*

Women (2002), use documentary photographs that show groups of women, veiled and unveiled together. The subtitles and cover text of Mehta's book anchor the preferred reading of this image: "Throw away clichéd ideas of Afghan women as passive, silent victims cowering under their burqas." The blurb, like the foreword alluded to earlier, protests at the "stereotype of helpless women, forced by the Taliban into silence and submission." The spatial organization of these covers uses a different aesthetic: there are groups of women, but they are differentiated, active, and resistant. These are expressive ethnicized bodies, and veiling is part of this self-representation.

These images emerge from that organizational framework that manages the commodification of images of Afghan women strategically: RAWA. There are other ways in which the organization participates actively in the circulation of Afghan life narrative. For one, RAWA benefits financially from the marketing of images of Afghan women in the West, very directly so through its website. However, it engages in cultural politics to contest the consumption of these images as exotic or primitive. In fact, these habits of thought are called into question quite deliberately. We see this in numerous ways. To return to an earlier spectacle, one example of this resistance is the exchange Zoya makes at Madison Square Garden. Zoya attends as a representative of RAWA, invited by Eve Ensler, author of *The Vagina Monologues*. It is Ensler who has written a poem called "Under the Burqa," and it is she who asks Zoya to bring her burka to New York "because she wanted to use it for my speech" (Zoya 2002, 211). Zoya remarks that, remembering how she feels wearing a burka in Kabul, she wonders how anyone can find poetry in it: "A woman in a burqa is more like a live body locked in a coffin" (209). But she accepts the exchange, accommodating Ensler's fantasy (a "fanciful longing" in Young's terms [1997]) of what it is like to wear a burka and indulging Winfrey's role as liberator; in return Zoya is able to speak to 18,000 women to gather donations and to inspire them to help RAWA.

Similarly, RAWA sometimes posts at its website and in its brochures poems from women in North Carolina or Montana fantasizing how it feels to wear the burka. The organization accepts and uses these imaginative appropriations of the veil as part of what Cheryl Benard calls its "postmodern sense" of the effectiveness of emotion as an affective conduit for political communication (2002, 220). Benard's interpretation of RAWA as a postmodern political movement seems a jarring act of imaginative appropriation—after all, features such as the strong collective ethos of RAWA, its promotion of a charismatic leader, the recruitment of members through schools and charitable services, the international network of supporters, and the ability to maneuver skillfully in asymmetric conflict might equally well be related to modernity: these recall strategies of the socialist collectives in the USSR, for example. Mohanty argues that the preferred autobiographical subject of Anglo-American feminism is not reproduced in these kinds of testimonial narrative, which privilege the collective and set out to document and record a history of popular struggle and resistance: "Testimonials do not focus on the unfolding of a singular woman's consciousness (in the hegemonic tradition of European modernist autobiography); rather their strategy is to speak *from within* a collective, as participants in revolutionary struggles, and to speak with the express purpose of bringing about social and political change" (2003, 81). Resistance by RAWA to the cult of the individual adopts techniques contrary to liberal humanist notions of individual agency and the private self: the idealization of the role of the martyr for the cause—effected through Chavis's biography *Meena* (2003), for example, and the self-representation of women as activists in the community, as warriors rather than wives and mothers. Zoya, too, is a patriot above all: "I have never had a private life, and I have no regrets about this. I do not see anything beautiful in me that a man could look at in a special way. I have never dreamed of a man looking at me, nor have I fallen in love. . . . Only if one day there is peace in my country, and a democracy in which men respect women can I think of marriage" (2002, 131).

This style of resistance is anchored in specific and small day-to-day struggles and practices of women as a collective. As Mohanty (2004), Sommer (1998), and Anzaldúa (1987) suggest, these testimonials of subaltern women challenge liberal humanist notions of subjectivity and agency. Life narratives of RAWA women have been taken up in American academic discourses variously. In *Veiled Courage,* they are case studies of postmodern resistance for Benard, an "expert in project design" (2002, 1). Alternatively, in *With All Our Strength,* Anne E. Brodsky uses community psychology to frame these life narratives as examples of resilience, helping the West to design effective interventions "from the outside" (2003, 7). Either way, RAWA takes every opportunity to elicit, use, reflect on, and deflect metropolitan demands for authentic life story. This is one model of communicative ethics at work, as Afghan feminist activists maneuver to pursue their needs and interests and to accommodate and respect what can be dramatically different investments by feminist activists in the West.

Grafts

The burka is a boundary where cross-cultural translation is always fraught with difficulty. The spectacle of Oprah Winfrey liberating Zoya into speech by stripping the burka away is a haunting one—it resonates personally, a reminder of my own recoil and consternation at first sight of the cover of *Latifa*. As something of a recent culture industry, life narratives by Afghan women have been taken up variously. The spectacle of the passive, captured Afghan woman plays on that fantasy of unveiling for Western metropolitan readers and spectators, and it is powerful propaganda in times of war. Nevertheless, life narratives have given the Afghan feminist resistance a powerful entry into the public sphere of the West, and they are able to use this to promote their campaign for a secular and democratic sovereign state. They do not hesitate to put to other uses fantasies of wearing the veil by Western women, and that equally ethnocentric moment of recoil from the burka is also useful to their cause. The cross-cultural translation of selves here is a complex one.

As Chandra Mohanty observes, the burka marks the limits and limitations of feminist thinking about agency and cultural difference. The figure of the woman in the burka returns to haunt feminism with seemingly intractable cultural difference. Given the rhetorical uses of the "girl in the blue burka" in the war on terror there is now renewed urgency in approaching her otherwise. In situations such as this, where perspectives and experiences are shaped by privilege and oppression in intractable cultural difference, there can be no simple reciprocity. So, for example, for all the good-hearted intentions of Ensler and Winfrey, empathic identification with Afghan women can lead to serious misrepresentation or the repetition of damaging stereotypes and ideologies: "When people obey the injunction to put themselves in the position of others, they too often put *themselves,* with their own particular experiences and privileges, in the positions they see others . . . the assumptions derived from their privilege often allow them unknowingly to misrepresent the other's situation" (Young 1997, 48). When members of privileged groups imaginatively represent to themselves the perspective of the oppressed, their representations can often carry projections and fantasies through which their own complementary image of themselves is enhanced and reinforced. The desire to strip Afghan women of their burkas is a spectacle that works in precisely this way. Two things are happening here. First, we fail to recognize the idioms of agency that are relevant for Afghan women. Second, we avoid "the sometimes arduous and painful process in which they confront you with your prejudices, fantasies, and mis-understandings about them" (Young 1997, 49). Young suggests that in moral humility one starts with the assumption that one cannot see things from the other person's perspective. Ethical relations need to be medi-ated differently, in conditions that recognize both a profound desire to communicate and reach understanding and the irreversibility of per-spective, experience, and idiom. With these cautions in mind, we might do more than recoil from the sight of the burka or fantasize that we can inhabit this space empathically. We might, for example, take up the ethical response of recognizing complicity through an owning of "the little perpetrator" (Sanders 2002, 4).

And so: you enter the bookstore and regard that massed display of veiled women. You wonder what extraordinary change of currents brought these lives into your habitat, which hitherto has paid so little regard to Afghanistan. You feel the unease produced by the crocheted face plate of the burka, and you feel the pull, the inexorable logic, of placing this as alien and Other. You look at it, barefaced, and wish it stripped bare, too.

How can you move forward from this otherwise and disrupt a con-ditioned response? Perhaps you take a detour and begin to translate the veil differently in order to move across cultures. Perhaps you choose to reinscribe the burka by thinking through the skin, also a boundary and a site of exposure or connectedness where borders between bodies are unstable, crossed by differences that refuse to be contained on the inside or outside of bodies (Ahmed and Stacey 2001, 2). Perhaps from here you can begin to translate the veil differently, to understand it as part of embodiment and an expression of boundaries of the body, the self, and belief understood differently to what you know. By rethinking inside and outside in this way you might no longer fantasize that the veil must be pierced for you to communicate across this boundary of cultural difference. You begin to translate the veil more transparently, as a fluid and ambivalent garment, an interface of skin, flesh, and cloth, which is a lived embodiment for Afghan women. In the war of words and significations attached to the war on terror, the faces of Afghan women mark a threshold in the struggle over how subjects become hu-man. That moment of recoil at the sight of the burka is an emotional and piercing reminder of my own tenuous and provisional grasp of my own self and its place to speak humanely.

THREE

Testimony Incarnate: Read My Lips

Perhaps, then, it should come as no surprise that I propose to start, and to end, with the question of the human (as if there were any other way for us to start or end!). . . . The question that preoccupies me in the light of recent global violence is, Who counts as human? Whose lives count as lives? And, finally: What *makes for a grievable life?* JUDITH BUTLER, *PRECARIOUS LIFE*

About Face

There is a famous picture that is usually described as "the Afghan girl." It has a familiarity, and a currency; it "lays down routes of reference" (Sontag 2003, 85). It builds our sense of the present in relation to the past, through recognition: "I know her!" This is a haunting picture, then, of an unveiled adolescent girl with sea green eyes, that was taken in Nasir Bagh refugee camp in Peshawar in 1984. It first appeared on the cover of *National Geographic* in June 1985 and has been reproduced many times since—for example on the cover of the January 2006 collector's edition of *National Geographic,* "100 Best Pictures." The photo was a sensation, described as "one of those images that sears the heart" (Newman 2002, 10). On its first publication it was framed as a condemnation of the Soviet intervention that inspired many who saw it to make gestures of support for Afghan refugees. The same young woman appeared on the cover of *National Geographic* again in April 2002, at the time of other foreign incursions. Now she is not a barefaced cover girl, but a shapeless silhouette covered by a purple burka, clasping the photographic image of her younger self. She is anonymous, but we "know" and recognize her still.

In January 2002 a team from *National Geographic* television returned to the refugee camp at Peshawar with the photographer Steve McCurry, to search for the girl. What follows is a classic quest narrative. There are long and perilous journeys: McCurry from the United States to the refugee camps in Pakistan, and finally the Afghan woman herself, who travels on foot from her village in the foothills of Tora Bora and across the border into Pakistan. Attaching a name and an identity to Afghan refugees is, the documentary reminds us euphemistically, like finding a needle in a haystack. Finally, after forensic examination, the Afghan girl is authenticated: she is Sharbat Gula, a Pashtun rural woman, and a wife and mother. There are 3.5 million refugees as a result of the Soviet and American campaigns into Afghanistan; this is the one we know: "Her eyes challenge ours. Most of all, they disturb. We cannot turn away" (Newman 2002, 11).

The urgency to return and attach a name, to personalize the Afghan girl, coincides with the appearance of Afghan women in those public spectacles in the Western media since 2001. As we have seen in chapter 2, Judith Butler describes this need of the American viewer to possess the face of Afghan women as symbolic: a "rationale for our violence, the incursion on sovereignty, the deaths of civilians" (2004, 142). Sharbat Gula emerges from Tora Bora (allegedly the refuge of Osama bin Laden), a region that was subjected to an intensive bombing campaign in the winter of 2001–2 in the first offensive of the war on terror: Operation Enduring Freedom. The *National Geographic* coverage remains silent on this point, although its resident journalist Cathy Newman writes at length on the devastation caused by the Soviet bombing that killed Sharbat Gula's parents: "By day the sky bled terror. At night the dead were buried. And always, the sound of planes . . . " (2002, 11). This is the world Sharbat Gula now inhabits again, and with her own daughters. It is photographer Steve McCurry who attaches symbolically the "recapture" of Sharbat Gula to the war on terror: "Afghanistan has been in the Dark Age for two decades. That she's resurfaced now is perhaps prophetic, a hopeful sign" (Newman, np). This is precisely what Butler means when she suggests that Afghan women signify a rationale for Operation Enduring Freedom.

But through her translator, Sharbat Gula recalls her anger that a stranger took her photograph in 1984. The cross-cultural transaction that secures a photograph of her unveiled face (which does not appear

on the cover) a second time is painful. What McCurry requires compromises the privacy and honor of this Pashtun woman and her family,
given ethnic and gendered customs of veiling and seclusion that are
essential to her identity. There is nothing liberating about her status as
an omen in the Western public sphere for Sharbat Gula; to the contrary.
McCurry recognizes that the photograph that has inspired so many is a
burden to its subject, and the negotiations with *National Geographic* to
establish an Afghan Girls Fund secures her reluctant consent. She agrees
to look into the lens of the camera but not directly at McCurry. Sharbat
Gula's face is now haggard, bearing witness to poverty, hardship, and
grief. Given the rhetoric of the campaign to liberate Afghan women,
what she has to say are some confrontational things. To her, the burka is
a beautiful thing to wear, not a curse; and for her life under the Taliban
was better, a time of peace and order. Sharbat Gula chooses to speak as
a wife and mother, representing herself as a relational subject. This is a
point at which discourses of Western humanism and selfhood have difficulty in capturing their subject.

In the *National Geographic* story Sharbat Gula's anger is neutralized
to "little emotion" and ethnicized to her Pashtun origins: "It is said of
the Pashtun that they are only at peace when they are at war, and her
eyes—then and now—burn with ferocity." Sharbat Gula's story resists
the psychologizing narrative that renders her expression "flat" and a
sentimental framing narrative that is unable (or unwilling) to translate
the decidedly unsentimental feelings of anger and grief that burn in
her. Ultimately, the connection the *National Geographic* team makes to
Sharbat Gula is again specular: the public eye of the lens, the eyes that
authenticate her identity, the eyes that are "haunted and haunting" and
yet refuse to look at McCurry, the eyes that "flash anger" as she subjects
herself to the scrutiny of strangers.

Moments when Afghan people are individualized and recognized in
this way are not prophetic; they are strategic. The "Afghan girl" story is
contained within the framework of humanitarian concern, which organizes the commodification of subaltern lives as appropriate subjects
for compassion. As the editor of *National Geographic* remarks in his discussion of the Afghan girl, "for us at the *Geographic,* that's the payoff:
When a reader says 'I understand. I'm moved. I'm inspired'" (2006, 47).
In fact, the reappearance of Sharbat Gula in 2002 did produce generous
donations to the *National Geographic* fund on behalf of Afghan women.
But, as Suvendrini Perera observes, the body of "the Afghan girl" is a
site at which the principles of security and humanitarianism meet, and
war and humanitarian aid are closely connected: "Her green-eyed gaze

legitimizes a new set of interventions—humanitarian, military, legal, socio-cultural, economic, political—in the war on Afghanistan" (2006, in press). The question of how and when "we" become emotionally attached to the bodies of Afghan children, women, and men is an important one. When do these lives matter? When do life narratives give face and authority to these lives? How do "we" become open to this haunting gaze? When do we look away (because of course we do)?

These questions about the absence of witnessing and the limits of testimony are the subjects of this chapter. They return to that struggle over how subjects become human through representations in the mass media, and how life narratives are engaged in this struggle for recognition. The quest trope recurs in journalistic memoir from Afghanistan in the recent past because it centers on that desire to locate and identify a single subject. In Christina Lamb's *The Sewing Circles of Herat* (2002), for example, it is the search for Marri, the young Kabul diarist whose first-person narration is interspersed with Lamb's own story. In *The Storyteller's Daughter* Saira Shah returns to Afghanistan to search for the three young girls featured in her documentary *Beneath the Veil:* "After 11 September, *Beneath the Veil* was shown again and again on CNN. Although we had made the film before the attack on the World Trade Center, Western politicians on all sides had used the faces of the three girls in Mawmaii to further their own ends. The girls' suffering was used both as an argument for bombing Afghanistan and for delivering aid to it. They, of course, were unaware that they had become icons. As far as we knew, they were still living on the front line" (216). Shah's narrative of the return to find Amina, Fairuza, and Fawzia, like Steve McCurry's search for "the Afghan girl" and Lamb's pursuit of Marri, draws attention to the ideological work of these Afghan icons and the limitations of Western humanitarianism that sets out to liberate on its own terms: "Afghanistan had confounded me, just as it has always confounded the West" (Shah 2003, 246). This turn to the impenetrable and unchanging primitive space outside modernity is repeated time and again in journalists' narratives. This is a long-standing codification of Afghanistan, and these icons become part of the currency whereby modernity produces its other, "verso to recto," as a way of at once producing and privileging itself (Gregory 2004, 4).

Arjun Appadurai's observations on the globalization of mass media and mass migration in the recent past draws attention to the commoditized trajectories of texts and images as a distinctive feature of modernity. These icons play a role in shaping what Appadurai calls a "community of sentiment": "A group that begins to imagine and feel things together" through the consumption of mass media product (1996, 8). Appadurai emphasizes that his approach leaves open the question of where modernity's experiments in electronic mediation might lead in terms of nationalism, violence, and social justice. However, Perera's point is the salient one here: the principles of security and humanitarianism, violence and social justice, converge in the processing of images such as "the Afghan girl." This "soft" genre of news that personalizes and humanizes its subjects—both the journalist and the subject of the quest. Identifying a face is a gesture that attaches a biography and (potentially) a celebrity status, a personality and subjectivity to people who are routinely denied these privileges—like refugees. The desire to shape empathic engagements drives these searches; this is a familiar ethics of recognition that carries life narratives across cultures.

Had Sharbat Gula and her daughters trekked out of Tora Bora to escape the carpet bombing of 2002 and moved beyond the refugee camps of Peshawar into the networks of trafficking in asylum seekers, they would have entered into a very different discursive field. They would have become alien subjects: faceless, stripped of the identity and life story that is assembled so assiduously in the iconic life narratives that are readily recalled by Western viewers. Time and again, Afghan people (like the father of the Mawmaii sisters in Saira Shah's memoir, and the RAWA activists such as Zoya) use their access to Western mass media and life narrative to draw attention to the terrible fate of Afghan refugees, a fate that threatens them all once they leave their homeland. This is the spectral presence that haunts contemporary Afghan life narratives. Erasing the humanity of refugees is a standard protocol in the mass media, and this too is strategic. Asylum seekers are routinely denied the "modest refuge provided by subjectivity," and they become something else: projections of fear and loathing. Dehumanizing the figure of asylum seeker, denying the human referent of face and body at all costs, is a response to threat: unwelcome strangers endanger the integrity of the nation. How do we witness the presence of these people when they lose face and become ghosts? How is life narrative invoked as human beings are denied subjectivity and become objects of fear and disgust in this way? These are questions that recur in this chapter. They require attention to two dimensions of testimony as it moves westward: first, the infrastructure and ethics of recognition that facilitate the movement of humanizing narratives into the Western media to powerful affect; and second, the fragility of emotions that are produced in recognition, and the strength of denial, when witnesses choose to look away.

Testimonial narrative does not always prick the conscience: it can languish unremarked and unwitnessed when its public becomes estranged and unsympathetic. This chapter asks why this is so by tracking the routes of asylum-seeker testimony. Sometimes testimony does not summon witnesses. When this happens, it has little to do with the experiences of trauma and dispossession that constitute the testimony. Rather, it is a matter of whose lives count, and under what circumstances. In fact, the recognition of testimony is a political and ethical act that "makes for a grievable life" (to use Butler's phrase). The mechanisms of cultural transfer that carry testimony into wider circuits are also at issue here.

Some life narratives and artifacts generate a demanding and haunting force that is able to pierce the skin and trouble a sense of self. On these occasions, testimony can summon its witnesses to *feel* that their lives and privileges are enmeshed in others and that interdependencies and responsibilities follow from this. The picture of the Afghan girl is one such testimonial artifact, it "sears the heart" and remains memorable. In these ways testimony "gets personal." The response to testimony calls on reason—the ethics of recognition—and also on the emotions. We are used to autobiography "getting personal" (the concept has Nancy Miller's signature) by speaking of the intimate and by bringing the private world into the public view (in Miller's case her father's naked body). But what happens when autobiography "gets personal" by registering the force of the public world on the privacy of the emotions? How do life narratives record the impact of history and move from outside in, to become witnessed and *charged* with feeling?

The Transit Lane

A testimonial literature emerged with the accelerated exodus of asylum seekers from Afghanistan and Iraq during the 1990s.[1] These bodies and the stories of them enter into global circuits of exchange. In fact, there are well-established conduits for the production, authentication, and cultural transmission of testimony, and these are available to nurture asylum-seeker testimony in terms of campaigns for human rights. This infrastructure has a precise postwar history, and it depends on nongovernment organizations (NGOs) and the moral authority of the United Nations. It draws on the Universal Declaration of Human Rights in 1948, the Geneva Conventions, and the construction of the "impressive battery of protocols, resolutions, and prescriptions for the treatment of refugees, minorities, prisoners, workers, children, students and women" that Edward Said calls "a new universality" in the late twentieth century ("Nationalism," 2002, 428). This allows individuals to initiate challenges to injustice variously: by telling stories to human rights advocates working for NGOs or by testifying before national inquiries and official or quasi-official tribunals, for example. In this global framework, individuals narrate their personal experience to invoke "rights discourse": "The teller bears witness to his or her own experience through acts of remembering elicited by rights activists and coded to rights instruments" (Schaffer and Smith 2004b, 3). This brings life narrative into circulation, and it has established a rapid and effective transmission of testimony into a global public sphere. Human rights platforms and mechanisms demand accountability on the part of nation states, international organizations, and compassionate individuals, who are prepared to take responsibility for the welfare of others. It draws on a humanist, modernist language of the rights of the individual to dignity, equity, bodily inviolability and freedom, and the responsibilities of citizens to respond compassionately.

Together these infrastructures and instruments nurture and harvest subaltern stories and represent them to multiple audiences through the Internet and in pamphlets, books, performance, and broadcast and print journalism. New technologies produce unprecedented venues for the production and circulation of refugee testimony through human rights activism now, and each of these sites has a distinctive dynamic and purchase. Occasionally refugee and asylum-seeker narratives are published as monographs.[2] More commonly, they appear in collections initiated and edited by activists.[3] Access to the narratives of asylum seekers moves beyond print, through the various and linked websites of human rights organizations: Human Rights Watch, PEN, Barbed Wire Britain, Refugee Law advocates, Asylum Support, Amnesty International, Asylum Seekers in America, among others. Specific detention centers sometimes have dedicated sites, and so do crises and tragedies involving refugees.[4] Professionals and public intellectuals take up asylum-seeker stories in various judicial, religious, literary, and therapeutic frameworks. These small shreds of life narrative are discontinuous and disembodied "voices from detention" that often elude search engines.

Asylum-seeker testimony (both print and online) is often gathered in composite text that is surrounded with peritext by authorized witnesses (writers, journalists, lawyers, academics). Characteristically a framing dialogue between those who testify and those who witness affirms the equal status of asylum seekers. For example, witnesses recognize the individuality of those who testify:

To the asylum-seekers—people just like us. (Tyler 2003, np)

The purpose of this book is simple: to give a face to the faceless; a voice to the voice-less. To show that people we hold in indefinite detention are human beings like the rest of us. (Amor and Austin 2003, v)

Listening to these voices is like looking into a mirror. They come not from strangers but from men and women who are already fellow citizens, close and clearly recogniz-able, of the same world we live in. (Malouf, quoted in Scott and Keneally 2004, front cover)

In response, those who testify assert their humanity:

My question: I am human and was foetus in my mother's womb and created from blood and flesh, with feelings and heart, and came into the world like anybody. Don't I deserve to live like other people? (Amor and Austin 2003, 97)

I WAS ON HUNGER STRIKE SEVERAL TIMES AND LAST MONTH I SEW MY LIPS. MY PRO-TEST WAS ABOUT FREEDOM AND BASIC HUMAN RIGHTS. THIS IS NOT MY CULTURE OR YOUR CULTURE BUT SOMETIMES SILENCE IS BETTER THAN TO SHOUT. (Amor and Austin 2003, 98)

I can't control myself, after that strip search in front of two officers. It is a very shame-ful thing for me; I cannot eat for two days. I thought about those two things [hand-cuffs and strip search] they have not any respect. I don't know why they treat us so bad; maybe we are not human because we are not white. (Refugee Action Commit-tee 2003)

Will we forever be locked up with this surrounding and dehumanizing?
We would also like our freedom and to live the way others live. It is up to you to decide what you should do about all this inhuman treatment and disrespect for hu-manity! (Yousefi 2004, 51)

These elaborate frameworks and protocols facilitate the transmis-sion, circulation, and witnessing of asylum seekers' narratives. Never-theless these continue to languish on the margins of the public sphere. Human rights discourse operates as a skeletal framework to nurture and support these most rudimentary forms of testimonial life: fragmentary, often anonymous, serial and inconclusive stories of suffering and injus-tice. These are disembodied: they are generally required to be stripped of personal, geographical, and other information that might identify indi-viduals as part of the formal processing of claims for asylum. Subsumed in the collective identity of the asylum seeker are vastly different ethnicized, gendered, class, and generational experiences; these individuals are now alien to themselves as well as to others. This testimony has few proper names and no single face or heroic presence. Crucially, it also has few who will give witness. This, too, is part of the war of words and significations.

Narrative Thresholds

Human rights discourse remains a benevolent and Western framework that manages testimony. It stands for a code of social justice and equality that claims international jurisdiction. This infrastructure can elicit testimony but it cannot guarantee the ethical and political conditions that secure an appropriate response: empathic witnessing. Testimony is a speech act that demands recognition and a response in terms of social action and social justice. In their overview of the 1990s as a decade when life narratives were instrumental, Schaffer and Smith (2004b) consider a series of campaigns in dispersed national contexts where testimony attracted international recognition of human rights abuses and commanded recognition: the Truth and Reconciliation Commission hearings in South Africa, the narratives of "comfort women" in East Asia, and the Stolen Generations narrative in Australia, among others. For testimony to become a social and political force in the public sphere that commands recognition and ethical response from both individuals and institutions, there must be an appropriate cultural and political milieu. Mobilizing shame has been essential to this human rights discourse. It suggests that institutions in the public sphere—governments, agencies, militias—can be made to respond to the force of public opinion and that they are psychically or emotionally structured like individuals and vulnerable to feelings of embarrassment and disgrace (Keenan 2004, 436). What drives this economy of affect is a matter of faith in a logic of ethical response: if mass violations become known, the world responds and reacts as an ethical witness in good conscience. This faith in "mobilizing shame" secures the work of testimony.

The idea of an economy of affect is useful for thinking about the passages of testimony and our shifting responses to testimonial artifacts. It grows from Sara Ahmed's argument that the emotions are always on the move and circulating between bodies. Rather than associating emotions with individual psychological states or public institutions, Ahmed emphasizes the social and cultural work of emotions: "Emotions are not in either the individual or the social, but produce the very surfaces and boundaries that allow the individual and the social to be delineated as if they are objects" (2004, 10). This is useful for thinking about the dynamism of responses to testimony, its ebb and flow in relation to wider currents and constraints. Although the association of emotion and affect with the instrumentality of an economy may seem jarring, it suggests the kinds of transactions and the shifts in value that occur around and through testimonial discourse as it seeks out its witness. The currency of testimony circulates with different exchange rates. In the case of the Stolen Generations narrative in Australia, for example, there was a process of gradual formulation and reformulation that occurred over decades, where a narrative slowly coheres and gathers momentum and recognition—Bain Attwood calls this a process of "learning about the truth" (2001, 183). This long process of accrual in value will bring both those who testify and those who will witness testimony to the point where an uptake occurs and private and public discourses catalyze one another to produce a recognition that is of historical significance in its attention to human rights and social justice. Many things contribute to this process of accrual that results in coherent and authoritative testimonial narrative—oral transmission within communities, campaigns for social justice, discourses of history and memory in academic scholarship, authoritative figures as bearers of paradigmatic story, autobiography in various textual forms, human rights inquiries, and mediascapes and ideoscapes that circulate through and beyond national contexts (such as indigenous rights movements, the authority of human rights discourse, and strong feminist campaigns).

Although this infrastructure is installed in and through a global civic sphere, the point that must be emphasized about this process is that, almost without exception, the horizon of the nation must be engaged in the cultural and political milieu that enables accrual to continue. For testimonial narrative to achieve prominence and affective force, there must a supportive environment that enables particular narratives to be told and heard and demands that their "truths" be uttered. Attwood draws on Peter Novick's (1999) work on Holocaust testimony in the United States to emphasize this point: "Public discourse doesn't just shape private discourse, it is its catalyst; it sends out the message 'This is something you should be talking about'" (2001, 197). This reinforces the argument that, although the transits of testimony may seem to be secured in acts of faith and good conscience and an international infrastructure of human rights, the management of testimony is almost always strategic and in the national interest.[5] For example, if we look at the process of narrative accrual in the cases of the Stolen Generations in Australia, the

Residential School narratives in Canada, and the Truth and Reconciliation process in South Africa, the testimonies of the violent oppression of indigenous and black citizens was heard in a discursive framework of reconciliation that suggested that empathic identification and a "talking cure" could be harnessed to the regeneration of the community of the nation.[6] Reconciliation linked testimony to personal acts of civic virtue and the national good. Tragically, the emotional valency of testimony has little to do with the intensity of the suffering or pain that it carries, and it has everything to do with the cultural and political milieu it encounters and its capacity there to command witness. The empathic engagement of privileged citizens with the experiences of oppressed others as part of a process of self-identification, and a cultivation of humanity, fueled the power of testimony in the late twentieth century to command witness: "I must be willing to entertain the thought that this suffering person might be me" (Nussbaum 1995, 91).

What we can also learn from this process of narrative accrual is the transience of this power and influence—compassion, Susan Sontag reminds us, is an unstable emotion, and the strong emotions are also the transient ones (2003, 121). There is nothing inevitable about the coalescence of testimonial narrative; there is no necessary surfacing of submerged history. To prosper, testimony must find recognition from those others who will register and witness its truth. When this fails to occur, trauma can remain trapped as "unclaimed experience" within the individual psyche and within the shared confines of the immediate community. These are circuits of pain, loss, guilt, anger, and shame that can contain testimony and hold it close to home. This brings us back to the asylum seeker and to the circumstance in which faith in mobilizing shame turns out to be a poor investment.

To accrue value and jurisdiction, testimony needs fortune, history, and national interest on its side. Asylum seekers have none of these things. Thomas Keenan talks about a failure to respond ethically that he calls "becoming shameless" (2004, 438). This is not simply denial or indifference to the pain of others, rather there is abroad now a more fundamental shift: an open defiance of the mechanisms of shaming, and a public embrace of shamelessness. Perpetrators of abuse now defiantly fail to respond to the exposure of violence and deceit in the light of publicity, and the power of testimony to make a disturbing intervention through shame is diminished. Becoming shameless is, then, a shift in the public life of ethics and the emotions that denies testimony the conditions it needs to flourish: the affective response of witnesses who will respond empathically and intersubjectively and who will recognize the claim that recurs through testimony, "I am human. . . . Don't I deserve to be like other people?"

The Carceral Archipelago

Testimony is immediately affected by shifts and realignments in national interest. In the case of asylum-seeker testimony in particular, the appeal to human rights discourse is contested by renewed discourses of belonging: homelands, patriots, closed borders, and national security. This language of citizenship is a new morality; powerful and resurgent sentiments emphasize national integrity and identity based on cultural purity. The idea of human rights discourse as a necessary ethical engagement with the other is decidedly passé now. Rather, vigorous reterritorialization is intrinsic to the war on terror, and "borderpanic" (to use a term coined by Perera [2006]) reigns. In this order of things, asylum seekers and refugees in particular remain outcasts. Their testimony is epistemologically disabled and dissipates into darkness and oblivion: "lives in limbo." The ideoscapes of human rights discourse that facilitated the transits of testimony have been dramatically reconfigured in the process of the war on terror, and asylum-seeker testimony encounters shamelessness and "paranoid nationalism" (Hage 2003) in place of empathic engagement.

All of this is fatal, for witnessing is fundamental to the autobiographical contract established in testimony: "As a performative utterance testimony depends on an audience positioned at various historical and psychological removes of estrangement, resistance, identification, or receptivity to the events being recounted" (Brodzski 2001, 871). The point is that the audience can be "removed" to a point of estrangement, where receptivity breaks down and defiance intervenes; we look away from the signs of trauma and suffering in our midst. The notion of compassion fatigue suggests this can happen in exhaustion, from affective overload through the mass media. However, there is a presumption of interiority and fixed referents here that needs to be called into question. If we understand emotions to be "on the move" to social and political effect, the withdrawal of empathy and the refusal to be shamed before asylum seekers is more than a psychic and individual phenomenon. It indicates a sliding of emotions from empathy to fear—not merely to fatigue and indifference. There is an important point here for thinking about testimony in particular. Sara Ahmed (2004) emphasizes that figures of hate do not have a fixed referent. This explains why, for example, we may be capable of empathic engagement with Afghan women when they appear on the cover of *National Geographic* magazine or in documentaries or when they are ceremonially unveiled in public pageants (the spectacle of unveiling discussed in chap. 2). In these contexts their humanity is recognized and affirmed in acts of empathic engagement, for they enter the circuits that remain available to testimonies of abuse of third world women in the third world. At the same time, men, women, and children from the Middle East become objects of hate when they approach the borders of the nation as asylum seekers. A different set of emotions and valuations come into play, and it follows that their testimonies coexist in very different and contradictory transits at one and the same time.

New procedures and spaces produced by an obsession with separation and classification, patriotism, and citizenship define and contain detainees and asylum seekers in the process of the war on terror. It follows that testimony from refugees and asylum seekers fails to achieve sustained recognition in the national community or the community of nations. In these times, their testimonies are faint and unreliable traces of bodies that appear despite brutal and strategic interdictions to categorize, contain, and silence detainees. Here, now, there are relatively few who are prepared to stand and give witness. Those who refuse to look away are themselves under the threat of being shamed and deterritorialized in the wider community of citizen subjects. In these circumstances, it takes scandal to bring detainees and their plight into the public eye. For example, the incontrovertible photographic proof of abuse and degradation of detainees at Abu Ghraib that was broadcast in April 2004 showed images of a triumphant U.S. military taunting naked Iraqi prisoners who were forced into humiliating poses. The photographs seem not to have been random but rather part of a dehumanizing interrogation process that was used in Afghanistan and Iraq (Hersh 2004, 38). Similarly, images of asylum seekers are used to dehumanize and shame them. One of the poignant refrains in refugee testimony gathered by Amnesty International is the self-consciousness of asylum seekers about the capture and networking of images, for they well know what can be done when they are represented as dehumanized bodies in abjection: "It seems important to recognize that one way of 'managing' a population is to constitute them as the less than human without entitlement to rights, as the humanly unrecognizable. . . . 'Managing' a population is thus not only a process through which regulatory power produces a set of subjects. It is also the process of their de-subjectification" (Butler 2004, 98).

A carceral archipelago stretches from Guantánamo in Cuba east to the United Kingdom "Detention Estate" and across to Lampedusa and, farther east, Abu Ghraib and Bagram airbase; it turns south to remote detention centers in the Pacific. Privately managed sites circle the global arena of the war on terror. Bizarre things happen to bodies and spaces as the status of territories and citizenship become strategic and open to revision in new antiterrorism legislation. New regulations have been introduced to modify the boundaries of national citizenship and qualify the obligations of democratic nation states to attend to human rights, even as they go to war for democracy and social justice. Derek Gregory (2004) argues that in these times Said's "imaginative geography" needs to be radicalized. He turns to Giorgio Agamben's notion of *homo sacer* ("sacred man") to decipher the politics of exclusion, which turns not on inclusion and belonging but the creation of spaces of exception and figures that are "the mute bearers of . . . 'bare life,' deprived of language and the political life that language makes possible" (Agamben quoted in Gregory, 63). Agamben's thinking emphasizes the volatility of borders that occur in juridico-political orderings of space. In this bizarre world, all is contingent: "security" reshapes the jurisdiction of national and international law, and the political frameworks that underwrite social life are continuously open to negotiation and strategic adjustment.

In a series of "riffs" triggered by Agamben's work on the camp as a "state of exception" that secures the extraordinary metamorphoses of space and identity in the politics of the war on terror, Perera draws attention to category dissolution and invention: denationalization and deterritorialization (the boundaries of national belonging and citizenship are reconfigured), strange oxymorons ("unlawful noncitizens"), and uncanny repetitions (whereby asylum seekers "become" terrorists, for example). In thinking about testimony, and the denial of asylum-seeker narratives, one slippage among all these is critical—the perceived gap that opens between the categories of the human and the citizen:

> The structure of the camp as a "dislocating localization" that exceeds the political system of the state is a space where the "national" is placed in suspension. . . . This space of the camp, where the category of "citizen" is no longer operative, also is the space where the claims and limits of the "human," what remains as a residue of the "citizen," are tested and revealed in lethal form. The figure of the refugee or "stateless" individual exposes the purchase of "the human" and its rights once divested of the rights it bears as a citizen. (Perera 2002a)

The stateless persons of the carceral archipelago reveal the limited jurisdiction of human rights and the ethics of recognition it secured. The reemergence of modernist categories of citizenship bring a renewed emphasis on "others." This is (to continue the theme of uncanny repetitions) a return to the past, for this tense relation between human rights and citizenship emerged originally in the eighteenth century. This is discussed at length by Hannah Arendt (herself a refugee following the Second World War), in her book *The Origins of Totalitarianism* (1958). Arendt argues that it is the refugee, the displaced person, who brings thinking about human rights into crisis. The category of the human broke down and became impotent in the twentieth century "at the very moment when those who professed to believe in it were for the first time confronted with people who had indeed lost all other qualities and specific relationships—except that they were still human" (Arendt quoted in Balfour and Cadava 2004, 280). As Balfour and Cadava observe, following Arendt, "it is precisely when the noncitizen appears, when the human is divorced from citizenship . . . that rights are lost" (281; see, too, Dixon 2002; Hage 2003; Perera 2002a).

In summary, then, the renewed emphasis on homelands, citizenship, and national sovereignty deprives asylum seekers of access to the codes of human rights discourse that have comprised the lingua franca for the production and reception of testimony. The availability of testimony is fundamental to the protection of human rights and (to return to Butler) to the question of "what makes for a grievable life." For the asylum seeker now, the opportunities to testify and find a believing witness are few. Although it may seem to be the case that testimony is the vehicle of "speaking truth to power" fueled by rights and the knowledge or consciousness of terrible experiences, in fact the ebb and flow of testimonial discourse also responds to national interests and international circuits of power and influence that shift and shape its witnesses. We can see this by following the movements of asylum seekers and noting the limited jurisdiction of their testimony.

Extremities

What happens to testimonial utterance when it struggles to command response as its witnesses move away, to shamelessness, estrangement, and resistance? Some asylum seekers now resort to body language and wound culture. They write graffiti in blood, carve words on skin, and speak with sutured lips. This is a language of desperation and last resort. It meets, in general, revulsion and disbelief: this behavior thus confirms the otherness of the foreigner, and it is unintelligible. When testimony falters as it does now, we must remember to question the silence and to probe the absence of story; in short, we must extend our vocabulary to read the unintelligible. Joseph Pugliese calls this language of self-harm "testimony incarnate" (2004, 33), referring to Cathy Caruth's argument that the traumatized carry an impossible history within them, or "they become themselves the symptom of a history that they cannot entirely possess" (Caruth 1996, 5). By its very nature, testimony ultimately carries criticism to the limits of autobiography as it struggles to possess history and register acute crisis and loss.

Testimony incarnate, above all, brings this to crisis because it makes extraordinary demands on how we grasp relations between self and other and forces us to a reckoning with testimony as a distinctive engagement and experience of narrative. And so, for example, Pugliese (2004) necessarily begins to reflect on himself as a secondary witness as he watches the film of a young Afghan refugee self-harm in the coils of one of the razor wire fences at the Woomera detention center in South Australia. This film, which includes footage taken by surveillance cameras, was broadcast nationally in the closing scenes of the teledocumentary *About Woomera* (2003). How is Pugliese to receive and give due recognition to this "suffering inside" of the refugee? "How can I begin to account for a trauma that exceeds all of my frames of reference? How can I begin to situate this violence within a schema of reason and law without perpetuating further violence? In the face of these anguished questions I attempt, in the first instance, to trace my position as witness to this violence" (2004, 25). In Pugliese's case, the act of writing becomes, in turn, performative and a further testimonial effect, which transmits and transfers the testimonial weight of suffering and pain in order to make Afghan lives and deaths matter: "There is an excess of flesh to this body, as every square inch of his skin is exposed to the tears of the razors. With every turn he cuts. Every gesture solicits a wound. . . . . He lunges forward, ensnaring himself further into the razor wire, and begins crying 'Killing myself, killing'" (24). Here is the Afghan body we cannot bear to see, hear, and feel. What is to be done, when regarding the pain of others in this way? Predictably, most viewers do not respond to these images with benevolence and a sense of moral obligation to address the suffering of asylum seekers; to the contrary.

As a language of last resort, testimony incarnate works on the body of those who give testimony and, in a profoundly different way, on those who witness.[7] This signification of the incarcerated body is shaped precisely by the forces that detain it and by the government and media discourses that represent it (Pugliese 2002). In this sense, its eloquence is consummate: lip sewing is a mutilation that allows the mute to speak.

Following Pugliese, then, who recognizes these terrible sights as an injunction to bear witness, we must attend to the precarious life of the Afghan refugee whose laceration at the boundaries of the detention center speaks so profoundly of internalized abjection, and who testifies to being the outcast: the object of our disgust and fear. He marks the boundaries of citizenship and belonging in our name, at the precise razor edge of detention, where the nation and citizenship fall away into the spaces of exception. For many of us, this is the world of our presence as citizens, and quite profoundly so: asylum seekers are definitively "not us," and they endanger what is "ours" in civic rhetoric of sovereign subjects and the newly energized national body.

What kind of vocabulary and emotional response can follow testimony into these darkest places where its intelligibility is open to question: the language of pain? How we move, and are moved, or remain immovable in response to it, is at issue. Engaging with the outcast in our presence requires that history move in us—the politics and rhetorics of the war on terror can "get personal" through the haunting presence and eloquence of testimony incarnate—for example, the lacerated asylum seeker witnessed by Pugliese or those who bear the scars of sewn lips. Powerful emotions are attached to them and intensified through their self-harm—fear, disgust and hate, and shame. These figures trigger passionate engagement and estrangement alike. In mapping "the cultural politics of emotion," Sara Ahmed (2004) and Elspeth Probyn (2002, 2005) make a phenomenological turn for the times by formulating the relations between bodily sensation, emotion, and judgments in ways that privilege the "sensational" and the performative: the immediacy and urgency of feeling in and through writing. This breaks with the cognitivist approach that emphasizes the connections between emotion and judgment, appraisal and attitude, and associates compassion with practical reason and civic virtue. If we are to engage with testimony incarnate it must surely be through the emotions, with all the risks that accrue—it does lack the efficiency and predictability of the transit lane, and its ethics are always open to question. It is in these extremities that a new engagement with ethics emerges in contemporary theory. The turn to Levinas, by Butler and Pugliese among others, is an attempt to formulate a new ethics of recognition that can engage with these times. Butler argues that in response, now, there must be a renewed attention to our fundamental dependency on anonymous others and a new imagining of political and ethical responsibilities that begins with an openness to narration that challenges the first person.[8] Here a different vocabulary of reading comes into play. In place of empathic engagement through the narrative imagination—an epistemology that draws heavily on readings of Anglo-American novels—is an encounter with testimonial narrative that produces a shattering sense of the limits of our own self and its place to speak humanely.

Testimony is a political act that works on the emotions, and as a carrier of affect; it shapes how emotions move and shift relationally; it produces and conducts what moves us and makes us feel; it travels on ripples of emotion. Testimony incarnate emerges literally and figuratively from those spaces where the claims and limits of the human break down in disarray. It is profoundly eloquent, and yet writing on the skin breaks with language to the point that it risks erasing the subject altogether. How then can it be witnessed? Is scarred skin readable as testimony? It is the very shudder and recoil, the revulsion and visceral emotion produced by testimony incarnate, that can relocate its witness into a self-shattering moment of recognition and embodiment: here "the loss of all comprehension becomes the condition of possibility for testimony, since this acute disorientation forces the reader to make a social and political context for both herself and the testimony" (Kilbey 2001, 130).

When testimony is written on and through the skin it takes an extraordinary toll on the body that writes and the bodies that witness. At this point, emotions do not represent history; they take us into it to catalyze an emotional response that cannot be denied. Testimony incarnate calls on an extraordinary leap of faith: that it can come alive in and through its witness regarding pain. At this point, where life is at its most precarious and humanity at risk, it follows that so, too, is testimony. Here we have moved a long way from the ethics and the emotions of our engagement with the image of "the Afghan girl." But we know her differently now. She is Sharbat Gula, and her face is scarred by grief and pain. If critical work has something to say about or to the present situation, reminds Butler, it may well be in the domain of representation where humanization and dehumanization occur ceaselessly (2004, 140). A criticism that speaks to this can begin with testimony and by insisting that Sharbat Gula and the young refugee ensnared in the razor wire are held together as images mobilized within the same field of representation. They are placed at the precise points where the human emerges and vanishes, and where we know and feel the limits of representation in a new world order, after the fall.

FOUR

Branding:
The Veiled Best-Seller

There is no denying it—as a topic, the harem sold books. From the eighteenth century on, whether you wrote about living in one, visiting one, or escaping from one, any book that had anything to do with the harem sold. Publishers knew it, booksellers knew it, readers knew it and authors knew it . . . they cannily entitled their books with the evocative words "harem," "Turkish," "Arabian" or "princess," and pictured themselves in veils and yashmaks on the front cover.

REINA LEWIS, *RETHINKING ORIENTALISM*

It would be naïve to imagine that we can directly confront Empire. Our strategy must be to isolate Empire's working parts and disable them one by one. No target is too small. No victory too insignificant.   ARUNDHATI ROY, *THE ORDINARY PERSON'S GUIDE TO EMPIRE*

The Blank Page

Military occupation, an act of trespass and conquest, delivers a "blank page" at the conclusion of Jean Sasson's best-selling biography *Mayada: Daughter of Iraq:* "This was only the second time in the history of modern Iraq that a blank page had been opened on the nation's book—a page on which the annals of history waited to be written, a page that would describe Iraq's future. Mayada gazed to the east as she prayed, 'May Allah guide the hand that writes on that blank page'" (2003, 270). This apocalyptic version of the occupation of Iraq in 2003 recalls Coetzee: it is the "new men of Empire . . . who believe in fresh starts, new chapters, new pages" (1982, 24). What is the work of romantic life narrative in this new imperium? What are the connections between grand strategies of geopolitics (decisions made in corporate boardrooms and centers of command) and "the spatial stories told by the lives of ordinary people" that circulate in the popular media? (Gregory 2004, xv). In this chapter, the connections of life story and book markets to geopolitics are scarcely veiled at all. Fabrications of self, space, and time are linked to the modalities of political, military, and economic power. In the "veiled best-seller"—popular and romantic biographies of Muslim women like *Mayada* that are syndicated globally and sold in vast quantities—one particular space exerts fascination. As Reina Lewis (2005) reminds us in the epigraph to this chapter, it is the harem that sells books. We are often blind to the more banal forms that deliver stories shaped by the colonial present, and veiled best-sellers are a case in point: they reproduce haunting and exotic oriental fantasies and engage our consent to trespass without shame.

The fantastic conclusion to Jean Sasson's *Mayada* suggests epic terms for the American intervention in Iraq in the northern spring of 2003, an offensive that preceded the publication and promotion of this popular nonfiction best-seller late that same year. In *Mayada* the devices of romantic nonfiction ostensibly celebrate the Western intervention in Iraq. However, the narrative is also hostage to fortune, and subsequent events in Iraq ricochet back to alter readings of the book. The processing of best-sellers like *Mayada* is an ongoing story. Critics rarely visit these regions of popular life narrative, although many readers do. To understand how life story links into the ideological work of consent and critique, the distinctive techniques, devices, and desires of the best-seller need to be considered.

The "Note from the Author" at the start of *Mayada*, which follows here, sustains the metaphorical connection between the invasion of Iraq and the writing of Sasson's book: "In 2002, Bush determined that the Iraqis had suffered enough under Saddam Hussein, and in early 2003, coalition forces removed Hussein from power. That year, Mayada decided she wanted the world to know the truth about Iraqi life, the truth as told by someone who has seen Iraq from every angle, from Saddam's palaces to Saddam's torture chambers. . . . Mayada asked me to write the story of her life, and I agreed" (xxi). As the appointed biographer of an authentic Iraqi woman (a ghostwriter of sorts, although the book is in her name), Sasson charts a path into Iraq, imagined as a welcoming space: it invites interventions from the West that are literal and metaphorical, military and literary, that will liberate Iraqis from their oppression. Through synecdoche, the author Jean Sasson becomes the nation: the American traveler to Middle Eastern lands finds people "always extended a welcoming gesture, cheerfully opening their homes and hearts" (ix). Sasson's visit to Iraq in 1998 is presented as an epic precursor of the campaign by U.S.-led forces in March 2003. The parallel between literary and military expeditions in the author's note is an autobiographical authorization and a preemptive insertion of *Mayada* into that space of "the blank page" of Iraqi history.

Mayada al-Askari, a Baghdad journalist and a member of the Iraqi elite, was imprisoned and then exiled to Jordan during the Hussein regime. She asks Sasson to write her life story, and the resulting biography anoints Mayada as a daughter of Iraq and an authentic inheritor of the traditions and glories of Mesopotamia. In this story of the Coalition Occupation, Iraq will be restored to power and influence in the form of a modern democratic nation state—guided (yet not ruled in the way of fundamentalism) by Allah, restored and given back to the Iraqi people by the benevolent invader. The production of the book itself personifies and naturalizes these transactions: these two women are situated through and in relation to each other as biographer and biographical subject, but in an unequal contract. A letter of authentication from Mayada al-Askari at the website establishes the links between the American author and her Iraqi subject: "Jean wrote my story, the story of my grandfathers, and the story of other innocent Iraqis. I am amazed at how she took the facts of my life and so perfectly captured the emotion in my heart" (Sasson, n.d.-a). The fate of Norma Khouri's hoax life narrative *Honor Lost,* a generic sibling of *Mayada* and a contemporaneous publication, is a reminder of how important this assertion by a genuine native subject must be. Al-Askari's affirmation serves as a public guarantee that there is, in fact, a body that authenticates this testimonial.

Who has the right to tell the life stories of Iraqi women embedded in *Mayada?* Although al-Askari is a journalist, and a well-educated and cosmopolitan member of the Iraq intelligentsia, she needs Sasson to render her life and relay the testimonies of other women for a wider readership. The narrative structure of *Mayada* is a complex series of life narratives that circle around the oppression of women in Iraq. Sasson narrates Mayada's life story, which, in turn, is a framing device that encloses the embedded testimonies of "shadow women." These are the women who shared a prison cell with Mayada in the Baladiyat Prison in Baghdad toward the brutal end of the Hussein regime, and the book is dedicated to them. These prison narratives are organized in a manner reminiscent of *Scheherazade:* a series of stories are told in darkness and captivity among women to sustain life and hope. Sasson uses the first person for these shadow testimonies. In this way there are a variety of women who testify, and these shadow testimonials are presented ostensibly as addressed to Mayada herself. Each is a story of terrible oppression under the Hussein dictatorship, and intermittently women are taken from the cell, abused, tortured, and interrogated and then returned with shocking injuries.

The presence of these subaltern first-person testimonies in the biography is important, for Mayada has led a privileged life and it is only her imprisonment and witnessing of these stories (and her shame that she has hitherto known little about Iraqi society beyond a privileged and wealthy enclave) that qualifies her to give testimony. What happens to Mayada in Baladiyat is a process of education and politicization that integrates her into a community of Iraqi women. Sasson dedicates the book to these shadow women, but readers have been quick to recognize that their presence remains spectral (rather like the "girls" in *Reading "Lolita" in Tehran*, which also invokes *Scheherazade*). When Mayada is captured and taken to the cell at Baladiyat it takes a moment for her to recognize these dark forms are in fact other women, and it is only the act of giving testimony that brings them to light. However, their presence is fleeting. These subaltern women are left in Baladiyat, unable to gain access to the networks of power and influence that allow the well-connected Mayada to negotiate her freedom, escape to Jordan, and revive her contact with her ghostwriter and friend Jean Sasson. In epitextual commentaries about *Mayada* readers look for some closure to these embedded testimonies of the shadow women and find the experience of reading the book limited because these stories are unresolved to their satisfaction. This might be an unrealistic and unsophisticated readerly expectation in more realist genres of life narrative, where unresolved plot and characterization can be marks of authenticity and truth; however, in the fantastic realms of popular nonfiction these desires for closure are legitimate and remain unmet.

Peritexts to *Mayada* suggest exactly what this style of life narrative has to offer Western readers. These recommendations draw on Sasson's reputation established by the *Princess* trilogy a decade earlier:

A book to move you to tears. (Fay Weldon)

Anyone with the slightest interest in human rights will find this book heart-wrenching. It is a well written, personal story about the violation of human rights. . . . It had to come from a native woman to be believable. (Betty Mahmoody, best-selling author of *Not without My Daughter*)

Absolutely riveting and profoundly sad. (*People*)

Epitextual commentary by readers confirms this anticipated and highly emotional experience of profound sadness from reading *Mayada*. This is a readerly expectation established by its place in a series:

Another wonderful book by Jean Sasson. This book is a heart-wrenching, eye opening account of Mayada al-Askari's time spent in an Iraqi prison. The book will touch your heart as you empathize with Mayada and the other women of cell block 52 who were unjustly imprisoned with her. It is hard to comprehend the grief and despair these women suffered as they faced torture and possible death on a daily basis. The book leaves you angry at Saddam and his regime but in awe of the imprisoned women who rally around one another for support and strength as they struggle to survive this horrific ordeal. I am so hopeful that the war brought an end to the suffering for these women and they were able to reunite with their families. ("An Eye Opening Must Read," September 29, 2004. Reviewer: Pam, Georgia, USA)

The notion that the invasion of Iraq might be accompanied by propaganda generated through the veiled best-seller may seem bizarre; however, this genre of life narrative is well adapted to naturalizing an aggressive military strategy as a benevolent intervention. This was obviously timely for metropolitan consumption in the winter of 2003. Through the venues and resources already established by the Sasson Corporation (an established broker of life narrative about Muslim women that I will return to shortly) al-Askari is offered as the authentic native woman. In this role, during the promotional tours for *Mayada* both she and Sasson attest to the sight of advanced weaponry during their travels in Iraq, and al-Askari assures the American public that loyal Iraqis enthusiastically welcome occupying American troops as a liberating force. Both assurances have turned out to be misguided as a violent and protracted insurgency has emerged in Iraq and weapons of mass destruction failed to materialize, but they were timely in marketing life narrative to an American readership in the autumn of 2003. *Mayada* offers some hope for a smooth transition to a Western style democracy in Iraq. The story of the al-Askari family across several generations is used to revive the prospects of an Iraqi intelligentsia that is defined carefully as nationalist, not fundamentalist. This elite group has a long history of accepting colonial modernity, and sponsoring Westernization. In *Mayada*'s appendix 1, an extract from a speech by Winston Churchill, MP, in the British House of Commons in 1921 attests to the value of Mayada's grandfather, Jafar Pasha, to the British Empire during the First World War. Like his granddaughter, he was accomplished in seeking the patronage of power-

MAYADA

DAUGHTER OF IRAQ

One Woman's Survival in
Saddam Hussein's Torture Jail

JEAN SASSON

AUTHOR OF *PRINCESS*

4   Front cover design from Jean Sasson, *Mayada: Daughter of Iraq*

ful colonizers. *Mayada* infers that the remnants of this reforming elite can take up the collaborative task of writing on the "blank page" delivered to them by occupation: the reinvention of Iraq as a modern secular nation. In this way *Mayada* presents the invasion and occupation of Iraq as a revival (rather than a foreign imposition) of an alternative democratic and nationalist tradition. In this scheme of things it is the Hussein dictatorship that is alien and imposed, and there is in situ an authentic aristocratic and hereditary fragment that can reclaim its destiny.

The contrast between the generic veiled woman on the cover of *Mayada* (fig. 4) and the al-Askari family photographs in the book is striking. These women have been unveiled for several generations, and it is only during the Hussein dictatorship that Mayada begins to veil and practice her religion devoutly. It isn't unusual that photographs in life narrative problematize rather than supplement or document the narrative. In *Mayada* the pictures of the al-Askari family illustrate complex and hybrid engagements across cultures; this elite Arab intelligentsia was Westernized by the intervention of the British in the Middle East following the decline of the Ottoman Empire, and it has ever since occupied a space of contradiction. Mayada's childhood photographs from Baghdad and Beirut are indistinguishable from those of her contemporaries in Massachusetts or Middlesex in the 1950s, although the Harrods birthday baskets and designer fashions identify the al-Askari family as members of a cosmopolitan and wealthy Arab elite that migrated seasonally across Europe and the Middle East. The snapshot of Mayada's relatives at the Dorchester Hotel in London in 1953, dressed in Western formal attire at an "Arabian Nights" ball, is a reminder of the contradictions and mimicry that circulate around Orientalisms new and old, and they complicate notions of ways that Arab and European traditions have come into contact through the lived experiences of recent generations.

Distant Places

Romantic fantasy simplifies these relations and offers a powerful mythology of Iraq passively awaiting intervention to enjoy the benefits of modernity that would otherwise be beyond its grasp. This is a fantastic process of self-production. The "Letter from Mayada" at the Sasson website (n.d.-a) introduces Mayada as an inflected spokesperson who authorizes Sasson as a compassionate advocate, "Iraqis opened up to her . . . people asked me to send their love to her, I never had such an experience in Iraq." The author's note at the beginning of *Mayada* is filled with

Sasson's desire to enter a fantasy world of romance and nostalgia—the first words of the book are hers: "Distant places have always called me." The translation of Jordan at one and the same time as familiar ("roughly the size of Indiana") and remote ("distant places") in the author's note, effects Sasson's (and the reader's) own smooth entry into an estranged world of romance:

Twilight had set in, and the local desert plants projected their sharp outlines against a peony-pink sky. As is their custom, many Jordanians had driven to the outskirts of the city, where they spread their colorful Oriental rugs on small mounds of dirt for their evening picnics. Dozens of small fires blazed, lighting up the shadowy silhouettes of women grilling chicken on spits. Tiny firelights flashed as Arab men gestured and emphasized with their lighted cigarettes, and small shadows scooted here and there as children played in the endless sand. I lowered the car window and heard the crackling of the fires mingling with the muted voices of family gatherings, and for a fleeting moment I wished to belong to one of those families. (xi)

This is a different country to the Jordan of Khouri's *Honor Lost,* where "customs," "Arab men," and domesticity are taken up in a world that is equally estranged but displaced into the dark fantasies of horror rather than the peony pink of romance. These are estranged Arab worlds colored by longing. In the veiled best-seller the contemporary Arabic society (Jordan, Iraq, Palestine) is tethered back to Bedouin customs, Nabatean tombs, and T. E. Lawrence. Nostalgic fantasies like this are a classic example of "fanciful longing": the desire to compensate for a perceived cultural poverty and the absence of custom and tradition in Western urbanized society (Young 1997, 43). In the autumn of 2003 the emotions produced by this fantastic, contradictory, and estranged literary engagement with Iraq were seamlessly linked to the war on terror and taken for real.

When texts coincide with warfare, the uses to which they are put are called into question. In *Mayada,* the occupation is justified: as the progress of civilization and modernity on behalf of the oppressed. This nostalgic insertion of a colonial past into a colonizing present is highly accomplished through devices that are specific to the best-seller. Ken Gelder remarks that popular fiction can on occasion be hooked into the ideological work of speaking to urgent global realities, and this is clearly what happens in *Mayada*. This relation is not just a matter of textual content, of plot and characterization. As a literary field, the popular is distinguished by the whole apparatus of production, distribution, advertising, promotion, and consumption. These comprise the logics of the field as a culture industry. Popular fiction and nonfiction alike are caught up in the mechanisms of the marketplace, they are conscious of their readers and determined to please them. Writers in this economy of the best-seller are prolific, and they become brand names: readers can anticipate features of a serial product that will reliably produce certain pleasurable effects. This explains the presence of the Sasson Corporation as a broker in the marketing of women's life narrative. These writers often sustain a sense of intimacy with their readers and use new technologies to sustain an active engagement with their fans and to sell more books and associated merchandise by endorsements.

As Gelder emphasizes, the logics and practices of popular "literature" are production, output, sequels, and craft—all resolutely opposed to the singularity of "Literature." Whereas Literary culture celebrates originality and the cerebral work of reading (captured brilliantly in Azar Nafisi's *Reading "Lolita" in Tehran*), popular literature gives itself over to fantasy and adventure, excess and exaggeration. The peony-pink shades of Sasson's landscapes find their origins in the generic rules and precedents of harem literature. The ideological framework of romance in the veiled best-seller is obvious in the social and moral map Sasson constructs: romance writing is based on the idea of an innate emotional justice— good people are recognized and rewarded. The fascination with a latent aristocracy and the "exceptional" character shapes the biographical narrative of the al-Askari family, and this is characteristic of the conservatism of the romance genre.

These logics of the popular as a literary field establish a critical vocabulary for understanding "the Sasson effect." As a literary celebrity, Jean Sasson embodies and promotes an exotic engagement with the Arab world. The genres of popular fiction (and I am extrapolating to nonfiction as appropriate here) require something fundamental to be installed at its core: "an attitude, a sensibility, a paradigm" (Gelder 2005, 64). *Mayada* is a romantic life narrative in a series in which Sasson establishes a highly ideological worldview. The Jean Sasson website presents a conglomeration of links and information. There is an engaging picture of Sasson herself surrounded by books and Arab artifacts, and there is an immediate and autobiographical appeal to a public that is gendered, classed, and given permission to read: "Anyone who has ever known me well acknowledges that I am a terrible housekeeper. . . . While I'm busy fondling my books, a lot of dust collects." Lists such as "What I'm Reading" and "Ten of My Favorite Books" further establish Sasson as an arbiter of the good fast read, with a passion for the exotic. These links can also be used to merchandise new and associated products—sometimes fatefully, as we see with the Norma Khouri hoax, *Honor Lost*. A "conversation" with the writer offers autobiographical details that link together Sasson's history as a Southern belle—born and raised in Alabama as "an intense humanitarian who was naturally drawn to situations involving inequality"—and her fascination with history, adventure, and the Middle East. The website features reading guides and discussion questions for Sasson's books designed by an educational consultant to facilitate (and promote) circulation in book clubs and schools. Sasson monitors and contributes occasionally to discussions of her books at the site, which gathers responses from readers. Many of these are "fans" who testify to how they are moved emotionally by the books. There is also a section called "Information on Frivolous Lawsuits," which has been used by Sasson to reply to an allegation of plagiarism, and this reply includes an extensive calendar of when she wrote her books and when she has been in the Middle East.

The commodification of these narratives is linked to a readership with distinctive tastes, needs, and values. The author herself models a deportment, which is available for emulation by middle-class women with a passion for books and reading: a desire to encounter other cultures by proxy. Sasson presents Arab women as romanticized figures, noble and refined; for example, even amid the brutalities of Baladiyat Prison, Sasson characterizes Mayada and the shadow women in a sentimental fashion, and without psychological complexity. A fascination with royalty as embodiments of the history of ancient and/or remote cultures—Persia, Mesopotamia, the Ottoman Empire—is a recurrent feature of the Sasson brand. As a style of cross-cultural engagement this connects "intense humanitarianism" and passionate commitment to the rights of women globally with a "fanciful longing" for a richer and aristocratic culture that compensates for a perceived lack in Western urban culture and society.

The logic of identity here approaches the relation between self and other as mirroring, which engenders an empathy with others insofar as one can see them as like oneself. Implying that all women have a common identity, and imagining a homogenous collectivity of women across cultures, almost always assumes that Western values are the basis of the transaction; Euro-American feminist theory and rhetoric tends to be ethnocentric in its analysis of gender, experience, and oppression in this respect (Young 1979, 13). These are the grounds for extending the jurisdiction of Western feminism and human rights discourse to incorporate Muslim women and for campaigning on their behalf. When Iraqi women are represented as powerless victims—for example, the shadow women whose narratives are unresolved in Mayada's story, or the representation of Mayada herself as rendered eloquent by Sasson—they are being required to stand as other to Western women. This is the readily available conduit for life narrative to move westward and become a valuable commodity in the feminized metropolitan readerships for life narrative, and peritexts actively position readers in this way.

Product Placement

The production and reception of these best-sellers defines this literary field. These relations are dynamic. Often this is taken to mean these books are transient, ephemeral things, and given that the economy of the popular often works on the basis of the series and the branded product rather than on any single canonical text, this may well be appropriate. However, like all commodities, texts can strike the unexpected—given the dynamics of the mass market, they can be recycled and revived. Alternatively, they can reach a use-by date unexpectedly. At one extreme they can be recalled and removed from the shelves as a bad product (back to *Honor Lost* again). Sometimes, they can enjoy a prolonged shelf life—for example, Betty Mahmoody's *Not without My Daughter* has been continuously in print since 1987. Readers (often thought of as collectives rather than autonomous individuals when it comes to "literature") may be loyal to a brand but they are nonetheless discriminating. Gelder (2005) makes a critical point in characterizing the readers of popular genres: they may be leisured, fast, believing, and enchanted consumers, but they are not unthinking, uncritical, and undiscriminating (Janice Radway [1987] came to a similar conclusion in her study of romance readers). These readers can be disturbed by scandal, for genre shapes but does not fully determine reader response. The veiled best-seller is at risk when it engages with contemporary events as directly as *Mayada*, most particularly as it attempts to contain the occupation of Iraq.

We see this in the ongoing processing of *Mayada*, where it is clear that the conflict and rise of insurgency in Iraq impinges on reader responses to the ideological work of the book. Later developments, such as violent resistance, the ongoing deaths of civilians and military, and the struggle among factions within Iraq, call into question Sasson's vision of Iraq as the blank page awaiting inscription. Mayada's status as an authoritative inflected spokesperson on behalf of the Iraqi people becomes less convincing as it is clear that differences of allegiance to various religious, regional, ethnic, and gendered issues are constitutive of Iraqi politics, and a widespread cynicism about the motivations of the Coalition occupation calls into question Mayada's assurances of welcome. It is hard to impose a readymade docile Iraqi aristocracy into a position of eminence from afar. In particular, a different uptake of *Mayada* begins to emerge in the wake of scandal in 2004. Epitextual commentary suggests that, for some readers, the images and stories of atrocities against Iraqi prisoners at the hands of the American military at Abu Ghraib prison in Baghdad taint their reading of the book: "Army Pfc. Lynndie England probably didn't read this book before she became a guard at Abu Ghraib prison. But Jean Sasson's retelling of the prison experiences of Mayada, a prominent Baghdad journalist, has become a different reading experience as a result of England's (and others') alleged prisoner abuse at Abu Ghraib. The dim and squalid world of Saddam Hussein's Baladiyat prison that Sasson portrays resonates all the more unpleasantly since the media publication of pictures from Abu Ghraib" (Rayburn 2004). In the romantic framework of *Mayada* there is no moral ambiguity; the overwhelming drive of the narrative is to validate explicitly the assertion of pro-Western experience and values in Iraq. However, recent scandals and narratives of abuse from Abu Ghraib relocate readings of *Mayada:* empathy is replaced by irony (the death of romance!) and ethical boundaries blur. The elaborate fantasy of cross-cultural engagement in *Mayada* is overshadowed by (to use Rayburn's term) "unpleasant resonance." Scandals are affairs that destabilize the dynamics of the production and reception of even seemingly remote and mundane texts, and matters of impropriety in the public sphere can call their authority into question.

Of course, the most readily available epitexts are linked to book promotion activities and inclined to endorse the normative reading. Yet scandal can relocate a text into an alternative regime of value, and the structure of identification established for the implied reader is no longer tenable. Romance may be otherworldly, but it is not insulated from current affairs. Both Jean Sasson and Mayada al-Askari respond to criticisms of *Mayada* and use the Amazon.com website to reinforce their intention that "this book makes readers admire and respect Arab women." The veracity of *Mayada* anchors campaigns on behalf of social justice for Iraqi women. This jousting indicates the now turbulent passages of the book, and it suggests that Gelder's argument about the importance of genre in shaping readerly expectations is astute. Readers of the veiled best-seller will forgive fantasy, lack of psychological depth in characterization, and an estranged reality—all of which mark *Mayada* as true to generic type—and they will display strong loyalty to Sasson on the basis of past acquaintance with her work and her commitment to social justice for women. Nevertheless, fans police genres vigorously. Best-sellers become hooked into urgent global realities at their peril, for processes of commodification are never fully complete, nor are the effects of life narratives in action entirely predictable: "Given their imbrication in the flows of global capital and the commodification of suffering, stories are received and interpreted in unpredictable ways by those whose attention they seek and garner" (Schaffer and Smith 2004b, 27).

Recitations: The Spaces of the Harem

On the one hand, then, *Mayada* is afloat in a highly volatile and unpredictable set of circumstances, and its political investments become less convincing as the occupation of Iraq continues. At the same time, it is anchored in the well-established traditions of harem literature, which enable women writers to intervene in debates about gender and modernity and the relations between Occidental and Oriental cultures and societies. The whole business of writing, marketing, and reading best-sellers turns on precursors, sequels, precedents; these are the guarantees of generic consistency that secure reader loyalty. The veiled best-seller is a citational genre and intertextual relations are explicit. Gelder (2005) makes an important point in distinguishing the dynamics of the best-seller: individual authors may stand out in the field of popular writing and become brand names (as Jean Sasson does), but it is because of the genre they write in, and best-sellers characteristically broadcast generic affiliation. For this reason, publishers insisted on the generic picture of the veiled woman for the cover of *Mayada,* rather than a picture of Mayada al-Askari. Sasson discusses this decision at the Amazon.com website as a process of commodification controlled by booksellers.

About the cover: Once the author sells the rights to a book, he/she has little input about the covers or about anything much to do with the book, including publicity. Publishing is a business and publishing houses have large staffs to decide the best way to make their money back on a book. Dutton first had a cover with Mayada on it but when they took the book to market, the big booksellers protested the cover and said they wanted a veiled woman on it. At that time, the cover was changed. This was not the author's decision. (Amazon.com, September 24, 2004)

In fact, no image of Mayada al-Askari has appeared in the epitextual materials that circulate around and about her biography.

As a genre of popular biographical and autobiographical writing by women, harem literature goes back centuries: to the first Western woman's account of the inside of the harem—Lady Mary Wortley Montagu's *Embassy to Constantinople* (written in 1717 and first published in 1763). Since the eighteenth century, writers and readers turn to life narratives that sustain exotic images and titles featuring the veil, "harem," "Arabian" "concubines," "purdah." Western and Eastern women use the harem as a space for reflection on women's rights, freedoms, and desires. For Montagu, and other women writers, the sequestration of women in Islamic society suggested concepts of domesticity unavailable in Western traditions. It is by no means the case that women's writing about the harem tells a singular story of the oppression of Arab and Muslim women through sequestration. There is an important point to be made here (and it is the central argument of Reina Lewis's recent work on Ottoman women [2005]): Western women's accounts of the harem are self-conscious, heterogeneous, and contradictory from the outset and, although they are constantly marketed on the truth factor of offering access to forbidden spaces ("hareem"), they cannot be read as realistic, unmediated, or unembellished. Rather, they are historically contingent commodities. In the contemporary veiled best-seller, the war on terror hardens the lines of difference between cultures; this sharpens popular representations of women in the Orient as captives, victims of oppression and sexual cruelty. This is a contemporary example of a long-standing relation of harem writing to the vicissitudes of foreign policy and the changing fortunes of imperiums—Ottoman, British, and American.

Writers and readers have investments in the predictability of harem literature, and the peritexts of veiled best-sellers constantly direct attention to precursors and intertexts. As I have argued in an earlier chapter, reading life narratives from cover to cover—traveling on the routes suggested by epitexts and peritexts—allows us to track the textual cultures of life narratives. So, for example, Jean Sasson's earlier *Princess* trilogy authorizes *Mayada* on the front cover blurb. The trilogy has been brought back into print, released as a boxed set in 2004 "due to market demand," and in fresh (veiled) livery. They now coexist alongside *Mayada* on the shelves although they were originally published a decade ago. The war on terror secures their ongoing relevance and legitimacy. Sasson's fascination with royalty and the aristocracy emerges in these Arabian biographies, where she becomes the ghostwriter for Princess Sultana, a rebellious and spirited woman who is held captive by the "archaic traditions" of the House of Sa'ud. In *Princess* ([1992] 2004), *Daughters of Arabia* ([1994] 2004), and *Desert Royal* ([1999] 2004) stereotypes of a perverse sequestered society of Muslim women are renewed: the ultimate space of the Orientalist fantasy. Princess Sultana is a native informant, like Mayada she is a personal friend who asks Jean Sasson (who lived in Saudi Arabia from 1978 until 1991) to become her voice and tell her story, promising readers a "peek behind the veil and inside the palace walls" (*Princess*, 15). Authenticity is important: "The story of Princess Sultana is true. While the words are those of the author, the story is that of the Princess. The shocking human tragedies described here are factual" (*Princess*, 9). Sultana makes a direct appeal to Western women in a letter addressed to "Dear Readers of *Princess*": "We Saudi women have few possibilities for genuine change. We Saudi women need your help. Many of you live in countries where you can insist that your governments demand change from one of their economic and political partners, Saudi Arabia" (*Princess*, 20). The trilogy features terrible stories of the sadistic abuse of women in a community dominated by primitive customs, which reproduce women as victims and men as savages. Suicide and honor killing, infanticide and infibulations, rape and sodomy, polygamy, homosexuality, prostitution, and pornography—all are revealed in Sultana's narrative of the depravity of the Saudi royal family. The Western reader is gendered and placed in contradiction: she is a potential advocate for human rights on behalf of Saudi women, and she is offered the pleasures of the voyeur, with privileged intimate access to the sexualized and depraved harem.

Like Mayada, Sultana yearns for the benevolent American presence to initiate change: "The spark of life generated by material desire is hopelessly lacking in my land. Because of this, I despaired that the pages of history would ever turn in my land. We Saudis are too rich" (*Princess*, 90). In a commentary at her website, Sasson links the *Princess* trilogy to the events of 1991: "The reaction to the presence of the female Allied soldiers in the Persian Gulf war brought worldwide attention to the lowly status of women in Arabia . . . the idea began to form that one positive result of the war would be the loosening of the social customs that keep Saudi Arabian women relegated to the dark ages" (n.d.-b) But this simplifies the complex relations between Saudi Arabia and the West. Sultana's appeals for Western intervention on behalf of oppressed women are deceptive—Saudi Arabia is a key ally of the United States and crucial to military strategy in the Middle East. There has been ongoing American presence and investment in Saudi Arabia. The point is, this presence has not translated into a critique of Saudi customs, and it is very unlikely that this will occur.

The geopolitics that stall human rights campaigns on behalf of Saudi women can be traced further through recitations—a specific intertextual relation that connects Sasson's *Princess* trilogy to the notorious Western docudrama *Death of a Princess,* described as one of the most controversial television programs ever put to air. Originally screened by PBS in May 1980 and screened again in a special twenty-fifth anniversary celebration in March 2005, this story of the honor killing of a House of Sa'ud princess, Misha'al, in July 1977 presented a controversial image of the Saudi royal family as licentious, corrupt, and promiscuous. Sultana gives her version of the docudrama narrative in volume 2 of Sasson's trilogy, *Daughters of Arabia,* and it fits seamlessly into the representation of Arabs in the docudrama as by nature sensuous yet perverted by fundamentalism and tribal custom. The docudrama and the political controversy that ensued in Britain and the United States (involving diplomatic incidents, maneuvering by businesses with interests in Saudi Arabia, and pressure from special interest groups) challenged precisely that separation of foreign policy—economic and military relations among Britain, the United States, and Saudi Arabia—and human rights—the ongoing suppression of women in the kingdom.[1] Despite this public exposure of abuse and violation of women's rights, appeals to the international community have been in vain. The logic of Sultana's call for benevolent intervention is flawed: because Saudi Arabia is a powerful political and economic partner of America and its allies, there will be no concerted response for demands to change its gender relations and customs. Epitexts and peritexts confirm that the veiled best-seller travels on routes that are always inflected by broader geopolitical concerns. Campaigns for women's rights, in particular, are sensitive and taken up variously and strategically. In a new author's note to *Desert Royal* Jean Sasson observes that in the wake of 9/11 and the war on terror there have been public celebrations of the liberation of Afghan women from the burka and attention to the condition of women in Iraq; however, silence prevails about Saudi women. She looks for a campaign on behalf of women to take effect globally following the war on terror. The routes of the veiled best-seller itself reveal why this will not occur, for popular cultural forms are co-opted variously into more specific and aggressive geopolitical agendas, which always temper their global campaigns for human rights and social justice. To return to Butler: the rights of women in Afghanistan and Iraq were taken up as a "rationale for our violence, the incursion on sovereignty, the deaths of civilians" (2004, 142). No such rationale exists in the case of Saudi Arabia. Arundhati Roy makes the link succinctly: "It's being made out that the whole point of the war was to topple the Taliban regime and liberate Afghan women from their burqas. We're being asked to believe that the U.S. marines are actually on a feminist mission. (If so, will their next stop be America's military ally Saudi Arabia?)" (2004, 18).

Ultimately, the route of the veiled best-seller returns to Tehran and taps into the political and emotional legacies of the Iranian Revolution, a crucible in contemporary Euro-American representations of Islamic societies. The endorsement of Betty Mahmoody, coauthor (with William Hoffer) of *Not without My Daughter* (1987), is reproduced on all of Sasson's best-sellers. It is Mahmoody's story of her incarceration in Iran after the revolution that revitalized the captivity narrative in contemporary harem literature (and, incidentally, the legend of the innocent American confronted by fanatics): "Like most sheltered Americans, I had overestimated the power of my government in dealing with a fanatical foreign power" (165). In the period immediately after the overthrow of the shah, the hostage crisis produced the conditions for a virulent depiction of Iranian Islamism in the form of a captivity narrative to come into play, and Mahmoody's book is based on her own traumatic experiences as a wife and mother. It remains popular these days and, like Sasson's *Princess* trilogy, has recently been republished for a new readership. This fear of captivity is the dark side of harem literature: here is the horror of the white Christian woman incarcerated and subjected to the veil against her will. *Not without My Daughter* continues to be a best-seller, and Mahmoody's graphic description of holding a spittle-laden chador tightly to her face is not easily forgotten. The Iranian hostage crisis preoccupied the American public and U.S. foreign policy, laying a rich archive of images in popular memory for Mahmoody's own story to reach a wide and believing readership on its first release in 1987, which was later expanded with the release of Brian Gilbert's film of the memoir in 1991. Nostalgia for the Pahlavi monarchy of the shah lingers even now—quite explicitly in the epitexts that circulate around American harem literature. Like Mahmoody, Sasson, too, has strong feelings about the Islamic Republic in Iran and the republican revolution of 1979. At her website Sasson chronicles her reading in the spring of 2004, including Farah Pahlavi's autobiographical narrative, *An Enduring Love: My Life with the Shah*. This style of autobiographical romance from the now exiled pro-Western upper echelons of Iranian society promotes nostalgia: "I couldn't help but think how different the world would been had the shah not been overthrown. Certainly the horrific war with Saddam Hussein would not have occurred. . . . Who knows what the face of the Middle East would look like had the Shah remained in power? . . . I found myself liking the Shah a lot more than I could ever have realized" (n.d.-c).

The trope of captivity traces the attachment of life narrative to the politics of conquest and trespass. As Linda Colley (2003) points out in her brilliant history of captivity, the captive body is both symptomatic and emblematic, marking out the changing boundaries of imperial aggression: the frontiers where fears, insecurities, and ambiguities abound. Mahmoody and Sasson are vital to the processing of the contemporary veiled best-seller. Their endorsement in peritexts both identifies and polices the field, providing legitimation and approval. Their endorsement alongside the veiled image on the book jacket secures the brand (and so, too, does an Oprah Book Club choice, accorded to another captivity narrative about royal wives and concubines, *Stolen Lives* by Malika Oufkir, in 2002). To return to Gelder's (2005) discussion of the logics of this field: genre and branding works industrially and guarantees the content and the quality of the book. Endorsements, precursors, and re-citations register the new in relation to the history and traditions of the genre.

Reading this citational genre through its paratexts excavates a complex history of engagement in geopolitics. Alongside *Mayada* are recycled editions of Sasson's trilogy, originally produced in the wake of the Persian Gulf War, and Mahmoody's *Not without My Daughter,* a response to the Iranian Revolution a decade before that. These books signal their affiliation one to the other. Their copresence as harem literature and their campaign for social justice on behalf of women is traditional—part of the long history of women writing about gender across cultures with a desire to make compassionate connections. But the renewed value of the veiled best-seller as a commodity in the market now tells another story, one that marks the political vulnerability of harem literature: the cheap read that sustains voyeurism and propaganda; the selling of sensational stories of abuse in the guise of compassionate concern; and dreams of conquest that tie together violence and campaigns for social justice.

By focusing on the veiled best-seller, this chapter has become increasingly preoccupied with captivity, one way and another: shadow women remain captive in Baladayat Prison and interned in testimony by the autobiographical narrator Mayada; Mayada al-Askari herself, captured then liberated into eloquence and freedom by her American ghostwriter; Jean Sasson captured as a celebrity writer at her own website. There is also the jarring presence of Abu Ghraib Prison in Baghdad, and Rayburn's (2004) strange speculation about whether Lynndie England reads books like *Mayada.* There is the haunting presence of the events in Iran in 1979, which cast a long shadow in captivity narrative that I will return to in *Reading "Lolita" in Tehran* in a later chapter. Finally, there is the implied reader of the best-seller herself: conventionally figured as a mere consumer, enchanted, and captive. Much of this confirms the generally held view that best-sellers are enslaved to the crude geopolitics of capital-ism and imperialism. Clearly the veiled best-seller is a potent weapon in propaganda wars now. But I see it as a "soft" weapon, nevertheless: not because of its peony-pink tint but because of its susceptibility to taint. When romantic best-sellers take on the work of propaganda, it can be good business, but it is risky, for they too are hostage to fortune. Which brings us, finally, in the chapter that follows, to Norma Khouri and the aptly titled *Honor Lost:* the hoax that brings the brand into disrepute.

FIVE

Tainted Testimony:
The Work of Scandal

There is no testimony that does not structurally imply in itself the possibility of fiction, simulacra, dissimulation, lie and perjury. JACQUES DERRIDA, *DEMEURE*

And so in this stifling climate of laws, a modest beauty salon in Amman became the stage for an epic struggle between the almost blinding force of Islam and a fragile haraam—forbidden—love. NORMA KHOURI, *HONOR LOST*

Norma Khouri's fictional testimony is the hoax we had to have; the conditions are just right for life narratives by and about Muslim and Arab women to be "outed" in this way by a rogue trader with tainted goods. Two books, and an author with two very different identities, perpetrate this hoax; however, there is only one story to tell. In the United States, Atria Books (a division of the Simon and Schuster/Viacom group) published *Honor Lost: Love and Death in Modern-Day Jordan* in February 2003 (2003b). It remains available through Amazon.com as a "bargain book," although it has very publicly been withdrawn from bookshelves elsewhere. The creamy white jacket of *Honor Lost* promises entry into forbidden domains: the Muslim woman obscured by the veil, ancient ruins in the background, and Arabic decorative design are all trademarks of associations among gender, ethnicity, and tradition that drive the "veiled best-seller." Elsewhere, Norma Khouri's story appeared as *Forbidden Love. A Harrowing True Story of Love and Revenge in Jordan* and was also published in 2003 (through Transworld Publishers, a division of the Random

House Group in Australasia and the United Kingdom [2003a]). Random House ordered its withdrawal when it was outed as a fraud in July 2004 and maintains a website recording the extraordinary few weeks when it defended and then finally rejected Khouri as a trustworthy autobiographer.[1] In the meantime, Norma Khouri had taken up residence as a refugee in Australia and become a literary celebrity. The jacket of *Forbidden Love* is dark and gilded, the obverse of the pale palette of Atria's *Honor Lost,* but the same trademarks remain: the kohl-eyed veiled Muslim woman, and Arabic motifs suggesting enduring and ancient traditions.

Peritexts aside, there is a single story to both editions. It focuses on honor killing. This is the practice of retribution carried out by male family members when women bring dishonor to their families because of sexual indiscretions. Death is the most severe punishment; other forms of abuse and denigration of women are more common forms of retribution. Although the notion of family honor and shame is particularly important in Muslim communities, and the prohibition of sexual relationships outside marriage in Islam does not distinguish between men and women, in some countries women are singled out for punishment for sexual crimes. In their "Position Paper on 'Honor Killings'" (1999), the Muslim Women's League, which regards honor killing as a violation of Islam, suggests that this problem is not a problem of morality or of ensuring that women maintain their own personal virtue. Rather, it is a problem of domination, power, and hatred of women, who are viewed as nothing more than servants to the family. Like suttee and clitoridectomy, honor killing is an issue that produces moral outrage on behalf of women oppressed by archaic cultural practices.

In both *Honor Lost* and *Forbidden Love,* the same story of terrible retribution is told. Dalia and the autobiographical narrator are best friends, born in 1970 and raised in the tightly knit Jebel Hussein district of Amman. Dalia's family is strict Muslim, Norma's is Catholic, however the two women are persecuted by the "universal Arab creed" that oppresses all Jordanian women: the fierce and primitive Bedouin codes that are "always nagging at men's instincts, reminding them that under the Westernizing veneer, they are all still Arabs" (2). Unlikely as it seems, the two take advantage of the fact that Jordanian women can sustain careers in the beauty parlor business. They offer a service unique in Amman: a salon catering for men and women. N&D's salon opened in May 1990—or so the story goes. Dalia is beautiful in the way heroines of romance are meant to be: doe-eyed, perfect light olive skin and full lips, waist-length thick, wavy tresses. In March 1995 their lives change when Michael, a broad-shouldered handsome officer, comes into the salon. Unlike any

Arab man the girls have ever known or imagined (and they share a re-vulsion at the thought of being associated with Arab men), Michael is emotional, loving, and devoted. The doomed lovers and Norma risk their lives on a dangerous adventure "for simply a romance" (57). When the affair is discovered, Dalia is stabbed in her own home, the victim of an honor killing at the hands of her father and brothers: "Losing Dalia in this way made vivid to me something I'd always known but had man-aged to ignore. I could no longer hide my true emotions and beliefs in the hope my silent cries would be heard. In memory of Dalia, I vowed to transform my silence into audible screams for justice and equal rights" (145). This narrative is, then, presented as that "audible scream."

Now we know *Honor Lost* as a hoax, we are free to read it as a parody of the veiled best-seller, in which a modest beauty salon in Amman, Jordan becomes the scene for a clash of civilizations. Khouri, who claimed to have written the book secretly from exile in an Internet café in the West, connects this romance to the aftermath of September 11 quite explicitly. Honor killing, like the violent acts of terrorism against non-Arabs "that have made the Western world suddenly hungry to understand this alien place," becomes another sign of the call to war and violence that is em-bedded and codified in the Arab world (63). For Khouri, this primitivism and violence define a totalitarian Arabic society across the Middle East that persecutes women above all. In *Honor Lost,* this archaic misogynist society is defied by the essence of freedom: the spontaneous romance, "the Western idea of marriage for love" that animates the narrative as an "epic struggle."

It says a great deal about the climate for the veiled best-seller after 9/11 that Khouri's book was taken as fact rather than fiction, testimony rather than parody, despite its blatant stereotyping and logical inconsis-tencies. Her "insider story" of a society bound by barbaric rituals rooted in ethnic Bedouin tradition was very quickly recognized as a flawed ac-count by Jordanian activists in Amman. Ironically their campaign was triggered by hubris: at the end of *Forbidden Love* Khouri exhorts her read-ers to become part of the campaign against honor killing. She lists con-tacts in Jordan, including the e-mail address of the *Jordan Times* investi-gative journalist and activist, Rana Husseini, who has for over a decade written articles to stir public opinion against honor killing. It was the flow of e-mails triggered by her inclusion in the peritext of *Forbidden Love* that alerted Husseini to Khouri's testimony. Together with Amal Sabbagh, the secretary-general of the Jordanian National Commission for Women, she compiled an extensive dossier of errors in Khouri's book.

Their investigation established that no salon as described by Khouri had ever existed, and unisex salons are in fact illegal in Jordan; no one in what Khouri herself describes as a tightly knit Amman neighborhood had any knowledge of Khouri or her family or of the brutal murder of Dalia in 1996. Husseini and Sabbagh concluded that it is the timing of Khouri's book that is significant: between the 9/11 attacks and the Iraq war, the time was ripe for narratives emphasizing the primitivism of Arab and Muslim societies.[2] Sabbagh claims that the organization contacted Khouri's publisher, Random House, in September 2003 and warned it was publishing a fake book:

Actually, after reading the book we started investigating all the errors in the book. . . . And finally we sent them a letter on September 7 asking them very respectfully to review the book, have independent sources review it, and check the credibility of the book . . . we respectfully requested that the book be removed from the shelves and be stamped as a fiction book. It could have been written by someone with no knowledge at all of Jordan, its society. . . . But for someone to say she is a Jordanian, lived in Jordan all her life and just left the country it was impossible. (Quoted in Knox 2004b, 6)

The story unraveled very quickly once journalists were on the trail of fraud. By August 2004 the different identities of Norma Khouri were laid bare. Khouri is Norma al-Bagain Toliopoulos, and she lived in Jordan until she was three years old. She has a U.S. passport and has lived from 1973 to 2000 in Chicago, where some members of her family remain. Although Khouri is unknown in the neighborhood of Jebel Hussein in Amman, family, neighbors, and acquaintances recall her twenty-seven years of unremarkable suburban life in Chicago. In 2000, Khouri left Chicago, and she began another life as a refugee and autobiographer. The journalist Malcolm Knox links the fabrication of the life and the book: "She wrote the book and submitted it piecemeal to Christy Fletcher, a highly reputable New York literary agent. Fletcher edited it for fluency, but did not investigate the truth of Norma's story. He subsequently sold it to 16 publishers around the world, and it was comprehensively vetted by lawyers for Viacom in the United States and Transworld in Britain. None of this uncovered Norma's real life. Having sold the lie, she came to Australia, enjoyed a rapturous welcome from readers, and continued to act out the fabrication" (Knox 2004a, 1). By the time the lie on the page and in person was exposed, Khouri had petitioned the United Nations personally on behalf of oppressed Muslim women, her book was published in fifteen countries through global publishing networks, and Australians attended Khouri's dramatic readings in droves and voted her book one of their favorite one hundred books of all time.

Faddish Fibbing

When a hoax autobiography is outed in public, everyone becomes a literary critic, and the fraud is suddenly all so obvious.[3] "All autobiographies contain little lies, but Norma Khouri's may be one of the many that are one big lie. Khouri . . . had the usual formula for success in a world starving for fashionable victims. It goes like this: trade as a woman, if possible, who is from some tribe or oppressed minority, and has survived the cruelty of whites/colonialists/right-wing thugs/rich guys. And if you aren't any of all of the above, then fake it."[4] A scandal is a definitive event; it brings to light the social, political, and ethical investments of narrators, readers, and publishers in life narrative. A hoax brings autobiography out of the shadows and into the editorials, columns, and opinion pieces of the Sunday tabloid. "Write a book that tells of your woe, or trades on it. Garnish with New Age mysticism . . . and showtime! Teary readers! Big sales! . . . Just perfect for readers looking for the latest victims to weep over. In one shop I found [Khouri's book] next to four other books with near identical covers showing Muslim women peering sadly, but so fetchingly, from behind a veil." And so the tabloid columnist Andrew Bolt stitches together a "tradition" of minority life narrative from a different angle. Here is the dark side of autobiography in transit: "Why not lie, when it works so well that Rigoberta Menchú won a Nobel peace prize through her even more faddish fibbing in her *I, Rigoberta Menchú?* The Khouri hoax becomes the latest episode in a history of fakes, frauds and fibbers which links together a series of testimonies and autoethnographies in the recent past by those who bear the most sacred marks of victimhood, and particularly that ethnic thing."[5] In an article headed "Why We Love a Hard Luck Story," Bolt constructs a canon of fake lives: Norma Khouri, Rigoberta Menchú, Sally Morgan (1988), their fakery warning us we're pandering not only to self-pitying rage against the System but also to a romanticization of victimhood that keeps true victims in their place. The Jordanian activists, too, lament the effect of a fraud on their campaign against honor killing.

Scandal shadows contemporary testimony and autoethnography and draws it into disrepute, and at the same time it brings into view the expectations and contracts that bind readers, publishers, and writers of these genres. Bolt is a rogue critic. His canon of "fake" lives is tendentious, for it includes several of the most celebrated and influential literary testimonies of the recent past, Morgan's *My Place* and Menchú's *I, Rigoberta Menchú: An Indian Woman in Guatemala,* which have been the subject of intensive critical debate and are by no means generally labeled as hoax texts. In her discussion of the Menchú controversy, Leigh Gilmore discusses the complexities of testimonial speech, which bears witness to trauma and loss on behalf of a collective.[6] Gilmore points out that testimony tests crucial limits in autobiography, not only the one understood as the boundary between truth and lies but also the inflation of the self to stand for silenced others and speak on their behalf (2001, 5). Allegations of invention and fraud are especially troubling for minority life narrative, which is branded and sold in terms of authenticity and truth. Bolt places the marketing of Muslim life narratives crudely and cynically but astutely: this is how writers fake lives, trap publishers, and find a gullible readership. Bolt constructs this fakery as the latest episode in a gendered and ethnicized tradition, for in his account the hoax is the game of deceit played both by and on behalf of colonized women.

Bolt isn't the only journalist to make pertinent comments about these "hot" stories and faddish fibs. Hoax life narratives bring observations about the situation of contemporary life narrative out of the specialist academic journal and into the popular press. For example, the Khouri debate has led editorial writers, publishers, and journalists to speculate about the ways that memoir attends to a "psychological hunger" for learning about the lives of other people that is no longer met in contemporary fiction; Michael Duffy recalls Gertrude's Stein's prediction that the novel would die once we were able to read elsewhere intimate stories about private lives (quoted in Legge 2004, 2). Like the James Frey controversy of 2006, worries about "quality control" arose: why can't publishers police the boundaries of autobiography to maintain an authentic product? What are the rights of readers and the responsibilities of publishers? Are Khouri's readers entitled to a refund? Booksellers agree that the label of "nonfiction" was critical to the best-seller status of *Honor Lost,* as sales of nonfiction, from memoirs to autobiographies, fulfill a desire for facts and truth that is promised by the autobiographical pact. Finally, HarperCollins's publishing director, Shona Martyn, suggests Khouri's success benefited from a global post–September 11 demand for nonfiction, "particularly books which perpetuate negative stereotypes about Islamic men" (quoted in Legge, 2). The editorial in the *Australian* of July 30, 2004, concurs: "[Khouri] appeared to be a brave woman standing up for the rights of women in a brutal sexist society. In presenting Middle Eastern men as violent bigots, she had a plot custom-made for our times." It is the "custom-made" nature of *Honor Lost* that suggests this is the hoax that we had to have; this is the fake for which readers and publishers were ripe and ready. The empathic engagement that is withheld from refugees and asylum seekers is there in abundance for oppressed women in Islamic states. Khouri is the refugee who had a story to tell that we wanted to hear.

Discussions about the Khouri affair in the media bring into popular public discourse ways of thinking about autobiography that at other times may be disregarded as postmodern or postcolonial intellectualizing. The idea that life narratives enter the West from the East—Middle, Central, or Far—and circulate to shape public opinion, reinforce stereotypes, and present plots "custom-made for our times" suggests their potency as propaganda. Arguments about legitimacy and authenticity are critical in the trajectory of minority life narrative, and testimony is always subject to cross-examination; these arguments become heated and volatile as testimony gathers force and becomes authoritative. By identifying the hoax as the "dark side" of autobiography in transit I mean to suggest that allegations of faddish fakery and the questioning of authenticity are almost always present when a testimonial narrative reaches the threshold where it becomes an influential force in the public sphere, able to elicit empathy and awareness of human rights issues. We see from Bolt's scornful commentary how effectively testimony can be contained and discredited, and how powerful a hoax text can be in drawing down the whole industry. His pithy summary—"trade as a woman . . . who is from some tribe or oppressed minority, and has survived the cruelty of whites/colonialists/right-wing thugs/rich guys"—satirizes minority life narrative, and it touches on the scandals that have tainted other authoritative life narratives that speak of human rights abuses, such as indigenous testimony, Menchú's *testimonio,* Holocaust testimony, and now life narrative from the Middle East.

Scandal is good for publishing in terms of sales at least. Although *Forbidden Love* was withdrawn from bookshelves in Australia in 2004, the Atria edition of *Honor Lost* remains available in the United States, online at least, and the debate in the media has produced a rush of interest and sales. In fact French publishers refused to withdraw the book and exulted in its infamy and the increased sales that followed. Improbably, over 250,000 copies had been sold worldwide before the fraud was uncovered. "Improbable" because, as one Amazon.com reader delicately remarks (prior to the controversy): "Her writing may not be as eloquent and stunning as one may hope."[7] From the very first sentence of the prologue to *Honor Lost*—"Jordan is a place where men in sand-colored business suits hold cell phones to one ear and, in the other, hear the whispers of harsh and ancient laws blowing in from the desert"—it is clear that Khouri is not averse to stereotype and cliché, to doe-eyed heroines and savage Bedouins, and readers were quick to recognize these aesthetic flaws. The question of why readers valued this narrative despite the ethical flaws that follow from blatant ethnicized stereotypes is an important one.

There are other uses of scandal for, as Gilmore argues in her discussion of *I, Rigoberta Menchú* and *The Kiss,* scandalous self-representation brings into view how stories of private lives emerge and circulate to polemical effect in the public sphere. Gilmore uses the concept of jurisdiction to suggest that autobiographical self-representation is a forum of judgment, and it makes claims to certain kinds of agency and authority. By using the concept of jurisdiction to examine the power of life narratives in particular, Gilmore draws attention to how they offer nonlegal testimony and make claims to authority in the public sphere that cannot be made through more formal judicial processes: "Jurisdictions are forms and representations of legitimacy that confer status and identity on persons and acts" (2002, 597). Most useful for thinking about *Honor Lost* is the suggestion that the concept of jurisdiction illuminates the rhetorical strategies around self-representation, identity, and authority that are used to locate a personal history within the public sphere. Hoax aside, *Honor Lost* was always a controversial text, for it uses life narrative to bring to light the practice of honor killing, invoking quite explicitly an alternative jurisdiction to the Shar'ia courts that address the custom of honor crimes according to traditional Islamic law. In the peritext of *Forbidden Love* Khouri deliberately invokes an international court of appeal, an alternative jurisdiction on behalf of oppressed and silenced Arab women in Jordan: "the voices of people in Western nations."

Striking a Chord

The peritext of Khouri's book establishes a cross-cultural relationship that situates the reader as Western and female. The guarantee of authenticity by Jean Sasson, the author of the best-selling *Princess* trilogy, on both editions of Khouri's book also offers legitimacy. To establish a market prior to publication, Khouri's publishers sought Jean Sasson's patronage for the book. At Sasson's website we can still find her endorsement of the Atria edition.[8] The connection between Sasson and the readership Khouri pursues is explicit on the cover blurb, where Sasson promises "this extraordinary true story is well told, worth telling and impossible to put down." The affinity between Khouri's narrative and Sasson's series of popular biographies that feature the oppression of Muslim and Arab women by ancient tradition is clear. In the trade that circulates around and about life narrative by and about Arab women, the American writer Jean Sasson is a powerful broker, and a brand name that attracts a loyal readership. Her endorsement of *Honor Lost* was a sign to readers of its generic affinity with the nonfiction best-seller, which is "impossible to put down"—a mistaken endorsement, as it turned out, and Sasson herself can be regarded as a victim of lack of due diligence on the part of Khouri's literary agent and publisher.

The subtitle of *Forbidden Love* is *A Harrowing Story of Love and Revenge in Jordan,* and a statement on the reverse title page confirms its pedigree as authentic life narrative: "This story is true to my memory and experiences. Pseudonyms have been used and details altered to protect the identity, privacy and safety of people mentioned in this book." This statement is not reproduced in the American edition, *Honor Lost,* although the jacket commentary and dedication to Dalia affirm the autobiographical narration of testimony on behalf of a dead woman. The covers of both editions feature every-(Muslim)-woman, promising the kind of "pleasurable sadness" that is the stock in trade of Muslim life narrative (figs. 5, 6). The connotations of this image are confirmed by the cover blurb: "Shocking and dramatic, *Honor Lost* will strike a chord with women everywhere and is a testimony to the courage and strength of women who are prepared to defy generations of male dominance." The association of *Honor Lost* with campaigns for human rights is also explicit: "The author is donating a portion of the proceeds from the sale of this book to international women's and human rights charities." The very last page of *Forbidden Love* includes a supplement that asks "What can you do?"

A lot! A campaign is now underway to bring an end to honor crimes. Everyone can help by signing e-mail petitions, writing letters of objection or donating to United Nations approved organizations that are working for women's rights.

"In fact," says Norma, "the voices of people in Western nations are particularly powerful because Jordan is desperate to give the impression that it's a modern, democratic state. For this reason Jordan hides honor killing from the Western world but increased awareness and involvement by the international community will make it difficult for the Jordanian government to maintain that image and allow this practice."

5　Front cover design from Norma Khouri, *Honor Lost: Love and Death in Modern-Day Jordan*

NORMA KHOURI

FORBIDDEN
LOVE

A harrowing true story of love and revenge in Jordan

6   Front cover design from Norma Khouri, *Forbidden Love*

This call to collective action through nongovernment organizations (NGOs) is strategically important. The autobiographical Norma elicits the empathic response of a powerful gendered, secular, and humanist readership in the West: those who identify with democracy, feminism, and modernity and who are susceptible to the evangelical appeal to promulgate these values elsewhere. In this way, *Honor Lost* evokes empathy in a specifically targeted readership, and powerfully so, given its narrative of endemic and sanctioned abuse and violence against Muslim and Arab women. It seeks to channel this emotion into activism in the global arena. The representation of Jordan as a fundamentalist, patriarchal, and authoritarian society that presents a duplicitous front to the West is a story well crafted for these times and, as Khouri points out, a refutation of the carefully produced image of Jordan as a contemporary reformist Islamic nation that is nurtured by the Jordanian state in the Western mass media.

A particularly modern set of associations that connect life narratives to humanitarian campaigns establishes the jurisdiction for *Honor Lost*. The modernist language of human rights in the final decades of last century established a role for life narratives as persuasive global carriers of "rights discourse" (Schaffer and Smith, 2004a, 3). Life narratives promulgate this language as they legitimate personal experience as an agent of change and carry passionate and authentic appeals for social justice and sovereignty across an international civic sphere. This has driven the memoir boom, shaping cross-cultural engagements in compassionate and empathic terms. By appealing to this jurisdiction, Khouri produces a story pitched to an already well-established market for exotic life narrative in the West. The ingredients for the success of *Honor Lost* and the conditions of Khouri's rapid emergence as a literary celebrity in a variety of media are sketched succinctly by Schaffer and Smith, and these are all vital to the success of the Khouri hoax: at this historical moment, telling life stories in print or through the media depends on a Western-based publishing industry, media, and ownership; this dependence affects the kinds of stories published and circulated, and the appeals they make to audiences; interlocking media venues carry life narratives through print and electronic media with a recurrent interest in stories of suffering, survival, and individual triumph. In this way, life narrative is used as a means of staging trauma in a variety of media. The commodification of sensationalized life narratives by Arab and Muslim women is a well-established circuitry that was immediately available to Norma Khouri. Directed to a Western feminist reader or spectator, a large and well-established readership, these narratives draw on "rights discourse" to trigger empathic identification, benevolence, and a response to trauma in terms of a liberal set of values that are held above and beyond cultural difference. These stories, as Schaffer and Smith emphasize, are frequently sensationalized, sentimentalized and charged with affect, and they offer privileged readers the pleasures of empathic identification, which becomes "a means to the reader's own self-affirmation as an empowered agent, here an agent of social change and humanitarian betterment" (12).

In this way a set of conditions, established last century, is a transit lane that allows some stories of trauma to move from East to West, South to North, rapidly and to become highly valued commodities that find a "primed" readership. Khouri's book is able to "reduce" readers so powerfully *because* human rights discourse is situated as a universal and uncontestable ethics of cross-cultural relations, an inevitable and natural "moral grammar." As part of the doxa of globalization it seems both true and necessary. The representation of honor killing in *Honor Lost* shows why life narrative is such a powerful commodity in directing this traffic across cultures, for Khouri associates the West with freedom, human rights, reason, and democracy as opposed to an Arab world that is associated in equally isomorphic terms with barbarity, misogyny, and madness. She then proceeds to invite Western intervention in the interests of social justice. This interpellation of readers in the West as enlightened and powerful appeals to the coalition of women particularly: the spectacular success of *Honor Lost* and its charismatic author suggests how buying and reading life narratives becomes an act of solidarity through which women can understand themselves to be part of a powerful cross-cultural collective.

Appeals to an alternative jurisdiction on behalf of Arab women draw powerfully on feminist identity politics—the desire of women to identify with each other empathically across cultures. In *Honor Lost* Western women readers find both a reminder of their power and an invitation to intervene on the behalf of women who are silenced and oppressed by "primitive Arab customs." Identity politics accentuates the power and authority of rights discourse, and honor killing is an issue where the incendiary combination of gender, trauma, and cultural difference creates the infrastructure for a compelling life narrative to become part of activist campaigns. *Honor Lost* appeals to the global campaign against honor killing, and it recycles stereotypes of the endemic primitivism of Arab culture in Jordan as anxieties about Islamic fundamentalism are on the rise.

Trust

The conditions are ripe for a hoax to emerge through Muslim and Arab life narratives in the course of the war on terror. A hoax rides on the momentum of best-selling autobiography. In fact, the presence of a hoax can signal that testimony has reached a threshold of legitimacy and recognition in the dominant culture such that it can mask the pretender. There is a generic place on the shelf already established, as it were, and the hoax text signals its affiliation with this established tradition, sometimes quite extravagantly so. The hoax testimony is a parasite. This means two things: it travels on a dominant testimonial current, and it saps its power and authority by drawing all testimonial narrative into disrepute. Life narrative is vulnerable to co-option in this way. The autobiographical contract is susceptible to fakery, and testimony is above all genres of life narrative at risk, reduced through hoax to a display of "the most sacred marks of victimhood, and particularly that ethnic thing." The idea that testimony speaks truth to power on behalf of the oppressed is the source of its legitimacy; membership of the subaltern community is vital to the authority of testimonial discourse. Susanna Egan is right to point out that deliberate imposture barely figures in current theorizing about autobiography and ethics (2004, 15). In discussions of testimony in particular, imposture is inconceivable and beyond the pale as an outrageous abuse of faith and trust. For this reason, the hoax leaves a legacy of suspicion and taint in its wake that diminishes trust for testimony more generally.

The connection between testimony and human rights defines it as a hallowed act of life narrative. Cynthia Franklin and Laura E. Lyons (2004) suggest this sacredness of testimony quite explicitly by bringing together the forensic brushwork of excavating the bodies of victims of torture and murder, attending to the remains of human beings with scrupulous care and devotion to precise detail, and the production and witnessing of stories that "make these lives and deaths matter" (v). Dealing with testimony requires respect: "'Personal effects' refers to the belongings of the dead, and testimony constitutes a narrative remainder. In the context of struggles against human rights abuses, often what remains of victims and the stories that can be told about their work, their relationships, and what is known of their end" (viii). This very direct connection between testimony, abused bodies, and oppression situates the production and witnessing of testimony as sacred acts of remembrance.

Metaphorical associations between the bodies of testimony and victim, text and flesh, are faked quite specifically in *Honor Lost*. Norma speculates that Dalia's murder by her father and, perhaps, her brothers will remain a matter for the Islamic Shar'ia courts rather than the civil legal system, for laws pertaining to honor killing "stem from ancient beliefs that, by now, have been codified into law" (154). Furthermore she anticipates that Dalia's body will be subjected to the indignity of a postmortem to ascertain her virginity for her family and the courts. It is at Dalia's unmarked grave—where she is buried without ceremony and with no coffin in a "bizarre" place between Islamic and Christian burial grounds—that Norma and Michael, Dalia's beloved, meet and Norma promises to take action on her friend's behalf. *Honor Lost* is presented as that legacy, and it is specifically dedicated to the memory of Dalia: "I realize that she left me with a mission. It's a task I must undertake, a goal I pray to reach. I must find a way to expose honor crimes for what they truly are: legalized murder. To break through the official Jordanian code of silence and find a way to make all Arab women's silent cries for justice and freedom heard around the world" (207).[9] Under these circumstances, the faux testimony is an act of sacrilege: it tampers not just with property and truth (which are abused in all literary hoaxes) but also with faith and trust. It is an outrage to the reader, to the dead on whose behalf it seeks advocacy and remembrance, and the living who remain silenced victims of abuse. In *Honor Lost* there are two life stories told relationally, ostensibly based on a collaborative diary: the autobiographical Norma and the biographical depiction of Dalia. These stories stand (or fall!) together, and they are the affective core of the book.

We now know that there is no body to be carefully excavated by the brushwork of this testimony. The fact that honor crime continues is uncontested, as activists in Jordan point out, although they argue that Khouri vastly overstates its frequency for dramatic effect. What reduces this testimony to "Harlequin romance in a chador" is the misrepresentation in Khouri's own autobiographical story. There is no collaborative diary by Norma and Dalia, no meeting beside an unmarked grave for Norma and Michael, and (most important for testimony as a genre) there is dissent from the community of women in Jordan on whose behalf Khouri claims to speak. As a story of fraud and deception unfolded in mid-2004, the questions that became most pertinent were how a hoax of this order—the confection of Amman from Chicago—can be sustained now, when new technologies offer archival search engines and rapid global communications across diverse communities and when the manuscript was submitted to a reputable agent and subjected to legal scrutiny. Why did the publisher overrule the evidence of fraud that emerged from activists in Jordan soon after the book was published? As a faker Khouri doesn't belong to a literary tradition of "benign pretenders who set out to parody avant-garde cliques and politically correct fashions"; rather, she belongs to something more sinister: a "new breed of fakers that excels in the bizarre and disturbing business of fictionalizing not just words and authorship but entire lives" (Legge 2004, 2).[10] This fakery reduces testimony to propaganda: a canny manipulation of public opinion for personal gain.

Successful hoax can tell us much about reading communities, and the politics of reading, as well as the ethics of international publishing. Norma Khouri's performances and readings from *Honor Lost* at literary festivals and school assemblies "reduced" seasoned readers and schoolgirls alike to public displays of emotion on a regular basis. Ultimately, the worry following the outing of a successful hoax is not about where the money has gone, why publishers have seemed to exert no means of quality control, and whether readers can sue for their money back, although these are the issues that are of immediate interest to the media. The piercing issue is the susceptibility of the reading public to certain kinds of fakery and the absence of a "moral grammar" that can distinguish the sacred from the profane.[11] From the Khouri hoax we can learn, to our embarrassment and shame, that Western women readers and the literary intelligentsia more generally may be especially vulnerable to propaganda in the form of testimony and capable of an unquestioning acceptance of some categories of information about other cultures if it takes certain generic forms of address. Search engines can be fast and effective, but they need to be put in motion by questions, by doubt and suspicion. The cynical faking of testimonial genres may be a canny exercise in autobiographical performance for Western eyes, and it unveils testimony as a persuasive form of "soft power": an appeal to a natural and inevitable dominance of values, ideals, institutions, and ideologies that are seemingly above and beyond culture and history. It also suggests that the pleasures of empathic identification, and the kind of self-affirmation and empowerment a gendered reading public in the West may derive from testimony, is vulnerable to cynical and political manipulation in these times.

Unpalatable as it may be, the fact is that testimony can be a deeply flawed vehicle for cross-cultural communication and, what's more, a self-serving one. The hoax testimony targets and dupes a readership by manipulating a moment of consumption that is intended as a gesture of ethical and moral responsibility: the reader is buying truth, and declaring an openness to what is likely to be a difficult act of empathic engagement. Or is she? What happens when a testimony does not speak truth to power but, alternatively, might be seen to speak propaganda, a form of untruth, which serves power?

Fair Trade

These questions about the communicative ethics of testimony require a shift of emphasis. The hoax either misrepresents or confects trauma, with the effect that the social, political, and affective work of testimony is brought into disrepute. Questions about what testimony is doing here and now as a commodity that deals with cultural difference reroutes what may seem to be the appropriate ethical response to narratives of trauma and abuse. The graphic demonstration of the sacred and forensic work of producing and responding to testimony, which Franklin and Lyons (2004) offer in their discussion, indicates that the ethical work of testimony is a matter of witnessing, is a case of an open and sincere gesture of recognition and remembrance. To pursue questions raised by the commodification and consumption of testimonial discourse is to open another line of enquiry altogether, and this raises issues about the manner of representation, what attitudes and actions it embodies, and how it is being put to work as propaganda in a particular historical context.[12] It is only in the absence of Dalia's body that we can begin to raise these questions about *Honor Lost* with no risk of disrespect for the dead.

In the wake of a hoax it is critically important to decipher how testimonial forms of life narrative can be used to speak untruth in the interests of power, for this is what we can learn from fraud. In his discussion of the Sokal hoax, in which Alan Sokal set out to see whether a leading cultural studies journal would publish a nonsensical article if it sounded good and favored the editors' ideological preconceptions, John Guillory points out that scandals have the typical feature of erupting suddenly and disappearing quickly and nearly completely from public consciousness (2002, 470). This is a pity, for as we mull over the still warm remains of *Honor Lost* there is much to learn about the ethics of life narrative in these times; a hoax flushes these "uses" into the open. *Honor Lost* suggests how "rights discourse" can be open to manipulation in bad faith. This hoax could be sustained at a time of unprecedented information demand, exchange, and commerce around representations of the Middle East because Norma Khouri satisfied the urgent need for the "inflected representative" who is chosen by the media to speak on behalf of a group. She appeared to have authentic local knowledge about Jordan, but she was also Western, educated, and sympathetic to Western values. Those who had the authentic knowledge to call Khouri to account lacked the cultural capital to intervene. For a short time Khouri became an expert witness, an authoritative interpreter of Arab culture in terms of a binary logic that privileges the West as representative of universal values—human rights, democracy, free speech—and uses human rights discourse to assert these rights across cultures. If we examine the discursive grid of globalization after the events of September 11 with a particular interest in the politics of affect, representations of women emerge as the most highly emotive images (Schirato and Webb 2003, 180). As a self-appointed spokesperson for Arab women, speaking as a political refugee, Khouri's performances in person and on the page were brilliantly targeted, for what she had to say associated the violation of human rights in general and misogyny most particularly with the most powerful and lived traditions of Arab culture: "[The] fierce and primitive [Bedouin] code is always nagging at men's instincts reminding them that under a Westernizing veneer, they are all still Arabs" (2003b, 2). This version of Amman "as dense-packed and tight-knit as a nomadic camp and filled with descendents of the original tribes" was, for a time, a powerful use of testimony to validate Western values and interests in times of crisis (Khouri 2003b). Descriptions of readers and audiences at literary festivals and in school halls being "reduced" to tears by this book are common; the idea of "reduction" suggests a loss of moral integrity and emotional excess not just in the general public but among gatekeepers in the intelligentsia: writers, teachers, critics, academics, and journalists.

Honor Lost has been followed by what is in some respects a more sensational and awful testimony about honor killing: *Burned Alive* by "Souad" (in collaboration with Marie-Thérèse Cuny). This is a translation of the original French version, *Brûlée vive*. The subtitle of the hardcover U.S. edition of 2004 is reminiscent of Khouri's book: *A Victim of the Law of Men*. In May 2005, a paperback edition appeared in the United States: *Burned Alive. A Survivor of an "Honor Killing" Speaks Out*. The cover of all editions features a sinister variation of the generic veil imagery (fig. 7): a woman's face covered with a white surgical mask (although the narrative itself indicates that Souad has a pretty face and the terrible scarring is visible elsewhere on her body). *Burned Alive* is promoted in peritext as the "*first true* account ever published by a victim of an honor crime," "the shocking, true story of one woman's escape from an 'honor' killing." Souad is the pseudonym of a woman who grew up on the West Bank. In her account, she is a victim of a crime of honor

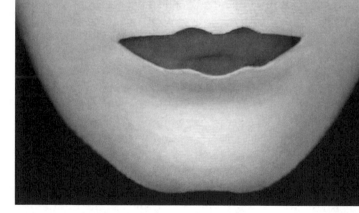

SOUAD

Burned *alive*

The shocking, true story of one woman's escape
from an 'honour' killing

7 Front cover design from Souad, *Burned Alive*

when her brother-in-law set her alight after she became pregnant before marriage. Severely burned, she was abandoned and left to die by her
community and rescued with her baby son by a European aid worker,
Jacqueline Thibault, who negotiated their removal to Europe. Souad testifies that she has lived as a wife and mother in obscurity until called
on to testify on behalf of the NGO that saved her life. As with *Forbidden
Love,* the final page makes an appeal for donations for the organization.[13]
This book has all the signs, then, of invoking the jurisdiction of humanitarian values against scandalous criminal customs in Arab societies. In
this return to honor killing, it is the victim herself who gives testimony
in the first person, she is the body in the text, and there is no surrogate
narrator as in the case of *Honor Lost.* However, other features of *Burned
Alive* are familiar: this is a sensational testimony solicited by human
rights activists and circulated to benefit an NGO, the Surgir Foundation.
The network of rights discourse defined by Schaffer and Smith (2004b)
establishes the expectations: readers will find in *Burned Alive* a story that
is both familiar and strange, shocking yet true, generating that affective
experience of "pleasurable sadness." Epitexts suggest that readers rapidly
took up Souad's testimony as further evidence of the epic war between
worlds since 9/11.[14]

In *Burned Alive* tactics that dramatize the speech situation of Souad's
narrative invite a self-reflexive reading of the book, for they perform the
negotiations of power between those who testify and those who witness
what they have to say—Souad, her amanuensis and patron Jacqueline
Thibault, and her European audience. A scarred and damaged body authorizes testimony in *Burned Alive,* an authentication that eluded *Forbidden Love.* The signs of trauma and abuse are the guarantee of authenticity, and they are there for all to see in Souad's narrative of her first
testimonial performance, given when she had been in Europe for about
fifteen years:

Jacqueline asked me to bear witness in the name of the Surgir Association. She waited
until I was emotionally capable, after the depression that had devastated me. . . . I
was better, but I still felt fragile in front of those European women. I was going to
speak to them about a world so different from their own, about cruelty that would be
inexplicable to them.

I told my story sitting on a platform before a small table with a microphone.
Jacqueline was next to me. From the start I threw myself into it. And they asked me
questions.

"Why did he burn you?"

"What had you done?"

"He set fire to you because you spoke to a man?"

I never said I was expecting a child. I said that if you were only gossiped about in the village, you might end up with the same punishment as someone who was pregnant. I said nothing about my son . . .

A woman in the audience got up and asked: "Souad, your face is pretty, where are the scars?"

"I knew you would ask me that question. I expected it. I will show you my scars."

I got up and in front of everyone, undid my shirt. I was wearing a low-cut blouse and short sleeves underneath. I showed my arms, I showed my back. And that woman started to cry. The few men who were there looked uncomfortable. When I had displayed myself in public I felt like a sideshow freak. But in that situation it didn't bother me because I was bearing witness and I had to make people understand that I was a survivor. I was dying when Jacqueline arrived in that West Bank hospital. I owe her my life, and the work she pursues with Surgir requires a living witness to demonstrate to other people the reality of the honor crime. (175–76)

This returns to the grounds of testimony incarnate, the subject of a preceding chapter. Souad, like many subaltern women before her, resorts to "organic writing," the marks on her body, to convince her inquisitive audience of the truth of what she has to say. At the same time, she calls into question the very notions of truth that might be relevant for testimony of this kind. She recalls, for example, that in these public performances she said nothing of her son, and she had no qualms about concealing what might seem to be important aspects of her story and its representation of honor crimes. This says several things. First, it promises that this print version, *Burned Alive*, offers an account that has been withheld in preceding stagings of the testimony. Second, it suggests that what might be relevant as "authority" in testimony to trauma is the evidence of suffering—the marks on the body rather than the full or final revelation of verifiable fact. Third, it offers a clear recognition by Souad of the terms and conditions of her testimonial speech in Europe and how she might use it as an occasion for agency. She has the power to withhold and shape her speech even as she responds to the imperative to testify on behalf of Surgir. Souad has not given a single account of the events that led to her incineration. In fact, she has assembled a rationale for multiple and varied accounts—diverse stagings of testimony before audiences in France, alongside the aid worker who exerts a moral obligation to speak, and a long process of memory work that includes psychoanalysis and medication.

Souad both fulfills and rejects expectations of truth in testimony. Traumatic experience and troubled memories continue to affect how she represents her experiences as a wife and mother in the West—she is, for example, ambivalent about the child she conceived in disgrace, and she is alienated not just by the terrible scarring but also by the violent loss of her homeland and by those European expectations that reduce her to a "freak" and require her to strip in public view. Her narrative emerges as an example of "recovered memory," and this is used to justify her flawed recollection of events and even extraordinary developments, such as forgetting her language of origin. There is no pretense of a whole story here, for Souad remembers fragments and shards; images of her life in the West Bank "play out in slow motion, like films on television" (93). The narrative records a series of obsessions and hauntings: "This is how the pieces of my former life try to find their place in my memory. A green door, a sack, a father who wants to suffocate either my mother or me, my fear of the dark and the snakes" (53). These are all perfectly acceptable signs of recovered memory work, which licenses and authenticates a testimony that is halting and subject to change. What might seem obsessive and delusional under other circumstances—the childhood obsession with death and the father, the repetition of infanticide in her family, the wanton inescapable sadism of all Arab men, the forewarnings of incineration, and the estranged psychic landscapes of a West Bank village—can all be explained by the psychoanalytic model of traumatic remembering and suffering. In *Burned Alive,* then, the flawed conditions for testimony are acknowledged by Souad herself. From a psychoanalytic reading, the very taintedness of Souad's testimony might be regarded as signs of authenticity and verisimilitude. The slippages and memory work that mark *Burned Alive* can be taken as marks of the interiority and belatedness of trauma that is highly valued in subaltern stories of abuse elicited in human rights activism in the recent past.

But a hoax changes how we read; it is a reminder of the vulnerability of teary readers and gullible gatekeepers and a market invested in traumatic remembering and Muslim life story. In the shadow of the hoax, we must strive to become different readers. The boundaries between these two stories of honor crimes—Khouri and Dalia, and Jacqueline and Souad, *Honor Lost* and *Burned Alive*—blur, and so do distinctions between hoax and propaganda. *Burned Alive* was published through the same Transworld network as Khouri's book, although the book's editor, Sally Gaminara, has vouched for the book's authenticity and claims to have met Souad. Recently the historian Thérèse Taylor has raised questions that remain unanswered about the legitimacy of Souad's story, and she begins by explicitly invoking the Khouri hoax and examining the reception of *Burned Alive* in France, Britain, and the United States, where

Souad's story has been accepted and praised as an authentic artifact. Taylor's research draws attention to logical inconsistencies in the narrative: the lack of evidence for grave allegations, the faulty geography of the West Bank, the ignorance of the domestic customs of Palestinian women, and the contradictions in chronology. Are these explicable in terms of posttraumatic memory? As with *Honor Lost*, Taylor's research reveals that the local communities of women and activists against honor crimes in Jordan have misgivings about the work of NGOs such as Surgir, which removes women from their communities, with the effect that all familial connections and cultural traditions are generally lost. Most important, there appears to be no communal history that authenticates Souad's account, and this is a critical issue for the legitimacy of subaltern testimony on behalf of the oppressed. Taylor's research is a breaking story, and the status of *Burned Alive* is uncertain following her rigorous questioning. The possible fabrication of Souad's testimony and its timely appearance in print as part of the booming market for Muslim and Arab life narrative suggests that a cynical and highly politicized manipulation of life story is more than incidental to the war on terror and that in the battle for hearts and minds tainted testimony is a powerful conscript.

Hoax, scandal, and impropriety haunt testimony, and this is a good thing. In their wake, we are free to ask questions that might otherwise seem improper. As parasites, hoax texts draw attention to the processes of syndication and legitimation of subaltern life story and the global economy and commodification of trauma and testimony. Honor killing is one of the paradigmatic stories that are selected by NGOs and activists to target privileged readers; these testimonies sell like hotcakes and trigger empathy and political responsiveness to human rights agendas. These processes of commodification remain entirely predictable and repetitive—in this sense, at least, the product is reliable, and the consumer insatiable. This is so self-evident that, to return to hubris, Khouri could risk making links to activists in Jordan who could immediately recognize the illegitimacy of her story but lacked the cultural authority in the West to question the jurisdiction of the book. Likewise, *Burned Alive* depends on contemporary theories of traumatic memory in the West to counter significant inconsistencies in Souad's story. Teary readers and big sales, faddish fibbing and propaganda are the stock in trade here. Popular life narratives move fast: they sell rapidly—although we are beginning to see that the shelf life can be a problem. But what if this doesn't matter?

In discussing the Khouri hoax I am often asked why do we need the fiction? Honor killing does happen, why does the story have to take this form before we care about it? If we read *Honor Lost* and *Burned Alive* together, one answer is that veiled best-sellers tell more than one story. First they quite rightfully draw attention to honor crime as an evil expression of domination and hatred of women, but as we have seen, the League of Muslim women and Jordanian activists such as Husseini and Sabbagh have a long history of campaigning against honor crimes in these terms. Their local campaigns are disabled by false claims that become notorious in the West. Second, these fictions also foreclose more historical and appropriate ways of representing Arab cultures, societies, and communities. By reducing contemporary and urbanized cultures, yet again, to an estranged ahistorical land of Bedouin custom and ancient tradition they renew the fantasies of Occidentalism. *Burned Alive* is one of the few life narratives to emerge from the West Bank in the recent past. Like Khouri's Amman, the community in *Burned Alive* is de-historicized, stripped of its name and status as the occupied territory "Palestine," and unfamiliar to the people who live there. Here Arab men and women exist in a primitive, premodern, and subhuman condition, not yet articulate sovereign subjects—Souad becomes human when she is removed to Europe.[15] Ironically, even as she ostensibly testifies on behalf of Arab women, Souad denies their humanity: "If I had lived there, would have become 'normal' like my mother, who suffocated her own children. Maybe I would have killed my daughters. I might have let one burn to death. Now I think that is monstrous,—but if I had stayed there, I would have done the same!"(177).

Souad suggests this "speaking out" is the "only weapon I have" to act on behalf of Palestinian women. Yet these "weapons" of traumatic autobiography produce significant collateral damage through this ongoing production of Arab monstrosity: a civilization eternally primitive, outside of time, and beyond history, its women destined to "accept beating as natural. No thought of rebellion occurs to us" (51). The recent English translation of Suad Amiry's *Sharon and My Mother-in-law: Ramallah Diaries*, with its richly detailed spatial and political grasp of daily life under occupation on the West Bank, suggests by way of contrast a more complex and contradictory experience of gender relations and Islamic traditions. Amiry was born in Amman and lives in Ramallah under Israeli occupation; her war diary emerges from the e-mails she exchanged with intimate friends. These spaces in Jordan and the West Bank, both reduced to abstraction in *Honor Lost* and *Souad*, emerge in Amiry's narrative otherwise: crowded and chaotic, complicated by dense neighborhood and familial networks, and shaken by the ongoing strife of the Intifada, the first Gulf War, the Oslo Peace Accords, and, since 2003, the

Separation Wall. Campaigns against honor killing that make a difference may well draw on life narratives, but they will be stories like this, which are recognizable and authenticated by their communities of origin.

This is to suggest that, as with other products, we might invoke the ethical terms of fair trade—the idea of a partnership and exchange between the producers and consumers of goods in global networks. Western consumers have learned to require some reassurance of integrity when buying coffee, tea, sneakers, and other imported goods. They understand it to be in their own ethical interest to ask questions about how these commodities relate to their place of origin, what work they do there, and what exploitative relations might continue as these commodities are produced and consumed in other worlds. These are legitimate questions for the trade in life story, too. While we still "buy" that ethnic thing where (as Khouri memorably puts it) "the sand still blows in from the desert," we reduce ourselves and others, refusing the complex cultural dialogues and exchanges that make a difference to the rights of men and women.

SIX

Embedded: Memoir and Correspondents

I behold the breaking down of a world that has erased its borders: fainting away. The corpse, seen without God and outside of science, is the utmost of abjection. It is death infecting life. Abject. It is something rejected from which one does not part, from which one does not protect oneself as form and object. Imaginary uncanniness and real threat, it beckons to us and ends up engulfing us.
JULIA KRISTEVA, *POWERS OF HORROR: AN ESSAY ON ABJECTION*

The word memoir is linked etymologically to the idea of mourning through *memoir,* which carries meanings to do with mindfulness and remembering; the shadow left by the dead is as much the terrain of memoir as the quest for the self.   DRUSILLA MODJESKA, *TIMEPIECES*

New kinds of autobiographical subjects emerge in various shapes and forms, and social crisis is a catalyst in this process. Tracking the ebb and flow of life narrative, the dynamics of its production and consumption in a field of reading and writing, suggests how places to speak are shaped by the "urgent present." This is quite literally so in journalist memoirs from Iraq, where the spatial geographies of the campaign organized journalists' own self-fashioning. "Embedded," "unilateral," and "Baghdad reporter" are distinctive categories and sets of relations. This is one of the interests of this chapter: How do these memoirs engage with their "placement" in an invasion force? The production and consumption of life story is never a wholly private or aesthetic affair: it is determined by processes of authorization within the public domain; it is part of a constant struggle for jurisdiction in the public sphere; and it is subject to the operations of mass media and mass consumption. Spawned in literature, journalism, and ethnography, recent life narratives by professional journalists working in Iraq reflect personally with some anxiety and concern about the role of journalists as public intellectuals who have been scripted into a key role as witnesses in the war on terror.

Since the 1990s, as Leigh Gilmore points out in her discussion of the "limits" of autobiography, the age of memoir and the age of trauma have coincided to shape a fashion for self-representation energized by trauma (2001, 16). Gilmore argues that the recent expansion of self-representation and attention to trauma is driven by publishing concerns about valuable and marketable commodities as much as the reconception of language, agency, and the human subject following poststructuralism: "There goes Derrida; here comes Oprah" (18). However, thinking about the subject in terms of the performative and a constant questioning of the self and its place in the world draws attention to ways the self is put to work in and through crisis. The commodification and legitimacy of various selves in the market of life narrative at any one time is a gauge of the dynamics of contemporary culture and history. War sharpens and accelerates all of these things. And when the trauma of war is written of from the perspective of a conqueror, it colors these things.

Although this dealing in trauma and life narrative predated September 11, the Iraq campaign, and the war on terror more generally, the sense of crisis surrounding these events has shaped a different set of conditions for speaking about trauma. This has energized a flow of life narratives and a readership more receptive to testimony from Afghanistan and Iraq, as we have seen in preceding chapters. These testimonial narratives by resistant and marginal subjects coexist in a "mirror talk" with memoirs by those who are located as authorized and accredited witnesses to trauma and war and who need no introduction or endorsement by benevolent others. These two autobiographical forms of narrating a life in history—testimony and memoir—might be understood as diametrically opposed yet interdependent in the textual cultures of life narrative. The memoir is traditionally the prerogative of the literate elite; alternatively, the testimony is the means by which the disempowered experience enters the record, although not necessarily under conditions of their choosing. Both are preoccupied with placing the self in the records of public and official history. Quite different histories and experiences are brought into the public record by these genres. To date, many of these authorized witnesses of the war in Iraq are journalists, and journalism is often the first stage of writing to capture traumatic experience for the public record. In fact, in societies in the throes of traumatic conflict, journalism can be a powerful and preferred means of intellectual work (Singh 1994, 211) that deals in and through testimony. Since 2003, memoirs by journalists who arrived in Afghanistan and Iraq as fully accredited interpreters of the war have appeared in a surge of publishing activity. These memoirs are marketed as more "accurate" and "immediate" accounts than earlier reportage, and they both consolidate and reflect on the renewed status of the journalist as an information broker in the war on terror. The notion that trauma can be generalized, shared, and vicariously experienced through media representation is a powerful assumption in the recent past (Bennett and Kennedy 2003, 5), and in this chapter, the effects of graphic accounts of trauma in war journalism from Iraq is an important issue, and this is where the implications of journalism in dealing with testimony become evident.

Memoir is a distinctive space for autobiographical writing. As a metatextual account—a reflection on the self in process and in history—it offers the possibility of incorporating "immediacy" and more authentic truth into life narrative. "Immediacy" and "authenticity" are elicited by reporters on the prowl for an "untold story"—a highly valued commodity. At the same time, memoir can be used to incorporate subjective responses that can call the truth, authority, and ethical responsibilities of the narrating autobiographical "I" into question. When journalists use memoir as an opportunity to reflect on their craft, an important site in the production and circulation of life narrative comes into view. How is this war zone in Iraq used as an opportunity for autobiographical performance in memoir? How is it made personal, and to what effects? How does the media industry and competing global, corporate state ideologies and interests shape it? What is the economy of the "mirror talk" between memoir and testimony here?

Trading in Trauma

When journalists write memoirs they draw on and enhance their established place and professional reputation in metropolitan networks of print and online and broadcast media. These autobiographers need no introduction, for their names, voices, and/or faces are often familiar. Memoirs trade on this. Sandra Silberstein argues that, in the new set of discursive transformations that have formulated the war on terror, the news coverage itself has increasingly become the story (2004, 161); so, too, have the lives of correspondents, who are both licensed and required to speak more personally in these times. Memoir reflects in a confessional way on the ethical practice of journalism and makes public worries about witnessing trauma. This is not new. But this surge of memoirs indicates some changes in the way in which journalists work, in the economic and ethical factors influencing what they write, and how they obtain material in the war on terror and the Iraq campaign in particular (Bailey and Williams 1997, 371). Most important, these memoirs indicate how reporters are occupying new professional identities produced for war journalism by the military intervention in Iraq in 2003. A number of categories of authorship have been devised to analyze the news coverage from Iraq, and these are coded entirely in terms of the reporters' location: embedded reporter, Baghdad reporter, unilateral reporter, anchor, Qatar reporter (Lewis and Brookes 2004, 285). These locations flow through into journalists' memoirs rhetorically as a primary influence on their self-representation. These categories are taken up in professional identifications and are used in memoirs to shape various disciplines of views, and to argue for superior ethical integrity and insight. Anxiety about the conduct of the Iraq campaign and its aftermath is palpable in these memoirs, which reflect continuously on how war reportage became responsible for justifying a military intervention that divides the international community.

The ethical and intellectual work of the profession itself is an urgent issue in a war zone where shame and humiliation abound and rebound. The conduct of the war on terror has raised many questions about the proper relationship between government and the Fourth Estate, and these memoirists reflect on the control and regulation of public intellectual culture in the present crisis. In Iraq a strategy was designed to place the media rather than the Pentagon as the messengers; "the war was seen through the eyes of journalists" (Hess and Kalb 2003, 12). This is a rhetorical move. It nurtures personalizing narrative that has the potential to mask or distract from more systemic and critical representations of the military and political domains in the conduct of war. For example, systemic corruption can be contracted to personal culpability, and discussion of foreign policy is reduced to a series of carefully managed media "opportunities." The demise of investigative journalism and the wavering of public commitment to principles of justice by public intellectuals have been identified as an early casualty of the war on terror (Butler 2004, xi). This concern for truth is not unique to the Iraq campaign (after all, Phillip Knightley calls his study of war journalism *The First Casualty* [2003]), but the prospect of the strategic management of Western journalists and journalism in Iraq and the alternative perspectives emerging through al-Jazeera led to widespread speculation about the corruption of the craft. The policy of embedding in particular, a formal and controversial initiative of the Iraq campaign, places a new emphasis on the personal: the role of the correspondent as the authorized eye and witness to trauma.

These memoirs are, of course, highly marketable commodities and part of a sequence of products that might be cynically described as moving through a series of genres from breaking news to the human interest sidebar, the news analysis, the lengthy magazine piece, and then finally the book (James Carey quoted in Schudson 2002, 38). These books hold the promise of more truth and the confession of previously forbidden authentic and intimate detail about war and trauma that is edited out of preceding genres of report. Publishers' blurbs promise, for example, the "enthralling, deeply personal and utterly authentic" from Garrels's *Naked in Baghdad* (2003), which is marketed online along with *Embedded*, a collection of short memoirs edited by Katovsky and Carlson (2003), which is promoted as "deeply personal and highly emotional accounts of the Iraq War . . . an emotional window to war and reporting." These offer a "more personal, gripping story than the bombing missions and flag-raising reported on the nightly news during the invasion."[1] The personalizing of coverage of the Iraq war through the placement and perspective of the individual journalist, both in memoirs and in earlier reportage, is a reminder that although memoirs personalize history, they do not necessarily historicize the personal to reveal the discursive shaping of "news" and the role of the journalist.

Helen Buss's definition of memoir (2001) distinguishes it from autobiography on the grounds that memoir writers seek to make themselves part of public history. One could say this about testimony, too, of course; however, these two forms of history writing empower very different subjects. Recently journalist memoir has emerged as a genre of life narrative given to haunted and fragmented accounts of the professional self as it deals with testimony and trauma in quite specific historical contexts. Because memoir makes history and crisis personal, as a style of self-fashioning it can be an effective vehicle for ethical self-reflection. Alternatively, it can offer a flawed understanding of historical forces. For example, Antje Krog's memoir *Country of My Skull* (1998) is a controversial consideration of her own role as Antje Samuel, a journalist and witness "covering" the Truth and Reconciliation Commission for the South African Broadcasting Commission from April 1996 until January 1998. Krog's memoir absorbs testimonies given at the commission and reflects on her own complicity as an Afrikaner and a public intellectual—some would say it is seriously flawed and it continues to use testimony inappropriately.[2] Others see it as an example of Mala Singh's observation that journalism is available as a means of radical and powerful responses to conflict (1994). Memoir and testimony coexist (in "mirror talk") as forms of life narrative that carry longstanding and generic associations with authoritative and subaltern knowledges respectively: each presents very different ways of addressing a public and capturing a public presence, legitimated by alternative sources of cultural authority and different traditions of self-fashioning. To return to Susanna Egan's sense of the active relation between autobiographical genres as mirror talk (1999), it should not surprise that where we find subaltern testimony and trauma we also find troubled memoir by those who witness and bear the responsibility of disseminating testimony.

Krog's literary memoir, with its splicing of fiction, testimony given by participants at the Truth and Reconciliation Commission, and her response as a witness, is a pathbreaking study of how the journalist is both witness to trauma and complicit in the damage as a benevolent other. Although more literary than any journalistic memoir to have emerged from the war on terror to date, *Country of My Skull* has triggered the debate about the trauma trade in journalism and lays the groundwork for reading the recent memoir by correspondents in the Middle East and Central Asia as the work of engaged and anxious professionals. As a metatext, memoir can become a style of personal writing that alters the original framing devices of the story: the selection, presentation, and emphasis in the witnessing of events is different this second time round. Memoir can explore the taintedness of sources that was papered over in the first account; it can suggest the subjectivity of expression, the presence of propaganda, the limits of the authority based on presence and "eyewitnessing," and the politics of identity building that shaped the original frame. Here journalism can move into a different analytical mode: what Barbie Zelizer describes as the "fundamental self-doubt" of the profession comes into view in a self-conscious way (2004, 191). Or, alternatively, the memoir can reduce the complexity of historical forces at work in war to the personal frame, and it can contribute to the cult of celebrity that is also a mark of contemporary journalism.

Nomadic Reportage

Journalists' memoirs from Baghdad rapidly take up performatively the spatial organization of news coverage: embedded/unilateral/Baghdad reporter, and so on. This is extended in memoirs to become a grid that indicates different regimes of truth and authenticity, most particularly claims to superior ethical insight. For example, in his memoir *Travels in American Iraq* (2004), John Martinkus appropriates a nomadic identification to place his perspective as more authentic and sensitive to local Iraqi experiences of the invasion. Martinkus deliberately avoids the carefully managed circuits that convey journalists to preselected "opportunities" under high security. He frets about how the insurgents learn to stage spectacular, suicidal, and symbolic attacks close to the two hotels where foreign journalists are based in Baghdad: the al-Hamra and the Palestine/Sheraton compound (163). As a gesture of independence and a desire to assert himself as an investigative journalist in search of the more authentic and adversarial story (rather than a docile subject incarcerated in the hotel), Martinkus sets himself up with other reporters in a suburban home in Baghdad. This has fatal consequences. Insurgents kill their translator and force the reporters to scurry back to the safety of the fortified hotel, where they are safe, contained by its discipline of views. The worrying implication is that the curtailing of independent investigative journalism, and the staging of carefully managed "live" media spectacles designed for metropolitan consumption in the United States and Europe, is the objective of both Coalition forces and insurgents alike. In part, *Travels* is a polemical reflection on how an independent and investigative style of journalism that is pursued through "going native" can be sustained in this carefully policed war zone. It is also, as we shall see, a thoroughly stylized rhetorical presentation of a professional identity. As a unilateral reporter, Martinkus is a writer who has to produce and market a commodity in a highly competitive industry where the freelancer is not necessarily at an advantage.

Memoir is marketed as the definitive and superior journalistic account. This is a necessary rhetorical strategy: How can these memoirs create a distinctive place in an economy of news already saturated with product? *Travels in American Iraq* is promoted on the cover blurb as "more immediate, more intimate and more skeptical than other writing from the war-torn country." What does "intimacy" mean here? More to the point, how can memoir claim a distinctive place among the various news media in these times? How can print journalism lay claim to "immediacy" given the arrival of "live feeds" from embedded reporters, online journalism, and war blogs—all "real time" modes of communication? What memoir offers is not immediacy but intimacy; not new information but self-reflection on acts of witnessing trauma; not seamless delivery but a presentation of the apparatus of contemporary journalism in a war zone. In Martinkus's memoir, "intimacy" means attention to the local networks and factions in Iraq, as well as the people on the street, which respond to the American presence variously. There are two worlds in Iraq, and they are mutually exclusive: the occupier and the occupied, and Martinkus is trying to engage with both sides. He is an avid collector of testimony, although he is careful to include the necessary presence of the translator who is the conduit of information and a good shepherd: "Sala wasn't paying enough attention to translate properly because— unbeknownst to me—people were threatening as we walked past" (79). Martinkus uses his memoir to bring into view the careful management of information and the trading of story that occurred between these two "worlds." For example, he gathers enough Iraqi testimony in the vicinity of Abu Ghraib to scent a story: "I needed more solid evidence to break such a story. Although I had no doubt abuses were occurring, the only supporting evidence I had were the Iraqi testimonies that other journalists had poured scorn on" (114). Again, the idea of a threshold for testimony is useful to grasp how subaltern story must accrue authority and find the right "carriers" to break through and become authoritative. In the case of Abu Ghraib, Iraqi testimony alone was never enough to secure the story; it took the incontrovertible evidence of photographs from the American military itself for the story to break open.

There is an indication at the very outset of *Travels* that immediacy incorporates an embodiment of the reporter in and through trauma. In italics on the first page of the book is an extract from a first person eye-witness report of a scene of terrible atrocity, which Martinkus describes in visceral detail. This account of the Ashoura bombings at Karbala in March 2004 includes specific detail routinely censored in standard Western reportage, and its syntax is designed to produce a powerful statement of witnessing in the first person:

I reached the bomb scene not more than a minute after the explosion. . . . I saw what was a severed small child's hand, half-shredded and wet, lying on the blood-covered road. There was no sign of the rest of the body. I was shaking and trying to hold my camera still. Under my foot I felt something slippery and my heel skidded. When I looked down, what I saw was unmistakable. It was part of a human brain. I gagged and my eyes filled up with water as I tried to steady the camera and not throw up. (1)

The distinctive place and "superior immediacy" of memoir is produced by this inclusion of the witnessing subject, the autobiographical "I" of the embodied journalist. The repetition of the first person subject accentuates the rhetorical effect: this is an account of the journalist in shock and trauma, which situates the reader as a secondary witness. This returns to the questions that have been raised by Krog's *Country of My Skull:* What are the ethics of using memoir to bear witness to trauma? What rights do journalists have to craft a powerful and professional self through witnessing in this way? When do they become complicit by trading in the damage? By placing the self autobiographically, Martinkus becomes a proxy for the reader, crafting a shocking account that sets out to overwhelm "compassion fatigue" and produce an appropriate ethical and humane responsiveness to civilian deaths in Iraq. At the same time, the inclusion of this kind of graphic detail as a rhetorical device also characterizes Martinkus as a unilateral reporter: independent, adversarial, autonomous. An Australian in the employ of no single network (in the John Pilger rogue reporter tradition), and in fact on the hunt for news as a commodity to sell, Martinkus is obliged to carve a niche for his memoir as a distinctive style of polemical reportage. Located outside the frames sustained by the media networks, and unconstrained by American patriotism, he suggests he is free to arrange events in terms of an overarching rhetorical frame that challenges the plots of the official story of the Iraq campaign. In this version, Americans are perpetrators not liberators; Iraq is invaded and occupied, not liberated. "Unilateral" becomes a style of autobiographical performance in *Travels,* a professional status defined over and against its "other": the embedded (and implied docile) reporter. *Travels* is a nomadic memoir: processual and unresolved. Constantly in transit, frequently disoriented and "rattled," Martinkus moves around the country in a series of encounters and translations that map a space of his own invention: American Iraq.

By representing himself as nomadic and traumatized in *Travels,* Martinkus uses memoir to practice a style of witnessing, a reportage that brings into view the body of the journalist who is recording, reeling in response to what he sees and hears, and contaminated by violence. In discussing the photographic representations of trauma in war reporting, Zelizer points out that the sides of the war that do not fit the prevailing interpretive assumptions are excluded by widely accepted protocols: "In most wars there are few or no images of human gore, one's own war dead or POWs, military operations gone badly, or the effect of one's own war on civilians of the other side" (2004, 116). By using his memoir to alter the frame and invoke images of gore and the dismemberment of children, to signify otherwise unremarked (Butler [2004] refers to "ungrieved") civilian death and the disintegration of moral authority in Iraq, Martinkus is breaking taboos to bear witness. Yet what are viable representational strategies for representing the trauma of others in journalistic memoir? The use of texts to transmit trauma and elicit empathy is at the heart of debates about Antje Krog's performance of trauma through witnessing the suffering of others in *Country of My Skull* (1998).

There is a critical difference, though. Krog is using the testimony of others and taking their voices into her own in a process of witnessing at the Truth and Reconciliation Commission. Taking the trauma of others into narratives of the self raises fundamental questions about the ethics of memoir. When journalists are installed as proxy witnesses of trauma on behalf of their readers, they achieve a visibility and a status as powerful individuals. As we have seen, gathering Iraqi testimony does not necessarily allow Martinkus to "break" a story, but first person eyewitnessing reportage does. The war on terror has created a new market for the production of celebrity journalism, and by infusing reportage and the personal, journalists' memoirs both confirm and accelerate this process. Zelizer and Allan argue that integral to this altered status of the journalist in the very recent past is the intense pressure to serve as conveyor, translator, mediator, and meaning maker of trauma on our behalf (2002, 2). In that succession of news "products" that carve out different approaches and perspectives of the same event, it is precisely the space of the personal and confessional and the freedom to include graphic descriptions of trauma that is expanded in memoir. To return to the example of Martinkus's report on the Ashoura massacre in *Travels:* it is in memoir that he is free (or required) to get personal and graphic with the body of the reporter and the bodies of others: "In Baghdad that night I went out on the balcony to smoke a cigarette and finally worked up the courage to take off my boots. In the worn-out heel of one of the boots there was a small cavity where stones often got stuck. I just knew something horrible was stuck in there. When I looked, I could see it was a piece of brain or flesh from the street in Karbala. I flicked it out with my pen and began to gag. I stood up, leaving my boots, and went inside to bed" (71). For unilateral reporters like Martinkus, autobiographical representation of the self becomes part of a process of commodification: the construction of a viable career through the astute distribution and sales of the authentic eyewitness story only they can tell. Armed only with a pen, the reporter conveys information and (as we see here) becomes part of a process of witnessing.

This is a haunting narrative. What kind of textual economy organizes the public circulation and consumption of this writing that dehumanizes the corpses of the Ashoura massacre over and again? Who is authorized to speak on behalf of the Iraqi dead—the Western reporter? What becomes palpable here is the absence of testimony and the presence of memoir as a tainted thing in its place. As Chris Hedges suggests, the words of the vanquished and the humiliated Iraqi citizens come later, and these journalists do not grasp and cannot feel the rage, humiliation, and indignation that pushed Iraqis to turn their country into an inferno (2004, 7). Perhaps some of this is muttered to Martinkus as he walks the streets of Baghdad, but it remains untranslated. There are Iraqi testimonial accounts and representations of the atrocity at Karbala and other carnage that has followed the occupation of Iraq. However, to date these remain contained in the local, vernacular, and private artifacts, circuits, and practices of narrative and grieving in Iraq that are not available for mass-market consumption in the West. As Bennett and Kennedy emphasize, the idea that trauma will be expressed and shared in textual forms familiar to a Western market ignores the way that post-traumatic memory is always a cultural construction, which both draws and innovates on available cultural frameworks and traditions for dealing with guilt, shame, and humiliation (2003, 12). The eyewitness accounts of journalists that are attendant on the occupation of Iraq are surrounded by gaps and silences that are also signifiers of trauma. In his writing about the politics of mourning, Derrida (1994) suggests that any speech after death is impossible, and yet it is also necessary as a practice of remembrance and pursuit of justice on behalf of the dead. The ethical responsibilities of producing testimony from death are all the more acute in times of war when, as is the case with Martinkus, there is necessarily a complicity and contamination. The description of the mass killing of Iraqi civilians by insurgents at Ashoura is both personal and professional, and it might be construed as an act of guilt and expiation in Martinkus's own interest. Nevertheless the visceral sign of contamination that is carried so powerfully in Martinkus's memoir extends the ripples of mourning following these civilian deaths, which are so often rendered as "collateral damage."

Crucial to the experience of trauma are the difficulties that arise in trying to articulate what is by definition a self-altering, self-shattering experience. By including this story of contamination, Martinkus writes of abjection, out of the fear of returning from scenes of carnage into civilized society with some visible mark of death on him. In her discussion of abjection, Julia Kristeva describes the abject as a violent and sudden emergence of uncanniness, and a crushing and sudden descent into "the weight of meaninglessness" (1997, 230). In abjection the boundaries of the body, the spaces between subject and object, the self and other break down, and there is a fall into the abyss at the borders of identity. Kristeva identifies the corpse most particularly as an object that generates abjection: "Corpses *show me* what I permanently thrust aside in order to live." The dead flesh that he carries with him from the Ashoura bombing casts Martinkus into abjection: he reacts viscerally—he gags, he shakes. It is this scene that calls into question—and to account—the rational consciousness of the unilateral reporter, the skeptical and acute eyewitness, that is the ostensible professional subject of *Travels in American Iraq* as a travelogue. Abjection makes slaughter intimate; the living are necessarily contaminated and haunted by the violently dead in an ongoing and self-shattering confrontation with "those fragile states where man strays on the territories of animal" (Kristeva 1997, 239). One way or another, journalists in Iraq are embedded in this narrative of shame. Martinkus's experience of abjection is infectious, and it travels powerfully into the experience of reading this account. It overwhelms all his attempts to be something other than "an American" in Iraq.

This appearance of what Modjeska (2002) calls "the shadow left by the dead" in Martinkus's memoir is an intrusion of the unanticipated and the unexpected—*Travels in American Iraq* is after all presented as a coolly rational and independent account, and Martinkus flicks the dead flesh from his shoe with his pen in an act of masculine bravado that accords with his appropriation of a nomadic independent presence in Iraq. And yet all of this is at the same time undone by the sheer overwhelming force of disgust in this contact with dead flesh: "through disgust, bodies 'recoil' from their proximity, as a proximity that is felt as nakedness or as an exposure on the skin surface" (Ahmed 2004, 83). In extending a reading of disgust beyond "gut feelings," Sara Ahmed suggests that a profoundly disturbing intercorporeal encounter is crucial to this emotion: the contact between sticky surfaces engenders the intensity of the disgust affect. As we have seen earlier, in chapter 3, Ahmed's phenomenological approach to the cultural politics of the emotions emphasizes the movement of emotions between bodies; emotions are associated with the impressions of one surface on another and they are always relational. The dead flesh that clings to Martinkus as he moves away from the Ashoura carnage adheres in memory as testimony incarnate and is carried as emotional affect—as an ongoing and indelible reminder of contamination and implication.

Naked in Baghdad

The spatial geographies that organize journalist memoirs from Iraq are taken up in narratives that are gendered as well as nationalized. Anne

Garrels arrived in Iraq and lodged at the al-Rashid Hotel, ostensibly beginning the journal notes from Baghdad in October 2002, which were revised and published as her *Naked in Baghdad* in 2003. *Naked* is written as a relational autobiography, splicing the journal notes of Garrels with the e-mail bulletins her husband, Vint Lawrence, circulated to their friends as "The Brenda Bulletin." As Garrels explains in her introductory note, "I reported the war and he reported on me." The autobiographical Vint has the first word:

BRENDA BULLETIN: OCTOBER 19, 2002

Well hello again,

Just when we were all getting used to the idea that our Annie was going to be more or less gainfully employed organizing the linen closet or darning socks by the fire, the damsel is off again this time to Iraq. . . .

Remember that intrepid comic book character of our youth, Brenda Starr, who was always getting into and out of impossible scrapes? Well someone the other day dubbed Annie "Brenda of the Berkshires," a reference to our remote abode up here in the hills of northwest Connecticut. It fits, and it has a certain ring, so I have appropriated it. (3)

Garrels's first entry also emerges from this domestic and relational space: "Vint and I took our usual farewell walk with the dogs just before the taxi came. It was a spectacular autumn day and we talked about all the garden projects we want to do next spring. We talked about everything but Iraq" (6). *Naked* is an American story for an American audience: promoted as an insight into "our" war; the memoir begins and concludes at Garrels's place of belonging: the homelands of the Connecticut farm.

As we have seen, Martinkus's self-representation in *Travels* begins with the bloody scene of the Ashoura bombings, and this is vital to the narrating "I" of the memoir and to his performance as an eyewitness and unilateral nomadic presence in a war zone. Although *Travels* is personal, it is not in any way domestic—to the contrary. In the linked diaries of *Naked* Garrels becomes visible differently; she is marked at the outset in terms of multiple relational identifications: Vint's partner, an American, and a fan of a professional avatar, the mythical reporter of American popular culture Brenda Starr. Most important, Garrels also elevates her minder and translator, Amer, to a relational status in the memoir, and it is Amer who becomes the testimonial presence and proxy of the Iraqi civilian. The diary structure that organizes *Naked* is sustained as a series of chronological entries, and these later include some feedback from readers about Vint's mock heroic tone, and his "appropriation" of Brenda the cartoon character in his contributions to the journal:

> A number of you have written of late questioning the continued use of the Brenda alias. Some have suggested that although amusing at first, the device has become stale, bordering on shtick. Others have written to say that the use of the name Brenda somehow demeans and belittles what she has done and where she has done it. I, too, was wondering about this. . . . The long and short of it is that Annie likes Brenda. It gives her a needed distance, a character to play to, and allows humor to seep into situations which, if reported straight, might well bring tears. (76)

As Zelizer observes, it is not unusual to find that reporters cherish the attention paid to the profession in popular culture, use it to sustain their enthusiasm about the field, and they are intrigued by the representation of journalists as characters in fiction, film, and television (2004, 199). In *Naked* Brenda Starr is (like the autobiographical Vint) a narrative device that reflects back on Garrels's awkward location in Baghdad. In a series of remarks about "our Annie" later in the journal, Vint points out that the journalist community at the Palestine Hotel is a "guy's world," divided between print journalists and TV types. This introduces glimpses of the larger Western media networks and interests that carve up the broadcast space in Baghdad, and it confirms the masculinist culture of war reporting. Garrels is a public broadcaster for National Public Radio in the United States, and so she is neither print nor television, "too old to be a babe, to serious to be dismissed" (144). The layers of identification and interrelationship that feature in *Naked* are (as Vint's readers point out to him) disconcerting, and it is no wonder that Vint has to intercede to offer instructions for reading the stereotypically gendered relations between the two diaries. But his suggestion that Garrels doesn't quite fit into the available and highly gendered professional characterizations of "girl reporters" that circulate in popular culture is compelling, and it is a reminder that the role Martinkus adopts as the independent nomad reporter also draws on well-established masculinist conventions. Vint's ironic and politically incorrect diary (which includes, for example, condescending remarks about young "bimbo" women journalists in Baghdad as well as "our Annie") is supplementary to Garrels's entries. Both narrators in this memoir are in the process of projecting a self that occupies unconventional gender roles in public at least (Vint, after all, keeps the home fires burning in Connecticut).

The question of how women who are journalists might occupy a position in the celebrity culture that has surrounded the profession since the war on terror is an important one. Garrels's voice is familiar to many American listeners of National Public Radio, and her memoir proceeds to capitalize on this profile. As one of the primary witnesses of the occupation of Iraq, broadcasting on an almost daily basis in real time, she witnessed traumatic events with a distinctive voice and an emotional force that, for many Americans, are intrinsic to the story of the occupation. *Naked* is true to form in that the promotional blurb promises more intense, intimate, and uncensored responses to the war filtered through a familiar personality. Given Garrels is a radio broadcaster and a woman, predictably the illicit knowledge suggested by the title brings her body into visibility: she confesses that in order to evade the surveillance of Iraqi authorities in the search for satellite phones, she broadcast naked from her hotel room in the dead of night—the girl reporter stripped bare. Again we only need to compare this to Martinkus's account to appreciate how differently men and women are placed in memoirs of professional correspondents.

But the Brenda Starr alias tells us this as well. Although this alias ostensibly appears as a gesture to an intrepid and resourceful cartoon character, a woman reporter who is cynical, funny, and tough, Brenda circulates in contemporary popular culture as a mark of ongoing ambivalence toward strong and independent career women. In his discussion of contemporary journalism films that feature female reporters in prominent roles, Howard Good (1998) finds the same awkward conjuncture that marks the relational nexus of *Naked in Baghdad:* the struggle between public and private, professional and domestic worlds that is often resolved by the female reporter being "tamed" to domesticity. Despite Vint's guidance on how to read these diaries, and the usefulness of the Brenda Starr persona to Garrels personally as an alter ego, author intention does not protect "The Brenda Bulletin," a report on the reporter, from invoking those other texts where the female reporter is humiliated and cut down to size to fit alongside her man on the farm. This is (as Howard Good suggests) an American story. Although memoirs may draw more directly from life, they are not insulated from the tropes and stereotypes of the profession in contemporary culture. Also an American story is Vint's final word in the "Brenda Bulletin," describing "Annie's" homecoming. In *Naked* the relational style of life narrative turns to a homeland security that can continue to sustain the heterosexual romance as a domestic retreat from violence: the ménage in remote Connecticut is romanticized and sealed away to counter the horrors of the war in Iraq (which of course occur in the defense of homelands such as this, rhetorically at least).

CHAPTER SIX

The Palestine Hotel

Garrels's diary brings the media circus, which orchestrates the unilateral war reporters in Baghdad, into clear view. Quarantined by a system of visas, minders, and translators that carefully regulate access and without a knowledge of place, language, or people, Garrels emphasizes the truth of the journalism business is anchored in relationality rather than heroics: "We are only as good as the people who work with us" (2003, 92). The paraphernalia of contemporary journalism crowds into the scene within the hotel in *Naked:* the business of setting up satellite links for live broadcasts; the testy relations among crews of different nationalities and various media (print, radio, television); the "celebrity effect" and the (highly resented) fleeting presence of media stars like Dan Rather and Christiane Amanpour. In his webdiary of May 2003, Salam Pax, the Baghdad Blogger, includes a withering snapshot of the self-centered fraternity of journalists in Baghdad: "Pool side at the Hamra hotel. Where every journalist wishes he had a room reserved. If they sit long enough there they could just forget that there was a war going on outside the hotel fences. Jennifer Lopez squeaking out of the speakers and cool $5 beers with over priced burgers and salads. . . . I don't swim. I sat reading a borrowed copy of the *New Yorker.* An article about the new X-men movie. All systems on autopilot" (May 23, 2005 [Pax 2002–4]). Pax sees the journalists who parachute into Baghdad as aliens and voyeurs, even as they see him as the "amiable native." It is Pax who describes talking with journalists as selling his soul to the devil: "I talked to Rory from *The Guardian* . . . when Raed saw me after 'the talk' he said I looked like someone had violated me. So there is a bit of guilt" (May 22, 2003).

It is almost inevitable that sightings of foreign correspondents occur in and around the public spaces of the hotel: the pool, the lobby, and the bar. Garrels chronicles the constant business of locating and relocating in the war zone: from one hotel/floor/room/minder/vehicle/visa to another. New technologies lend resonance to this obsessive focus and orientation to Euro-American time and place: some hotel rooms allow satellite phones better access to receivers, for example. Garrels relishes her move from the sixth to the eleventh floor of the Palestine Hotel in Baghdad: "The room looks out over the Tigris and the Republican Palace with access to the Atlantic Ocean East satellite, which does not seem to be as congested as the others" (124). Correspondents find their drivers, fixers, and translators in hotel lobbies; this is, after all, where Salam Pax was finally "outed" by the journalist Peter Maass, who was in search of a translator there. The importance of the hotel as a key site in the management of journalists in Baghdad cannot be overestimated. It has been suggested that one of the iconic moments of the invasion of Iraq, the toppling of the statue of Saddam Hussein in Firdous Square, was staged to the benefit of correspondents in a nearby hotel. For the correspondents, all routes begin and end in the hotel, and the maps of central Baghdad included in *Naked in Baghdad* dutifully locate the key coordinates of this professional habitus. In memoir, we learn about the plumbing in the al-Rashid and the Palestine, the "drinking hole" at the al-Hamra, the poker games in the *Washington Post* room at the Sheraton. This is an extension of the militarized landscapes of Baghdad that Derek Gregory describes as endemic and routinely emptied of the presence of civilians and signs of domestic habitation. Journalists are part of the occupying forces.

James Clifford's (1997) work on the transnational passages of people, commodities, and ideas focuses on the hotel as a rich chronotope of cultural interaction—a setting that organizes time and space in a representable whole form. The chronotope is usefully extended by Gregory's (2004) dovetailing of physical and conceptual spaces in Iraq as "spaces of occupation." Conceived in this way, the hotel is a place of fleeting and arbitrary encounters, of connection and juxtaposition—and, as it happens, the habitat of some five hundred war correspondents in Baghdad. By entering the hotel as a conceptual space, we approach both Salam Pax and the foreign correspondents in terms of their copresence in a complex field of cross-cultural engagements shaped by the enterprise of reporting the war on terror. Clifford apologizes for his preoccupation with the hotel; it is, after all, necessarily focused on the metropolitan centers (33). But no apology is needed here. As a device for capturing the particular and historically grounded habitus of the foreign correspondents "parachuted" into Baghdad, the hotel is unsurpassed as an organizing image of their location as an elite and empowered group of public intellectuals. The chronotope may be limited, as Clifford suggests, by the class, race, and sociocultural privilege of an archetypal bourgeois space, but in this, too, it captures the specific, limited cosmopolitanism of the correspondent, who remains closely linked to national and corporate interests and a resident of the first world.

Journalism, as we have seen, has been characterized as, among other things, a style of ethnographic writing: the best ethnographic writing and good investigative journalism draw on a wide range of sources of knowledge to draw carefully detailed and incisive representations of communities. Most recently, Ulf Hannerz draws on the similarities between journalism and anthropology as professional disciplines and parallel crafts: like anthropologists, news media foreign correspondents report from one part of the world to another through circuits dominated by North American and European interests, and they share the condition of being professionally located in transnational contact zones, engaged in reporting, translating, representing, and interpreting—managing meaning across distances (2004, 3). There are of course significant differences—the hotel is less satisfactory as a chronotope for the discipline of anthropology, which works its way forward from Malinowski's tent! Perhaps too, as Hannerz argues, "we have more knowledge, but they have more power" (4). Nevertheless like ethnography, journalistic writing is part of that congeries of "traveling" nonfiction that responds well to readings in terms of space and subjectivity as effect, as production, and as performance. This syncopation of place, space, and subjectivity that characterizes Clifford's work (like Said's "imaginative geographies" in *Orientalism* [1995]) captures what Gregory calls the "co-production" of culture and power and the production, circulation, and legitimation of meanings through representations, practices, and performances that "enter fully into (rather than reflect) the constitution of the world" (8).

This is to take a turn, and to read journalists' memoirs in terms of specific disciplining (or crafting) the self: a reflection on the professional identity and vocation of the autobiographical narrator and a text that both creates and authorizes what it perhaps only seemed to describe. For example, Clifford's work (1997) on the hotel chronotope draws attention to the ethnographic quality of Garrels's memoir. Among other things, *Naked in Baghdad* offers a valuable thick description of the correspondents' world, using the tools, customs, and technology of Garrels's craft to autobiographical and ethnographic effect. Likewise the nomadic processual prose of Martinkus's *Travels* (2004) responds well to Clifford's thinking about "routes" and the performative dimensions of travel. Questions about how these memoirs are disciplined, how the craft of journalism functions as a technology for shaping the autobiographical self in memoirs by journalists, and whether the professional identity of the narrating subject is stabilized or threatened through self-representation are all relevant here. In fact, this performative dimension of memoirs and their role in creating a historicized professional identity are heightened by the uptake of the Iraqi war in self-fashioning. To pursue this point further: it is through memoirs now that those categories—the unilateral, embedded, and Baghdad reporters—continue to circulate and become sedimented as discrete and meaningful locations and professional identities. Memoirs work, retrospectively, to claim superior ethical responsibility and professional prestige for one or the other. Unilateralism and embeddedness, in particular, are constructed as either ends of a spectrum from which different perspectives on the war are established. But what is the evidence that this is in fact the case? As Martinkus realizes when he scurries back to the security of the Coalition enclave in the green zone of Baghdad, a carefully contained media pack is in the interests of both insurgents and the occupying forces. This insight about the careful management of war journalism can be masked by adopting embedded and unilateral as alternative professional identities—an example of the important distinction to be made between personalizing history and historicizing the personal.

Captive

I began this chapter by talking about crisis and the emergence of new autobiographical subjects and genres. Memoirs by journalists in Iraq indicate unilateral and embedded journalism are in the process of producing professional identities that are taken up performatively and polemically in self-representations. It has been widely remarked that the occupation of Iraq was accompanied by a "journalistic invasion," which included a "slick new public-relations concept known as 'embedding'" (Katovsky and Carlson 2003, xi), and this produced a heated debate about the incorporation of journalists into a public relations exercise that would facilitate the production of propaganda rather than independent journalism. As we have seen, both Garrels and Martinkus use memoir to adopt unilateralism rhetorically, as a badge of independence and autonomy. They define their professional identity as journalists in Iraq over and against the embedded reporters who, according to Martinkus, are captives of the American military machine. For Martinkus it is a badge of honor that he has no access to the American military at all, and he is unrecognizable to them and at some risk from American marksmen in the streets of Baghdad and Karbala. We know from his casual asides that he is immediately recognizable as an 'American' to the Iraqis on the street. As autobiographical narratives begin to emerge from embedded reporters themselves—and to date, these are principally in the form of fragmentary oral accounts in edited collections—it is clear that embedded reporters traveled variously, and their accounts need to be read with specific and changing dynamics of authorship in view. Embedded journalists wrote for various readerships and regional markets, they used a variety of media technologies (print, television and radio), and their experiences were shaped quite differently according to their military location and host. Their situation is no more singular that the unilaterals or the Baghdad reporters, and in fact the differences among these situations can be called into question—all journalistic coverage of the war by Western reporters was carefully contained one way and another.

The embedded journalist preceded the Iraq campaign; however, coupled with new communications technologies, embedding did promise unprecedented immediacy and intimacy in coverage of war.[3] The idea of the embedded reporter was promoted as a distinctive feature of media coverage of this war. It appears that "immediacy" is initially translated as providing more graphic scenes of trauma, and these do gain an immediate positive feedback from readers. For example the embedded *Detroit News* reporter John Bebow points out that all he could do was "give really detailed, if possible, gut wrenching snapshots of what's going on . . . and that's why I wrote about dead bodies quite often. They were the stories that really hit people. . . . the stuff that really left a lasting impression was the dead body scenes" (Bebow 2003, 7). Here again we return to what Gilmore calls the limits of autobiography, that point of tension when the speaking of pain and trauma emerges from contexts that "are themselves impure" (2001, 2) with effects that remain uncertain. It has been suggested that the more graphic coverage from embedded reporters was part of the propaganda war in Iraq, serving to hide the essentially simulated and mythical nature of the one-sided conflict (Keeble 2004, 50). Embedded journalists often reflect that their location gave them "slivers" of history: intense experiences but with almost no sense of the larger context. These reporters agreed to a list of contractual conditions, including a long list of things on which they could not report. Oliver Boyd-Barrett includes dead bodies in this list (2004, 31); however, given Bebow's account it may be that the contracts were routinely ignored, or it was reporting on American bodies that was forbidden by the Pentagon contract and civilian bodies were another matter altogether. Graphic detail of the eviscerated civilian is an iconic scene that marks embedded reporting, and the discursive authority of journalists reporting on war must be gauged by both the contextual problems of determining what can be seen and how their accounts use graphic images to contribute toward understandings about the war. The shift of register to memoir allows a recoding, and how embedded journalists take up this now notorious location and respond to the demand for more graphic and detailed coverage of death is a breaking story.

Given its close relations to ethnography, historiography, and literature, the resources for recoding war narrative in journalistic memoir are rich, and timely. Some of this recoding will be surprising—for example, the satirical approach of Chris Ayres in his memoir *War Reporting for*

Cowards: Between Iraq and a Hard Place (2005). The practice of embedding reporters is clearly problematic given journalistic writing is traditionally understood in positivist and functional terms that privilege objectivity and a referential and unmediated reality. The reporter traveling in the soft-skinned Humvee, for example, is vulnerable to influence and is a long way from a newsroom. However, the more critical and self-reflexive dimensions of the craft—its subjectivity of expression, the politics of identity building, and the grounding of these in specific sociohistorial contexts and practices (Zelizer 2004, 176)—come into view in memoirs. The practice of embedding, in particular, brings the association of journalism with ethnographic writing to the fore, as the embedded perspective is intrinsic to the "human-world understanding and perspective" of ethnography as a discipline (Richardson 2000, 254). The worries about embedded story are, one way or another, worries about lack of discipline. The reporter will lose the objectivity of the journalist to tell the whole truth fearlessly, as well as the responsibility of the ethnographer to guard against "going native" in a military unit; they will be literary in taking license with textuality and in turning to imagination and interpretation rather than discourses of realism. Such license will produce a mongrel, which confounds protocols of reading and interpretation based in any of its constituent disciplines. These worries are borne out in Evan Wright's *Generation Kill* (2004), which takes all of this as opportunity. Wright is not unknowingly seduced out of objectivity and reason; he discards them as inappropriate to the representation of this war. His mongrel memoir is designed to bite and to break the rules of engagement that shape readerly expectations of war memoir. Wright gives up the chase for "truth" as a privileged access to the experiences of Iraqi civilians, and he finds his ethnographic subjects close to home.

Evan Wright was embedded with a platoon of Marines for six weeks, driving in a Humvee from Kuwait to Baghdad at the forefront of the invasion of Iraq in March 2003. He traveled with $12 Moleskine notebooks (marketed as a symbol of contemporary intellectual nomadism) in his back pocket. For Wright, the tools of his trade are important: low tech, Moleskines are "the latte of notebooks," "the old papyrus technology" that he takes back to its origins in Iraq (Katovsky and Carlson 2003, 332). The copious notes Wright took as an embedded reporter were first published as a series of articles in *Rolling Stone* magazine and, later, in a series of short chronological chapters in *Generation Kill* (2004). Wright practices a style of journalism that veers close to ethnography. The platoon is interpreted as a subculture, a community observed in precise detail as to manners, hierarchy, and rule-governed behaviors ordained by the Marine code of conduct; Wright's earlier experience as a journalist writing about the relatively amoral subcultures of the porn industry in Los Angeles and black skateboarders in Philadelphia is surely an important ethnographic precursor and influence. The sponsorship of *Rolling Stone* is significant, too. The magazine targets a younger, literate, American, and international demographic, and it seeks out alternative and more subjective styles of journalism that are colloquial and confrontational. It is the ideal venue for a radical and subjective uptake of embedding as a corrupted place for the authorship of war narrative from Iraq, and the series of three long essays Wright published in the magazine as precursors to *Generation Kill* were immediately recognized as a fresh look at the Iraq campaign.

What is striking about *Generation Kill* is Wright's relentless focus on a cell of Marines charging into Iraq as an ethnographic field—a place where he is at work in pursuit of a ground truth that is always going to be partial, troubling, and unreconciled. It is this troop that determines and organizes what the reporter can see and learn about Iraq—which turns out to be very little from some points of view. Whereas Martinkus and Garrels hold onto the ideal of gesturing to Iraqi experiences of the occupation as essential to truth in war journalism, Wright is embedded in a specific and rule-governed military community that can fathom very little from what it sees of Iraqi landscapes and people. The confused sense of Iraqi civilian presence is a mark of Wright's conscious projection of a militarized landscape in Iraq and the systematic destruction of domestic habitation and cultivation there. The ethnographic subjects of *Generation Kill* are not Iraqi civilians; they are the Marines of the Recon unit. Like Moleskine notebooks, the movement of the Humvee is an essential accessory to this narrative, and part of the apparatus that locates Wright as a participant observer who is in a process of personal and professional initiation—reflecting on his own growth through ordeals and savagery and finding the right literary and ethnographic tools and techniques to craft his memoir. *Generation Kill* includes a self-conscious reflection on his own dependency and need to assimilate into this group and on the processes of initiation and indoctrination that occur and impinge on his professional identity as a reporter. These are obviously the risks of embedding, certainly they are the matters that have been raised in critique of the practice (see, for example, Tumber 2004). Wright doesn't hesitate to take these into his memoir as conditions of authorship. But Wright uses embedding to develop a narrative technique that expands and amplifies the repertoire of witnessing by incorporating a rich and colloquial resource: the first-person responses of the Marines themselves. Wright captures his ethnographic subjects in the process of dealing with the shame and disgust at the horrorscape that they are in the process of creating, and he abdicates from the role of being the single witnessing subject. The Marines themselves worry over what happens to their humanity in this war, they lose respect for their leaders, reject the rhetoric of liberation, and agonize over civilian deaths. They do these things colloquially, idiosyncratically, and eloquently and their views displace the singular authorized narrative point of view.

Like Martinkus's transits through American Iraq, in *Generation Kill* Iraq is a space that is discursively mapped and corporeally experienced as chaotic and impossible to read or predict; here, too, the U.S. military is in the process of bringing anarchy and carnage, not liberation and freedom. Wright's memoir makes no pretence at humanizing or individuating the Iraqi civilians who have the misfortune to come within range of the Marines. He includes descriptions of degradation and carnage wreaked on the Iraqi population, which are almost fictional in their intensity and horror—the literary frame seems most appropriate. Joseph Heller's macabre *Catch 22* comes to mind, and so too does J. M. Coetzee's *Disgrace*. There are no illusions about a clean and precise war here. The breakdown between the primitive and the civilized, the animal and the human, is complete—perhaps within and certainly beyond the military cell. Along with the Marines, the autobiographical narrator learns to see his surroundings in the military terms of the ROE—rules of engagement—that "basically create an illusion of moral order where there is none" (Wright 2004, 176). Despite the latest technology and equipment, there are no grounds for recognizing and classifying what the Marines encounter as they campaign in Iraq, and the result is indiscriminate carnage and a license to kill. At the end of the memoir there is a reckoning:

In the past six weeks, I have been on hand while this comparatively small unit of Marines has killed quite a few people. I personally saw three civilians shot, one fatally with a bullet in the eye. These were just the tip of the iceberg. The Marines killed dozens, if not hundreds, in combat through direct fire and through repeated, at times almost indiscriminate, artillery strikes. And no one will probably ever know how many died from the approximately 30,000 pounds of bombs First Recon ordered dropped from aircraft. I can't imagine how the man ultimately responsible for all of these deaths—at least on the battalion level—sorts it all out and draws the line between what is wanton killing and what is civilized military "conduct." (347)

Although it has been alleged that once bonding occurs the embedded reporter will recoil from reporting the pleasure of the kill and protect the military that surround him (Tumber 2004, 192), the moral dilemma raised by *Generation Kill* suggests otherwise: the embedded reporter is not immune to the sublime experience of the kill himself—and perhaps this is where *Generation Kill* becomes bad ethnography and bad reporting.[4] Wright deliberately contradicts sentimental reports that American troops in Iraq are reluctant to use their weapons. They do so with alacrity. The autobiographical reporter is embedded so closely that he, too, experiences the adrenalin rush, the exhilarating transcendence and intoxication of armed combat.

This use of embedding is strategic on Wright's part. The idea that the reporter is a benevolent and liberal presence is a doxa of American war journalism since Vietnam. Wright discards this liberal humanism and challenges what he regards as the sanitized journalism that passes for truth in American writing:

For the past decade we've been steeped in the lore of *The Greatest Generation,* the title of Tom Brokaw's book about the men who fought in World War II, and a lot of people have developed this romanticism about that war. They tend to remember it from the *Life* magazine images of the sailor coming home and kissing his fiancé. They've forgotten that war is about killing. I really think it's important as a society to be reminded of this, because you now have a generation of baby boomers, a lot of whom didn't serve in Viet Nam. Many of them protested it. But now they're grown up, and as they've gotten older I think many of them have tired of the ambiguities and the lack of moral clarity of Viet Nam, and they've started to cling to this myth of World War II, the good war. (Wright 2005)

Wright turns to the adjacent disciplines of literature, film, and ethnography to shape his rules of engagement for war journalism from Iraq. From American fiction he takes the realism of Heller and Vonnegut— and Hemingway reputedly favored Moleskines after all, as did that other nomad autobiographer, Bruce Chatwin. One doesn't doubt that Wright witnessed dogs scavenging on human and animal remains from the back seat of the Humvee, but the generic protocols that suggest this graphic detail should be included for rhetorical effect in his memoir are not from the disciplines of journalism; they are literary devices to convey the disintegration of all civilized order. Like *Black Hawk Down,* the narrative point of view progressively develops from a depersonalized and mediated view to an increasingly on-ground, embedded ethnographic encounter that is steeped in violent death. In *Generation Kill* the progress toward Baghdad is a descent into the abyss that finds its apogee in the city itself, which is in chaos. The expectation of the Marines that they will work closely with the Iraqi community there and become a benevolent presence is dispelled entirely. One of the Marines is writing his own journal alongside Wright, an account of the war he calls his "Bitter Journal," which he will leave as his true account for his wife: "If they say we fought valiantly here, I want her to know we fought retarded. They haven't used us right" (Wright 2004, 283). A literary reading of all this might invoke Northrop Frye's dystopic genre of the antiromance, with its descent into a night world where demonic ordeals must be undergone, human creatures become inarticulate, and the distinctions between the human and the animal blur (1976, 118). Wright and his subjects hurtle through an abstracted space that is populated but dehumanized; they know nothing of local customs, languages, histories, traditions, and cultures. Their apprehension of Iraqi space is totally militarized and strategic. Beyond this, they are enclosed in a generational and distinctively American textual archive of popular culture that (along with the ROE) frames and encloses what they see and how they interpret their experience: *Black Hawk Down*, *Jackass*, *Doom*, Justin Timberlake, *Apocalypse Now*, *Hustler*, J. Lo. *Generation Kill* is an American story, and it is quite deliberately so.

The Bitter Journal

In a thought-provoking chapter on the role of war journalism in these times, Susan D. Moeller laments the absence of enterprise reporting from Iraq—the practice of journalism that would question the operating assumptions of foreign policy and the motives of the war on terror. The turn to a-day-in-the-life style coverage by embedded reporters has produced a docile media, in her view, which has turned away from its responsibility to cultivate a moral imagination and empathy in their audience by exposing the humanity of those civilians who suffer in war. Until the recent past, Moeller argues, "the human rights of distant strangers were reported on because the well-being of those strangers was understood to be relevant to Americans" (Moeller 2004, 74). Moeller is drawing on a communicative ethics that I have discussed at some length in earlier chapters, which privileges empathic connection to distant others. From this point of view, it is empathy that justifies the dealing in the violent deaths of others by the media—if social values are not engaged in an ethical way, then viewing the pain and suffering of others is mere voyeurism. Empathic engagement suggests that casual and passive spectatorship of violence and suffering becomes an ethical practice of witnessing, and the presentation of news should be constructed to direct audience feelings to produce this moral effect, rather than feeding complacency, prejudice, and ignorance or simply catering to vicarious pleasure. Elsewhere Moeller raises one of the problems in the graphic presentation of suffering in mass media to Western spectators and readers: "compassion fatigue," the title of her important study of jaded responses to journalist coverage of stories of famine and war (1999). News is a business, it must engage audiences, for these images are the products that it markets and sells. In her discussion of these issues Jean Seaton (2003) includes a useful historical perspective on the attention to empathy as an emotion that accrues particular social value as a framework for justifying the presentation of suffering for mass consumption. Seaton (like Schaffer and Smith in their study of human rights discourse [2004b]) points out that the commitment to human rights is itself a relatively recent development, a decisive shift in values encoded in the United Nations Charter of Human Rights. It is this that shapes an emotional economy that values empathy as a currency of cross-cultural engagement and that suggests that others are "just like us" with entitlements to the same democratic freedoms and rights. These are necessary arguments about various ways of historicizing the personal in memoir.

Empathy also shapes how news about trauma is constructed, and how it appeals to an implied audience (which, as Moeller unwittingly suggests, is broadly characterized as "American"). For example the place of the reporter as conduit and a receptor is vitally important: the reporter cultivates moral empathy by a subjective eyewitnessing account that responds to trauma performatively—sometimes graphically so, as we see in Martinkus's narrative. The autobiographical journalist in memoir is a point of moral and ethical accountability: he or she recoils and gags as a proxy, shrinking back in horror on our behalf. These memoirs by the authorized witnesses to the war in Iraq tap into powerful emotional and psychological responses to the war, and it is a consolation that the reporter can still find a place to stand, witness, and empathize. This is an important narrative device in how news about trauma is constructed, and it is powerful; eliciting empathy in this way involves using our feelings about ourselves to reach across to "distant others." Seaton points out that empathy is attractive, but there is something self-reflective about it, and because empathy makes us feel good, it is very easy to bear (2003, 53). A more difficult contract for dealing with trauma but a more timely one given "compassion fatigue" might refuse to place the autobiographical reporter as a stable and rational witness on our behalf, and it might complicate the notion that we can assimilate strangers and negotiate difference through empathic understanding. It could, for example, project intractable difference that must be negotiated in other ways. Alternatively it could take up Seaton's point that there is something self-reflective about empathic engagement and work with the self-reflectiveness using a different paradigm.

Generation Kill unsettles the doxa of empathic understanding in this way, and Evan Wright (who is writing about and for a younger and generational demographic) offers no "feel good" consolation or redemption in the witnessing of trauma. His approach suggests that the ideological framework of human rights discourse as a vehicle for war journalism is flawed and unable to undermine the rhetoric of this war, which, after all, uses humanitarianism as an instrument of state policy. Wright refuses to stand in the position of the ethical eyewitness that responds empathically to trauma: he sets out to recode war journalism by relocating the journalist from the position of the proxy ethical eyewitness to the position of observer who sometimes veers close to his subjects. A dismantling of the unified moral subject in *Generation Kill* occurs variously. The work of unsettling the moral imagination begins by making "home" a complicated, conflicted, and disturbing place. Wright brings the work of thinking about distant strangers closer by practicing the ethnographic techniques of close observation on the military force in Iraq. In this process it is the Americans who are made strange and unrecognizable—to themselves: "Culturally these Marines would be virtually unrecognizable to their forebears in the 'Greatest Generation.' They are kids raised on hip-hop, Marilyn Manson and Jerry Springer. . . . These young men represent what is more or less America's first generation of disposable children. More than half of the guys in the platoon came from broken homes and were raised by absentee, single, working parents. Many are on more familiar terms with video games, reality TV shows and Internet porn than they are with their own parents" (5). The dominant mythology that war turns on a generation's loss of innocence is no longer tenable, and Wright points out that few of the Marines would have been shaken to discover they were leading a grab for oil rather than a fight in Iraq to protect American freedom.

There is no stable, singular, personified point of "humanity" or human values from which to read and interpret the traumatic sights of degradation and death in *Generation Kill*. The reader, like the Marines and the autobiographical narrator, encounters Iraq intertextually, immersed in an ocean of other texts that mythologize mourning, death, and violence variously and inconsistently: *Black Hawk Down, Apocalypse Now,* the Creedence Clearwater anthems from Vietnam days, the computer game *Doom,* Elmore Leonard novels, Gordon Lightfoot lyrics, and Sergio Leone Westerns. All of these, and more, are intertexts that are invoked as frames of reference derived from American popular culture, which is the world these ethnographic subjects inhabit and carry to Iraq with them. In this Wright takes up the life world of his subjects, and it becomes a device for drawing all terms of stable reference and moral judgment based on liberal humanism into question. This is critical to Wright's attack on the moral clarity that the Brokaw generation sustained in and through war journalism.

One of the intriguing things about all this is that Wright's technique, which can be read as a sophisticated, postmodern, and thoroughly textualized representation of subjectivity and a turning to literature in the practice of journalism, is being taken up as a powerful and phenomenological grasp of what the experience of war is like for those who have served in the American military and their families in the recent past.[5] The question is whether this technique, which makes no pretense of engaging in an empathic identification through the suffering of Iraqi civilians, can respond at all to Moeller's requirement that war journalism should stir the moral imagination. The question would be too singular for Wright; it returns to a humanist ideology that blurs what Americans need to grasp about themselves and what is happening in Iraq. It is also a question that imagines that texts work consistently and predictably, and this blurs the different reading formations, interest groups, and markets that make the transits of texts a complex and unpredictable business. When all is said and done, *Generation Kill* is also available to be read for vicarious thrill, as the ultimate adventure, and there is no guarantee that readers will take the cover blurb of the first edition ironically, for the peritext promises: "It's another Iraqi town, nameless to the Marines racing down the main drag in Humvees, blowing it to pieces." This may seem heroic, and a perfectly acceptable real-life extension of X-box gaming. The circulation of militarized landscapes of the Middle East throughout Western popular culture works to reproduce these empty landscapes that invite militarized intervention.

Ultimately I want to suggest that Moeller's thinking is also too modest in what it imagines war journalism can do as a writing of history, subjectivity, and culture and as bearing witness to trauma in memoir. If we disengage a stirring in the moral imagination from the representation of distant strangers, then there is reason to think that *Generation Kill* is precisely placed to undermine the propaganda about homelands, democracy, freedom, and heroism that is part of the war of words in these times. We can see this by returning to the ethnographic and autobiographical dimensions of Wright's memoir. In interviews Wright describes himself as contaminated by Iraq: "haunted by the images of people that I saw killed by my country. There's no way around that" (2005). Yet, in what I earlier described as a "reckoning," at the end of the memoir Wright recalls rather dispassionately what he has seen in the past six weeks, and the blurring of judgments about the differences between appropriate military conduct and wanton killing. Unlike Martinkus, Wright offers no single sticky story to capture this haunting as emotion in his own narrative persona. When Wright writes of disgust, as he does, he refuses to offer himself as the proxy witness and moral compass that can contain the damage:

Dead cows, bloated to twice their normal size, lie in ditches. Human corpses are scattered about as well. It's now the familiar horrorscape of a country at war. Just before reaching the final Marine camp outside Baghdad, Espera's vehicle swerves to avoid running over a human head lying in the road. When the vehicle turns, he looks up to see a dog eating a human corpse. "Can it get any sicker than this?" he asks.

Person, however, has an entirely different reaction. Set back from the highway, gleaming like some sort of religious shrine, there is a modern-looking glass structure with plastic signs in front. It's an Iraqi version of a 7-Eleven. Though looted and smashed, it gives Person hope. "Damn!" he says. "It looks almost half-civilized here. (2004, 276)

Wright remains the intellectual nomad and, in this case, the ethnographer whose concern remains resolutely on capturing his subjects live. By turning aside from Tom Brokaw and the traditions of liberal humanism in journalist memoir, Wright refuses to contain and exorcise the telling of trauma in an emotional narrative of redemption that can somehow account for and contain the loss and suffering of "distant others" in apology or on our behalf. He refuses to mediate between the vastly different emotional responses here, for example, and offers instead that unreconciled coexistence of Espera's disgust and Person's hope.

The Iraq war doesn't yet have its anthems, films, and iconic narratives, but the art forms that emerge and do justice to the experience of the Americans in Iraq will, like *Generation Kill*, be shattering and self-regarding texts. In her recent study of how journalism enters the academy, Barbie Zelizer (2004) emphasizes how differently the profession is figured as it enters the domains of the social sciences and cultural and literary studies. By reading journalists' memoirs as autobiographical writing here (rather than as history, ethnography, or a form of extended news reportage) I mean to emphasize how the possibilities for speech and subjectivity in memoirs has become unsettled by what Kristeva (1997) calls the "death infecting life" landscapes of abjection in Iraq. From one point of view, the story that is to be told in war journalism from Iraq is quite simple: there was a rapid and overwhelming victory over forces that were in disarray and offered little in the way of resistance. New technologies and a strategy that incorporated journalists into the war zone allowed unprecedented access and immediacy in coverage of the conflict. The translation of this story into journalists' memoirs opens other perspectives and a recoil that is felt personally and professionally. A complex narrative emerges in memoirs, which are caught in the emotional and ethical aftermath that is the legacy of any war but that assumes distinctive forms in the war on terror. It is this that is opened up by questions intrinsic to autobiographics: the pursuit of the shifting elements of identity and truth that writers draw on to authorize themselves in acts of self-representation. Memoirs are a breaking story in which journalists continue to write to "do justice" to the war in Iraq. By reading these autobiographically I mean to suggest that this writing is part of the attention to emotions of grief, mourning, and loss that spills into the public sphere in the war on terror. The terrible and spectral presence of the victims of war are embedded in the American experience of Iraq, they carry into memoirs in sticky presence and ensure that the living will continue to be haunted by the violently dead and by those places where "man strayed on the territories of animal."

SEVEN

The Pangs of Exile:
Memoir Out of Iran

But will it do any good to appeal to even the best uses of the literary imagination in a political climate filled with prejudice and hatred?

MARTHA NUSSBAUM, *POETIC JUSTICE*

By the summer of 2005 Iranian memoirs were in vogue and circulating to critical praise and wide readerships in North America. One in particular was a best-seller, and it is the subject of this chapter: Azar Nafisi's *Reading "Lolita" in Tehran*. Also highly acclaimed were Marjane Satrapi's graphic memoirs, both translated from the French originals, *Persepolis* (2003) and *Persepolis 2* (2004). These are notable among a series of other recent memoir: Roya Hakakian's *Journey from the Land of No* (2004), Said's *Landscapes of Distant Mother* (2004), and Firoozeh Dumas's *Funny in Farsi: A Memoir of Growing up Iranian in America* (2004), among others. This is a generation of memoir, recalling the 1979 Iranian Revolution and its aftermath. They bring that traumatic memory back into the present, as troubled relations between the United States and Iran reemerge. The question of how we might read these memoirs and understand their contemporary currency is an important one. What is at stake when memoirs by Iranian exiles trade as best-sellers in these times? In what sense are these "Iranian" life narratives, and what is their relationship to Iran? What kinds of autobiographical subjects are emerging from the Iranian Diaspora, and what are the dynamics of the circulation and reception of these memoirs now? Negar Mottahedeh suggests,

"It cannot be coincidental that the memoirs by Iranian female authors now living in the West, such as those of Firoozeh Dumas, Marjane Satrapi and Azar Nafisi, have found such phenomenal commercial success at a time when Washington hawks would like the authors' country of birth to be the next battleground in the total war of the twenty-first century" (2004, 2). It isn't coincidence, and it isn't conspiracy either. Exilic memoir brings to the surface a long history of fascination, mourning, obsession, and a copresence that is an ongoing subtext in both Iranian and American imaginaries.

Iran and America are rendered together—both equally mythologized—in these life narratives that draw deeply on discourses of exile and displacement. Caren Kaplan (1996) insists that refugees, exiles, nomads, and travelers should be recognized variously and historically; they are producers of (rather than simply metaphors and tropes in) critical discourse. These Iranian memoirs occupy a specific subculture that is shaped by their origins in a turbulent period of Iranian history and culture and by the geopolitical grid of the war on terror that determines their production and reception as valued commodities in the United States now. As exilic memoir they reflect on and mystify history and place distinctively—both the past and the highly charged political present. Discussion of exilic writing emphasizes its characteristic tendency to erase the historically specific conditions of its production, dissemination, and reception (Kaplan 1996; Said 2002; Smith 2004). It is, then, the work of criticism to decipher the imaginative weaving together of "here" and "there" that shapes exilic thinking and to explore the precise sociopolitical contexts when memoir from Iran becomes popular in the United States. The interpenetration and entanglement, fascination and repulsion, of recent American and Iranian cultures and politics in dialectical relation suggest each makes an enemy of the other. As Slavoj Žižek (2002) and Derek Gregory (2004) point out, this process is imaginative and performative, and the lines of filiation and connection between them draw on complicated and mutable architectures of enmity (Gregory 2004, 16). Memoirs bring these always-relational productions and performances into view, personally speaking, and within the confines of individual lives and histories.

In *Reading "Lolita,"* Nafisi recalls that revolutionary Iran became obsessed with America in the 1980s. She draws on a variety of signs: the possession of the American Embassy in 1979 and the seizing of hostages, the Death to America slogans in the streets, the popularity of *Baywatch* and American classic films accessed through forbidden satellite dishes. Nafisi's mentor points out that she herself is very American, and the autobiographical narrator reflects that her children's memories of childhood lyrics and films in Iran will be the Doors and Michael Jackson rather than Persian songs. These different signs, drawn from both public history and private conduct and taste, suggest that relations between the United States and Iran are a critical issue for contemporary Iranians, both home and abroad. In *Persepolis* (2003) there is a chapter called "Kim Wilde," where Marji, the autobiographical narrator, recalls that her parents bring "hip stuff" back from Turkey by smuggling posters of Iron Maiden and Kim Wilde in the lining of an overcoat. In 1983 Marji puts on the latest Nikes, "my denim jacket with the Michael Jackson button, and of course, my headscarf" (131) and sets out for the black market on Gandhi Avenue, Tehran. More recently, Negar Mottahedeh describes driving north on the Sadr freeway in Tehran in the summer of 2004: "I came across a series of images covering the soundproofed walls of the opposite lane. The first panel from the left was a painted reproduction of the infamous photograph of the uniformed Pfc. Lynndie England holding a leash tied to the neck of an Iraqi prisoner who curls naked in a fetal position on the Abu Ghraib prison floor" (2004, 3). As Mottahedeh emphasizes, images of the United States in Iran, and vice versa, are densely networked and need to be read with precise attention to history and to changing relations among various states in the Middle East, including Palestine and Iraq.

Likewise, Americans are haunted by Iran. The Islamic revolution, and the hostage crisis of 1979–81 in particular, had ongoing repercussions in North America: it produced a mass exodus of Iranian intellectuals and accelerated the development of a strong Iranian exilic culture in the United States, and it left a residue of anger and bitterness that extended beyond the presidencies of Carter and Reagan. As I have suggested in chapter 4, the captivity narrative par excellence, Betty Mahmoody's *Not without My Daughter,* has remained popular and readily available ever since its paperback publication in 1987 (revived by Brian Gilbert's film of 1991) and draws on the lingering reservoir of contempt, bitterness, and fear. Contemporary memoir from Iran attracts American readers again now, and it revisits and folds the events of the Islamic revolution and its aftermath into the present one more time.

Roya Hakakian, a journalist for the American CBS network at the time of writing her memoir, indicates the subjective location and discursive trajectory of these exilic memoirs succinctly and rhetorically. For her, writing memoir is a revenge of sorts, for she suggests the greatest jihad of all following the events of 1979 was "the one against the 'self.'" Following the installation and hardening of the Islamic theocracy under

Khomeini, each citizen was expected to master by way of annihilation or regulation every desire and difference and was brought under ever increasing surveillance (2004, 201). After 1979, Tehran was transformed rapidly. Hakakian's autobiographical narrator buys maps of the city compulsively as neighborhoods, schools, and streets disappear. These are renamed and reconfigured to accord with a new reality, which erases the time, place, and mentality of her childhood as an Iranian Jew under the Pahlavi regime in favor of the new landscapes and ideoscapes of the Islamic state. Poignantly, the peritext of *Journey from the Land of No* includes these maps of an urban Tehran that exists only in nostalgic memory; this is the country of Hakakian's "lost" childhood. For women in particular, a vastly different spatial geography emerged as Iran was restructured into a totalitarian state under the Khomeini regime, which transformed relations between public and private space violently and in gendered terms. The imposition of the chador is one notorious sign of these developments that produce the "land of No"; another is a ruthless program of executions or imprisonment of dissenters that decimated the intelligentsia and drove others into exile. Through nostalgic memory Hakakian, like Nafisi, notes the disappearance of beloved places of childhood pleasure: the pastry shop, the bookshop, and the school.

Hakakian observes that a corollary of this "jihad against the self" was a silencing of individual histories: the end of autobiography. Several points need to be made about this. There is not a well-established tradition of women's autobiographical writing in Iran, for cultural reasons (a point discussed by critics of Iranian women's writing—for example, Najmabadi [1990], Milani [1992]). Keeping a personal journal is an important technology of the self in Nafisi's memoir, but this practice draws on Western traditions of individualism and self-improvement. The fact that it has taken almost three decades for a school of life narratives to emerge in English, and that they take the form of exilic writing, can be also attributed to the belatedness of traumatic memory and the place of these women in history: these memoirs are generational. Nafisi points this out: "My generation complained of a loss, the void in our lives that was created when our past was stolen from us, making us exiles in our own country" (76). Nafisi, Hakakian, and Satrapi are part of the class and generation of Iranian intellectual women who experienced the loss of freedom and the imposition of a radical code of Islamic conduct on the body personally and at a critical moment of becoming in their personal histories. These are women who were shrouded by the chador, and the trope of losing the land of their childhood to Islamic fundamentalism recurs. Hakakian and Satrapi were adolescents in 1979, and Nafisi was a recent graduate from an American university in Oklahoma, eager to establish herself as an academic in Iran. Nafisi acknowledges in her epilogue that the conditions she describes in her memoir have since altered significantly in Tehran; however, her recollections of a repressed and alienated society can seem wholly convincing and realistic to a Western reader in these times.[1] These autobiographies are narratives of trauma that remain preoccupied with an experience of estrangement, a "little death" of the self and a painful loss of the known world. The intensity of this death of a self and its habitus engenders resurrection through memoir as a Western metropolitan intellectual, and a Diasporic subject, with a troubled and ambivalent relation to a lost homeland and, it follows, to contemporary Iranian society and culture. Marjane Satrapi is very direct about this: "I am a foreigner in Iran. . . . Nowhere is my home any more . . . the book *Persepolis* I wrote for the other ones, not for Iranians" (Tully 2004, 2). These memoirs appear at one and the same time as unfamiliar and belated to contemporary Iranians, and familiar and welcome to contemporary American readers—a conjunction that signals their entanglement in complicated and mutable lines of filiation, connection, and commodification.

Another component of the discursive trajectory of memoir sketched in *The Land of No* is the curious and uninformed American readership eager to know about Iran and primed for stories of disenchantment by exiles. Like other autobiographical narrators—Souad or Zoya, for example—Hakakian describes the pressures to speak of the past and take up the role of native informant in the West. This sociopolitical context needs to be kept in mind to counter the idea that life narrative is a speaking cure for trauma that occurs according to the psychic needs and personal recovery of the traumatized individual and outside of political constraints and opportunities. Material considerations are important in shaping textual cultures. In *Journey from the Land of No* it is an American colleague who needs to hear what Hakakian has to say about Tehran and the Islamic revolution, and he is insistent and elicits the narrative despite her initial resistance. A fellowship at Johns Hopkins University in Baltimore gives Nafisi the time to write her memoir, and it is the war on terror that helps to accelerate not only the spectacular success of a memoir that was originally scheduled for a small print run but also the extraordinary and unlikely celebrity of a professor who interprets the world through a preeminent figure in the modernist literature of exile: Vladimir Nabokov.

Upsilamba

In the spring of 2004 Azar Nafisi appeared as an icon in the "Never Follow" marketing campaign for the Audi Corporation. The promotional image is riveting: Azar Nafisi floating on air amid a library of leather-bound classics (fig. 8). This teacher of Great Books is captured fantastically as the embodiment of freedom and transcendence; a banner, apparently in Nafisi's own script, flows across the bottom of the page: "Never let reality get in the way of imagination." This is an unlikely mantra for a woman whose professional life in Iran was cut short by the regime change to a totalitarian Islamist republic, but it signals her preoccupation as a professor of literature with the transcendent force of reading classic books. In *Reading "Lolita" in Tehran,* the autobiographical narrator introduces Nabokov's *Invitation to a Beheading* at the first meeting of her private class for seven of her best and most committed students in Tehran during the autumn of 1995. Then and there she introduces the iconic word "upsilamba." It is one of Nabokov's "fanciful creations," and for the narrator it means that moment captured for Audi: "the impossible joy of a suspended leap." "Upsilamba" becomes for the reading group "a symbol, a sign of that vague sense of joy, the tingle in the spine Nabokov expected his readers to feel in the act of reading fiction; it was a sensation that separated the good readers, as he called them, from the ordinary ones" (Nafisi 2003b, 21).

The commodification of Nafisi's image in the Audi campaign is a reminder of the recent rehabilitation and trendiness of the library, the bookshop, and the book in contemporary Western commerce. *Reading "Lolita"* has been carried on the wave of enthusiasm for reading as mass entertainment, which has been sponsored by Oprah Winfrey, among other prominent figures in the United States. The public campaign to restore reading as a recreational and communal activity, and the emergence of the book club as an important institution in the consumption of fiction during the past decade, is a precursor of Nafisi's appearance as a celebrity for Audi in the company of stars of football, film, and rock music: Freddy Adu, William H. Macy, and David Bowie. In the cover blurb for *Reading "Lolita"* Geraldine Brooks remarks that *Reading "Lolita"* is a "must read" for "anyone who has ever belonged to a book group" (fig. 9). This is canny marketing of Nafisi's book to a powerful niche market in contemporary book culture. Epitextual commentaries suggest that Nafisi's memoir has been a book of choice for many reading clubs, and the publisher offers questions to facilitate group discussion on the Internet. There are also assignments for sale at "Term Papers and

A special advertising section

Never let reality get in the way of imagination

"Many people find books like *Lolita* or *Madam Bovary* disturbing because they upset people's notions of who they are or who they could be. Many people don't like that. And that is why all great innovations, at the start, become great disturbances. It's only later on that we act as if they have habitually been there. But I look around me and I see a telephone or a car or an airplane. And I think, 'My God! How much imagination has gone into any of these instruments?'"

Azar Nafisi, celebrated author of Reading Lolita in Tehran. *Full interview and more at neverfollow.com.*

8   Image of Azar Nafisi from Audi promotion neverfollow.com

Essays" (AcaDemon.com, n.d.) that suggest American undergraduates are learning to read their own literary tradition through the prism of Nafisi's memoir: "Examine the theme of finding one's true self in *The Great Gatsby* and *Reading "Lolita" in Tehran*." For some readers and book groups it has not been a "choice" book, for they are taken aback by the

9 Front cover design from Azar Nafisi, *Reading "Lolita" in Tehran*

cultural capital required to digest the lengthy and didactic discussions of modernist writing in the memoir. This book is, for some, a disappointment, as the highbrow discussions of fiction in Nafisi's book don't quite translate into middlebrow markets; the absence of the upsilamba effect classifies some as "ordinary readers." For others, *Reading "Lolita"* is nothing less than an eloquent reinstatement of the pleasure of wholehearted reading and a confirmation of their status as "good readers." Nafisi's memoir both performs and requires an immersion in canonical literature for its avid reader, for reading popular page-turners does not produce the spine-tingling grace of upsilamba. *Reading "Lolita"* reflects the book group and the accomplished reader back to themselves in the most flattering terms imaginable. It suggests that reading the right books is a sign of aesthetic taste and cultivation, individual integrity and sensitivity. The advertising agency commissioned by Audi to design the "Never Follow" campaign trades on the link made between Great Books (and Audi vehicles) and commodities of elite status, which both confer and confirm the taste and distinction of the consumer. The Audi campaign highlights (and complicates) what is already a complex process of textual politics occurring in and around the reception of *Reading "Lolita,"* and it introduces an image of Azar Nafisi that suggests some of the complexities of her situation as an exilic autobiographer.

Although the Tehran connection is vital to the contemporary cachet of the memoir, there are other considerations in accounting for this best-seller. Nafisi's memoir is part of a phenomenon that Jim Collins (2002) describes as "high-pop." This is produced by a merger of what were previously taken to be mutually exclusive tastes and institutions, a renegotiation of relations between capital and "cultural capital" that has led to the popularization of Jane Austen novels in television and film, for example, or the marketing of the Ernest Hemingway furniture collection (both examples particularly relevant to Nafisi's canon of Great Authors). As Collins remarks, high art "has refused to stay put as a hothouse plant in the academy" in the recent past (2002, 3). The milieu of the book group in *Reading "Lolita"*—the living room with its lovely vista of the mountains surrounding the city captured in the mirror, the cream cakes and roses and good coffee, the committed and passionate teacher, and the bright young women who love to read to find in fiction "not so much reality but the epiphany of truth" (Nafisi 2003b, 3)—is a ritualistic setting for a discussion of how *The Great Gatsby, Pride and Prejudice,* and *Lolita* are to be consumed in highly cultured acts of transgression. The autobiographical narrator is didactic, and there is little in the way of dissent from her charismatic rendition of James, Fitzgerald, Austen, and

Nabokov. Only a succession of Islamist goons argue against Nafisi's po-lemical discussion of fiction, epiphany, and truth; these are male ideo-logues who lack the capacities for empathy that the "girls" practice and extend. Nafisi brings Western canonical literature, and modernist writ-ing most particularly, into a relatively accessible space, pulling books into the immediate range of the personal and private life of her girls. It is no wonder epitexts generated around *Reading "Lolita"* are so varied. They include testimonies from those who found the book difficult to master, on the one hand, and passionate fans who reproduce the milieu of Nafisi's living room in their own book clubs, on the other. The ac-quisition of advanced literary skills—the capacity for specific forms of reflection and imagination—and the grace of upsilamba involve a popu-larization of traditionally elite cultural competencies that is fundamen-tal to the high-pop phenomenon. In this way, *Reading "Lolita,"* like the BBC, Bollywood, and Karen Joy Fowler's *The Jane Austen Book Club* (2004), takes books that have been accorded canonical status in the academy to wider audiences, with the expectation that readerships can accumulate the skills required to enter into erudite conversation. As Collins remarks, the ability to deliver goods that were once the stuff of elite cultural plea-sures is a result of profound changes in not only delivery systems and commodification but also in the cartography of taste (11).

Book groups are part of this, and the relation of *Reading "Lolita"* to this implied readership takes the form of an elaborate conceit. As I have already suggested, the group milieu of Nafisi's book is orchestrated through a didactic pedagogy shaped by a charismatic professor rather than the more democratic ethos of contemporary book groups such as Oprah's Book Club (see, for example, studies by Farr [2005] and Long [2003]). Whereas Winfrey's project has been described as a middlebrow exercise in cultural democracy (Farr 2005), the dynamics of the tuto-rial prevail in *Reading "Lolita."* Nafisi's girls are exiles from the univer-sity; nevertheless its pedagogies survive in the memoir. The committed reader of *Reading "Lolita"* is positioned as an acolyte of the professorial narrator. We are drawn into the intimacy of her reading circle to acquire a high literary language and sensibility: "Please turn to page 148, and try to visualize the scene as you read the passage. . . . Now, please listen care-fully to that 'you'" (305). The literary curriculum is installed as a shap-ing principle, and it is a testament to this narrator's skill that American readers report turning to read Nabokov, James, and their own national literary tradition anew as a result of the passionate discussion of *Lolita* and *Daisy Miller* embedded in *Reading "Lolita."* Some find the original daunting in the absence of the autobiographical narrator, but as reviewers have remarked, this memoir has appealed to deep veins of bibliophilia (Nafisi 2004b) and a desire to acquire the cultural capital required to read complex literary fiction empathically, as suggested by the memoir.

Inhaling Experience

The appeal of *Reading "Lolita"* to American readers raises questions about what difference does it make to read *Lolita* "through" Tehran? How is Nafisi's Nabokov "irretrievably linked to this place, this land and these trees" (2003b, 338)? The memoir concludes metatextually, by reflecting on the circumstances of its genesis. The autobiographical narrator has decided to leave Iran and continue her academic career in the United States. It is June 23, 1997, and she writes in her notebook: "For my new book." Echoing in her mind is the last conversation with her mentor, and she writes:

I have a recurring fantasy that one more article has been added to the Bill of Rights: the right to free access to imagination. I have come to believe that genuine democracy cannot exist without the freedom to imagine and the right to use imaginative works without any restrictions. To have a whole life, one must have the possibility of publicly shaping and expressing private worlds, dreams, thoughts and desires, of constantly having access to a dialogue between public and private worlds. How else do we know that we have existed, felt, desired, hated, feared? (339)

The memoir is a record of a struggle to sustain these freedoms and a narrative about a profoundly troubled subjectivity haunted by the past and expressed in nostalgic memory. Like Roya Hakakian, Nafisi experiences the Islamic revolution as a jihad against the self that produces intense feelings of self-annihilation; this profound loss of self will, eventually, fuel memoir. These are the historical and psychological conditions that shape her appropriation of Austen, James, Fitzgerald, and Nabokov in Tehran, as her mentor points out: "This is the Austen you read here, in a place where the film censor is nearly blind and where they hang people in the streets" (338). Remarkably, the rerouting of Austen (and Nabokov, James, and Fitzgerald) via Tehran and the aftermath of the Islamic revolution produces a reading of these canonical texts that enchants many readers in the West. The diagesis of the narrative, and its specific mode of textual politics, seem natural in this vivid story of a reading circle that defies totalitarianism. However, *Reading "Lolita"* is a passionate and polemical narrative about the novel, the reader, and cultural politics.

To grasp the polemical and aesthetic edge of the theory of the novel in *Reading "Lolita"* we need to begin a rhetorical reading in Nafisi's reading room. As we have seen, it is a highly aestheticized space that turns its back to the street and its face to the mountains and the sky, which are mirrored and amplified through the room. The epigraph from Milosz's "Annalena" echoes this feature of mirroring and reflection that characterize this space, the work of reading and diary writing, and the nurturing of a private self in the reading circle. The hospital and the chaos of war outside the front door are displaced, cast off like the chador that the girls leave at the door. This opposition between "reality" and "imagination" is deliberate and sustained in the space of reading. An aura of "magical affinity" (57) produces peaceful coexistence despite political and ethical differences among the girls themselves. Here they become "naked on the pages of a book," a liberating experience of freedom that Manna, one of the girls of the story, recalls in the epilogue (343). This room is a wonderland (intertextual references to Lewis Carroll's novel *Alice's Adventures in Wonderland* are woven throughout the memoir), and it is a place of transgression, where curiosity and imagination rule. Akin to Woolf's room of one's own (also specifically alluded to in this book for bibliophiles), this is a withdrawal from hostile reality to nurture the self in fiction that needs to be understood in gendered terms. In this space, these women practice "an active withdrawal from a reality that had turned hostile" (11), and they will read only writers who have faith "in the critical and almost magical power of literature" (18); they are training to be good readers, in pursuit of upsilamba. Once they leave this room the return to reality is described as a return to alienation, and the lively characters become nondescript and colorless, with their individuality and uniqueness obliterated under the prescriptions for Muslim women produced by the Islamist theocracy.

The collective reading of Western classics, then, nurtures these women as fully *human* beings in the act of reading. Each text and author has a specific role to play in this process. *Lolita* is first. This text, and Nabokov more generally, are critical to the aesthetic vision of the memoir. The narrator reminds us not to take this reading of *Lolita* allegorically (a fixed mode she does not admire, for the same reason she turns aside from epic and romance as prescriptive genres inappropriate to their circumstances). Nevertheless, the relation of Nabokov's novel to Tehran and the revolution is highly symbolic. When read under these conditions, *Lolita* is not read from a feminist perspective, which would probably focus on the rape or improper seduction of the young girl. Rather, Nafisi and her girls read the novel as a critique of totalitarianism, and the assertion of an American democratic tradition: all individuals have the right to life, liberty, and the pursuit of happiness. Nafisi's girls read the novel to preserve their own life stories: "Like my students, Lolita's past comes to her not so much as a loss but as a lack, and like my students, she becomes a figment in someone else's dream" (37). As a writer, Nabokov himself is critical to the shaping of Nafisi's aesthetics of the novel. She uses Nabokov, a writer in exile following the Russian Revolution, to celebrate the power of imagination and curiosity—these are the essence of insubordination and individualism, and it follows from this that fiction is privileged as a point of entry into another world of "tenderness, brightness and beauty" (57). It is Nabokov who warns against complicity, the danger of "dancing with the jailer," and thereby participating in your own execution. The narrator returns frequently to the dance scene in Nabokov's *Invitation to a Beheading,* and the symbolic resonance of Nabokov's Cincinnatus is explicit: the "constant reminder of his uniqueness, and his attempts to write, to articulate and create a language different from the one imposed upon him by his jailers, saves him at the last moment, when he takes his head in his hands and walks away" (77).

A preference for "counterrevolutionary" writers and high modernism—Eliot, Plath, Nabokov, Fitzgerald—goes back to the narrator's years as a postgraduate student in Oklahoma in the 1970s before the Islamic revolution. The emphasis on the liberal imagination hearkens back to an earlier period of American literary criticism—Lionel Trilling, for example, who is also renowned as a brilliant teacher of the pleasures of the literary text and an admirer of Nabokov and literary modernism. In Tehran, and in response to totalitarianism, these preferences and practices of criticism become the basis of a full-fledged theory of the novel as generically democratic and subversive. Nafisi defines subversion using a favorite quotation from the German critic (and exile) Theodor Adorno that she writes on the board for her class at the University of Tehran: "The highest form of morality is not to feel at home in one's own home" (1984).[2] And so while intellectuals in Iran after the revolution turn to Gorky and Russian socialist realism, the narrator teaches F. Scott Fitzgerald and revels in his seeming irrelevance to the Islamic revolution. It is through Fitzgerald that Nafisi teaches her philosophy of reading fiction personally and phenomenologically: ideas must come through the *experience* of reading the novel empathically. Rather than an allegorical reading of *Lolita,* the novel is offered to the girls and to the implied reader as the sensual and subjective experience of another world: "You inhale the experience" (111).

As the spatial geographies of the reading room suggest, then, reading fiction through Tehran produces a spirited defense of the printed book and the Western canon in the interests of individual cultivation and a democratic community. *Reading "Lolita"* now recycles this knowledge and practice back into the West. Nafisi's memoir has become a best-selling vision of English literature as a transformative force. This is the aftereffect of Tehran, "this place, this land and these trees": a powerful celebration of reading as an act that brings fiction alive in what J. Hillis Miller calls the "interior theatre," produced by an allegro or "whole-hearted" reading (2002, 124). The surrogate readers of the Tehran circle lend a trompe l'oeil effect, an uncanny mirroring, to reading this memoir in books, and this is part of its extraordinary imaginative power. Miller's notion of allegro and lento reading is helpful in understanding the illusion. *Reading "Lolita"* reflects the accomplished and erudite reader back to herself in the most seductive and pleasurable way. This is the upsilamba effect produced by the register of the allegro reading: that wholehearted immersion in the virtual reality of narrative, a suspension in the pleasures of reading unselfconsciously and imaginatively—the reader response elicited most powerfully by *Reading "Lolita" in Tehran*. The lento reading follows and demystifies by asking questions and reversing the shape and dimensions of this fantasy. As Miller explains, there is an aporia of reading produced by the different counters of the allegro and lento, for each prevents the other from working. Nafisi's memoir is a disarming and formidable performance of reading in the allegro. Just as Miller and others reflect on the decline of the discipline of English and the death of literature in Western tertiary institutions, *Reading "Lolita"* produces a rebirth with an appeal to the alternative institutional network of the book club and the powers of reading empathically. Here the literary canon and the allegro reading travel as recreational pursuits, with less harassment from the lento reading practices and ideological critiques lodged in the academy.

To answer the question of what difference does it make to read Nabokov (and company) through Nafisi's Tehran, then, a first point to make is that via Nafisi we import what is to some extent a familiar discipline of English, revivified and made all the more powerful and poignant for our vicarious immersion "in a place where the film censor is nearly blind and where they hang people in the streets." In this way, *Reading "Lolita"* restates the value of the English canon in terms similar to American humanist critics such as Harold Bloom (1994), for example, who affirms that it is strangeness, a mode of originality, that makes an author and the works canonical. It is not a surprise to note that Bloom is allegedly an admirer of the blooming of the canon and the experience of aesthetic value in *Reading "Lolita."* Furthermore "aesthetics," F. Scott Fitzgerald, Henry James, and *Alice's Adventures in Wonderland* are, among other pre-occupations of *Reading "Lolita,"* included in E. D. Hirsch's (1987) list "What Literate Americans Know." It might, of course, seem unexpected that enhanced literacy in English and the Western canon might be promoted via a reading circle in Tehran. Yet, if we accept Derek Gregory's logic of architectures of enmity (2004)—which suggests that in fact Iran and America hold each other hostage, so to speak—then perhaps the export of an American literary canon and the reading practices of an earlier era to Tehran, and its subsequent recycling and importation with enhanced value, should not surprise.[3] *Reading "Lolita"* becomes another performance in a dance where seeming enemies are locked in exchange and caught in a hermeneutic circle generating ongoing and isomorphic fantasies of self and other. Nafisi herself resolutely denies this connection; rather, it is all imagination: "I did not write *Reading "Lolita" in Tehran* to tell Americans how we were deprived; I wrote this book to tell people how important imagination is no matter where you live" (2004a).

Exiles at Home

It is in the very nature of discussions about classic books that humanist and liberal precepts of individualism, culture, and civilization accrue what John Frow refers to as "a false glow of transparency" (1996, 131). As Frow suggests, the terms of sophisticated reading and the literary canon are the cornerstones of a hierarchy that organizes the most au-thoritative and entrenched practices of reading, although these practices are not always identified in terms of their precise histories and ideologi-cal investments. For this reason, the question of why *Lolita* or *Pride and Prejudice* or *Daisy Miller* are read in this way in Tehran seems redundant, for they are selected and interpreted in what Nafisi calls "disinterested faith" (2003b, 19). To lack this faith and instinct is a reflection on the self and its competencies, rather than on the book or the hermeneu-tic that understands reading in these terms. Frow argues that the only way to approach questions of cultural capital is to analyze discourses of value, so that the values (and faiths) of an intellectual elite, for example, are recognized as historically and culturally variable, and the meaning, value, and function of cultural practices are always the effect of specific and changeable social relations. From this point of view, we can begin to ask questions about how, and why, and under what circumstances Great Books and the literary imagination accrue value through memoir by Iranian exiles in these times, and how these memoirs circulate and are used in what Tony Bennett calls quite specific "reading formations" (quoted in Frow 1996, 145).

Following this, we might approach Nafisi's memoir to produce what Miller calls the lento reading: this takes it apart to see how an exilic politics and sensibility makes it tick (2002, 124). The work of historicizing the autobiographical subject of this memoir begins here. We can do this by returning one more time to the reading room in Tehran. At the very outset of *Reading "Lolita,"* when we enter this inner sanctum for the first time as readers, the autobiographical narrator points out that "more than any other place in our home, the living room was symbolic of my nomadic and borrowed life" (7). This introduces a thread that runs right through the memoir: the representation of the narrator and her girls as exiles in Iran. The room is, as we have seen, a place for curiosity, imagination, and transgression, a withdrawal from harsh reality through reading. Nabokov, the exile par excellence, haunts this space. Nafisi points out to her students that during the Russian Revolution the nineteen-year-old Nabokov would not allow himself to be diverted by the sound of bullets. It is this act of "disinterested faith" that Nafisi sets out to emulate in Tehran. Nabokov "kept writing his solitary poems while he heard the guns and saw the bloody fights from his window" (19). This is an emblematic scene. The reading circle discusses literature each Thursday oblivious to the hubbub of visitors who turn up to see the casualties of war in the hospital opposite. Quite deliberately, these realities are not mirrored in the reading room.

Tropes of exile recur throughout Nafisi's memoir. The autobiographical narrator recreates the scene of writing the memoir in Baltimore in 1999 with two photographs in front of her. In one, there are Muslim women, dressed in black robes according to the theocratic law of the Republic, only their faces and hands are uncovered. In the other, the seven women are disrobed in the private space of the reading room, and Mashid, Manna, Yassi, Azin, Mitra, Nassrin, and Sanaz (the girls of the story) become distinct individuals through the color and style of Western clothes and the length and color of their hair. Along with the mirror, the photography accentuates the theme of alienated self-imagery and the "schizophrenic" (74) situation of the women who are caught between the cocoon of the reading room and the harsh reality of the surrounding streets. All of these women lack a stable and coherent subjectivity. They take fiction for a reading cure and write journals as a deliberate technology of the self. But the diegesis of the memoir is shaped by the narrator's deepening sense of impotence and paralysis as the memoir unfolds, and she loses all sense of home and country: "I became again the child I had been when I would indiscriminately and waywardly pick up books. . . . If I turned toward books, it was because they were the only sanctuary I knew, one I needed in order to survive, to protect some aspect of myself that was now in constant retreat" (170). As in Hakakian's *Journey from the Land of No,* the theft of the self, a loss of language, and experiences of disembodiment are recurrent markers of exilic discourse— which is recalled, of course, in the Audi picture of Nafisi suspended in air in the library: "I notice . . . my growing sense that I was descending into an abyss or void. . . . I felt light and fictional, as if I were walking on air, as if I had been written into being and then erased in one quick swipe" (167).

Similarly, the representation of Tehran as an estranged landscape throughout the memoir is a motif of exilic representation. Like Hakakian, the narrator of *Reading "Lolita"* privileges a lost and prerevolutionary world of childhood in a city that is reduced to a series of symbolic spaces: the classroom, the room of the magician, the green door, and so on. In this way, remarks about the belatedness or unreality of Nafisi's Tehran seem to miss the point, for representations of Iran in the memoir are orchestrated not in relation to realism but to a quite specific discourse of estrangement. This is a lost "homeland" created by nostalgic memory. These memories draw on experiences understood as a pathological disorder: the experience of exile at home, "a feeling akin to visiting your old house as a wandering ghost with unfinished business . . . I had lost all concept of terms such as *home, service* and *country*" (169). These characteristic markers of exilic discourse recur in memoir as well as in what Hamid Naficy calls the "accented cinema" of the Diaspora (Naficy 1993, 2001). For realist representations of contemporary Iran, which capture what it is like to ride in a Paykan (an Iranian-made car) in Isfahan, for example, readers need to turn to memoir that engages with the country differently, such as Christopher de Bellaigue's *In the Rose Garden of the Martyrs* (2005). The contrast is instructive, for it helps to establish the particular space of exilic sensibilities in autobiographical representations of Iran.

Exilic sensibility shapes the specific fragment of the Western canon celebrated in the memoir. The autobiographical narrator tells us she is "like an emissary from a land that did not exist, with a stock of dreams, coming to reclaim this land as my home" (89). It is not coincidental that modernist writing is at the heart of these nostalgic dreams. Caren Kaplan's discussion of exilic literature links the aesthetics of modernism to quite specific political and economic practices, although she points out that the modernist trope of exile works to remove itself from politically and historically specific instances in order to generate ostensibly apolitical aesthetic categories and ahistorical values (1996, 27). To historicize the aesthetics and politics of this memoir is to read against the grain. On the basis of Kaplan's work we can begin to read Nafisi's memoir as a specific and contemporary version of a long-established practice of Euro-American modernist aesthetics and politics that draws on the exilic condition and its various incarnations in the work of Nabokov, Adorno, and Edward Said. At the conclusion of *Reading "Lolita"* is a classic and characteristic modernist embrace of exile:

That day, when I left my magician's house, the sun was fading and the air was mild, the trees a verdant green, and I had many reasons to feel sad. Every object and every face had lost its tangibleness and appeared like a cherished memory: my parents, friends, students, this street, these trees, the withdrawing light from the mountains in the mirror. But I was also vaguely elated . . . I went about my way rejoicing, thinking how wonderful it is to be a woman and a writer at the end of the twentieth century. (339)

Representations of exile and displacement recur in modernist writing, and the writer on the move is the avatar of literary modernism. Nafisi is drawing on a well-established tradition where producers of "high" forms of art and literature are inclined to see the outsider as an appropriate self-image (Smith 2004, 259). There are classic exilic formulations in this Tehran story: the writer as "unhoused," dislocated beyond all ideological constraints; a sense of nostalgia that both naturalizes the idea of belonging and home even as it celebrates metropolitan experiences; the narration of the past as another country that draws on a paradoxical relation between time and space; and, finally, the idea of aesthetic gain through exilic displacement as a privileged position, legitimating a point of view and constituting a point of entry into the professional domain of writing (Kaplan 1996, 36). In this way notions of exilic displacement are associated with ideas of creativity and artistic integrity in the West, a sensibility associated with Nabokov, James, Hemingway, Fitzgerald, and Adorno, among others (remember it is a quotation from Adorno that Nafisi takes as her mantra on the blackboard in Tehran). As Kaplan (1996) argues, the notion of exilic transcendence and artistic integrity is so thoroughly mystified and dehistoricized as to be normative, resisting attempts to place its discourses of value and literary expatriotism in historical context. This is, as I have suggested, one of the reasons why it can be difficult to get a grip on a lento reading of Nafisi's memoir. Readers are positioned with consummate skill to adopt the allegro reading, and from this perspective the memoir offers an extraordinary story that is a powerful humanist defense of reading, Literature, and resistance to totalitarianism. It offers a gendered critique of the Islamic revolution in Iran that takes up the literary language of second wave Western feminism—the room of one's own and the emphasis on the power of women to reconfigure and radicalize the private and domestic sphere—just in time to respond to a new phase of anxiety in relations between Iran and the West.

Accented Memoir

In my own allegro reading of Nafisi's memoir I imagine those discussions in Tehran had an accented quality that remains untranslated. The voices of Mashid, Manna, Yassi, Azin, Mitra, Nassrin, and Sanaz do not resonate in *Reading "Lolita"*; it is not until the last section, "Austen," that we learn about their personal lives in any detail. We glimpse the curls, the painted nails, and the shimmering earrings that attract the eye of Iranian censors and emerge from beneath the chador only when they enter the private room, but we do not hear the accented and hybrid languages that must ricochet around that room or the timbre of individual voices across generations of women, which ultimately include the narrator's mother and daughter in the rituals of the reading group. These are lost in translation. Are the discussions in English? How do these multilingual women shift and graft their written, read, and oral languages as they discuss and mark up their copies of *Lolita* and *Washington Square*? To be sure, Nafisi is innovative in shaping a free-flowing prose; conventional grammatical and typographical markers that distinguish between direct and indirect speech are absent in order to capture the dynamism of exchanges between speakers in a memoir that is shaped through dialogue and conversation. Nevertheless, this focuses attention on the didactic first-person narrator at the expense of polyphony and various points of view. The philosopher queen is always the focal point of the narrative. The girls remain in her possession and caught up in her story of alienation and exile.

Of course surrogacy is not the right concept to grasp the relation between American readers and the embedded readers, the young Iranian women who remain the collective: girls. Their reading is necessarily intercultural. The reading circle in Tehran begins with a Persian classic, *A Thousand and One Nights,* and they read the Great Books of their literary tradition alongside Western classics. The frame story of *A Thousand and One Nights* resonates intertextually with the story of the reading circle. The narrator is most intrigued by the three kinds of women portrayed there—all victims of the king's oppressive rule: there is the one who betrays and then is killed (the queen), those who are killed before they have a chance to betray (the virgins), and Scheherazade, the entrancing storyteller, who breaks the cycle of violence by choosing different terms of engagement: "She fashions her universe not through physical force, as does the king, but through imagination and reflection. This gives her the courage to risk her life and sets her apart from the other characters in the tale" (Nafisi 2003b, 19). The autobiographical narrator, too, is a Scheherazade, set apart, and the girls remain in her shadow, like the virgins who "have no voice in the story, [and] are mostly ignored by the critics" (Nafisi 2003b, 19).

Western readers emerge from the experience of reading Nafisi's memoir without being shaken or stirred by the rich traditions and repertoire of Persian culture. Only traces of Persian aesthetics emerge. For example, Nafisi's wonderful description of the elusive seduction of Sanaz's Persian-style dance links to her reading of desire by indirection in Austen; and she recalls her own pleasures of reading classical Persian literature— Rumi, Hafez, Sa'adi, Khayyam, Nezami, Ferdowsi, Attar, Beyhagi—in a small Tehran salon: "We would take turns reading passages aloud, and the words literally rose up in the air and descended on us like a fine mist, touching all five senses. There was such a teasing, playful quality to their words, such joy in the power of language to delight and astonish. I kept wondering: when did we lose that quality, that ability to tease and make light of life through our poetry?" (172). The modernist classics are not pulled into a cross-cultural space of translation and transculturation through engagement with Persian and Islamic traditions in *Reading "Lolita."* In his discussion of exilic popular cultural production Hamid Naficy argues that the globalization of American popular culture does not automatically translate into globalization of American control and values. He emphasizes that it can produce a shared discursive space where transnationals can localize, domesticate, and indigenize texts: "They may think with American products, but they do not think American" (1993, 2). But is this what happens through the globalization of the Western canon in *Reading "Lolita" in Tehran*? This is a critical question in thinking about Nafisi's memoir, which neither revises nor repudiates canonical texts of the Western tradition. To the contrary, canonical authority is renewed in a particularly imposing style.

In a recent discussion of the importance of teaching the humanities in classrooms beyond the affluent West, Gayatri Spivak (2004) argues for the value of literary reading. Like Azar Nafisi, she defends the attempt to develop in students the habit of reading, but differences are immediately apparent in Spivak's location of the teacher and the student. She argues that reading is about "suspending oneself into the text of the other—for which the first condition and effect is a suspension of the conviction that I am necessarily better, I am necessarily indispensable, I am necessarily the one to right wrongs, I am necessarily the end product for which history happened, and that New York is necessarily the capital of the world" (2004, 532). Spivak's defense of a specifically literary training as a slow mind-changing process is based on the idea that it can be used to open the imagination to other mindsets across cultures; literary reading is a training to learn from the singular and unverifiable. Here, as in chapter 3, we return to that idea of the singularity of the literary imagination, that capacity to produce what Attridge describes as an encounter with alterity and a "remoulding of the self that brings the other into being as, necessarily, no longer entirely other" (2004, 24). Spivak refuses to write from what she calls the "metropolitan middle-class side" of the cultural divide. The liberal idea of the narrative imagination producing a sympathetic identification or empathy across cultures suggests that "everyone feels the same complicated pleasures from a Dickens text" (Spivak 2004, 567), which Spivak rejects. She stands resolutely by the importance of taking pedagogy and cultural difference into account when literary texts travel across worlds—understood in terms of differences of class, religion, ethnicity, and nationality—and she regards teaching literature outside of the first world as a project that requires openness "to be othered by the subaltern" through a deliberate awareness of the task of teaching "in two worlds" that are asymmetrical (2004, 568). The idea that teaching literature across cultures is necessarily political is alien to the pedagogy of Reading "Lolita". Exilic discourse—masked as the authentic word of the native informant—travels into the West particularly well in these times for, as Nussbaum (1995) suggests in the epigraph to this chapter, appeals to even the best uses of the literary imagination can be co-opted in times of prejudice and hatred. This raises the other dimension of complicities in Reading "Lolita": What is the relationship of this memoir to the architectures of enmity that flow through the war on terror now? How does Nafisi position her contemporary readership to engage with the dynamics of the cultural construction of Iran in the West (and vice versa)?

Issues of complicity haunt Nafisi's memoir and remain unresolved and troubling. The narrator remarks that Iranian intellectuals themselves are complicit in the totalitarian regime of the Islamic Republic, for they fatally misread the dynamics and failed to see the importance of campaigning for democracy above all in the vital, brief interregnum between the fall of the shah and the installation of the ayatollah. She also suggests that every time the women assume the veil through anything other than choice and devotion it is an act of consent to totalitarianism, although dissent attracts terrible retribution. This links, of course, to Nabokov, the writer who is at the heart of her thinking through issues of freedom and justice and a more existential approach to complicity. Distinctions need to be drawn among the various invocations of Nabokov in *Reading "Lolita."* For example, the story of Cincinnatus is all about the attraction of pleasing the jailer. The autobiographical narrator teaches the girls that the circular structure of the narrative is determined by its understanding of the dynamics of complicity and consent: "The worst crime committed by totalitarian mind-sets is that they force their citizens, including their victims, to become complicit in their crimes. Dancing with your jailer, participating in your own execution, that is an act of utmost brutality" (76). Only by constantly reminding himself of his uniqueness and his attempts to write and create a language different to the one imposed on him by his jailers is Cincinnatus saved. Nafisi uses this story to project a complex network of identification between the perpetrator and victim in totalitarian regimes. From this point of view, complicity is not a matter of labeling or identifying perpetrator and victim independently one from the other; it is, rather, a process and a contamination of what seems to be an oppositional pair, one with the other. This is a remarkably contemporary formulation of complicity, in fact, and it carries within it what we might now recognize as a Derridian sense of the foldedness of oppositional pairs. At the same time, there is another Nabokov at work in Nafisi's text. This is a version of the autobiographical Nabokov, who inspires the dynamics of the reading room as a place apart; in this incarnation he is the writer in the tower who hears the guns and keeps writing his solitary poems regardless.

All of this falls from reading *Lolita* in Tehran and an exilic aesthetics that is driven by literary modernism. These are critical components of autobiographical subjectivity in Nafisi's memoir. When Edward Said writes that if we want to understand exile we need to forget Nabokov, one suspects he is turning away from that Nabokovian withdrawal from the world into the text that influences Nafisi so powerfully. Said's essay "Reflections on Exile" (2002) is concerned about the transformation of exile—a condition of terminal loss and the sorrow of estrangement—into a potent and enriching motif in modern culture. From this point of view, Nafisi's memoir is a recent and especially accomplished performance within a twentieth-century tradition that celebrates deterritorialization as spiritual and intellectual enlightenment. "Exile," argues Said, "cannot be made to serve notions of humanism" (2002, 174). *Reading "Lolita" in Tehran* is a reminder that it can do this, and powerfully so. As I have argued in this chapter, Nafisi's book renews a liberal humanism in American literary criticism and hearkens back to an earlier age to revive a literary canon and critical epistemology. But what Said means, of course, is that exile should not be used this way and that Nabokov's story of the virtues of maintaining the literary sensibility by looking away from the street is inappropriate for these times.

Said, characteristically, argues that by forgetting Nabokov we might remember (rather than mystify) history. This is an ethical issue for the present: "The difference between earlier exiles and those of our own time is, it bears stressing, scale: our age—with its modern warfare, imperialism, and the quasi-theological ambitions of totalitarian rulers—is indeed the age of the refugee, the displaced person, mass immigration" (2002, 174). Said's essay was originally published in *Granta* in 1984, and so his "present" is not quite ours. Nevertheless, Said's objection to rendering exile—"irremediably secular and unbearably historical"—aesthetically and humanistically comprehensible touches on ethical questions pertinent to Nafisi's memoir.

Adorno's work on the capacity of contemporary culture to commodify everything one says or thinks, as well as every object one possesses, is also useful, given the enthusiastic uptake of Nafisi as a celebrity and public intellectual in the United States. The success of Nafisi and her memoir in the American market is a spectacular example of the appropriation of exilic writing to set a vogue and to neutralize Iranian and Islamic difference as style: "The mainstream culture is dominant not because it obliterates all opposition but because it compromises and selectively incorporates the expression of alternative viewpoints into civil society through the rule of law, education, media, fashion, and consumer capitalism" (Naficy 1993, 34). Characteristics of the modernist exilic sensibility lend themselves to commodification as signs of discrimination and taste: the respect for imagination, supreme individualism, and the cachet of the aesthetic.

But of course Adorno is there in Nafisi's memoir, and his un-Nabokovian reflections on exile as damaged life are a troubled subtext. Signs of this are embedded at the scene of writing in Baltimore, where reality does get in the way of imagination. The autobiographical Nafisi writes with three mementos in her office; these are testimonial artifacts from the girls that trigger her memory work. Two of these are photographs: the girls in their public and private appearances, as they arrive at the reading room in chador and then as they inhabit it, as readers "naked" on the pages of the book. The other memory prompt is a folder Nassrin sends with her regards:

I have the folder here on this other desk in this other office right now. It is brilliantly colored: white with bright bubble-gum-orange stripes and three cartoon characters. In vivid green and purple characters it says: *Be Seeing You in Fabulous Florida. Things Go Better With Sunshine!* Inside the folder, Nassrin had transcribed every word of my classes during my last three terms at Allameh, neatly written in her handwriting, with headings and sub-headings. All the sentences and anecdotes were recorded. James, Austen, Fielding, Brontë, Poe, Twain—all of them were there. She left behind nothing else—no photograph and no personal note—except for one line on the last page of the folder: *I still owe you a paper on Gatsby.* (328)

These mementos are haunting things, and they unsettle rather than stabilize the possession of history through memory. Nafisi meditates on these issues quite deliberately in *Reading "Lolita."* She recalls worries that she does harm to the girls by creating a utopian fantasy world parallel to a dystopian present—a democratic West defined over and against a fundamentalist Iran: "[The girls] tend to look at the West too uncritically; all that is good in their eyes comes from America or Europe, from chocolates and chewing gum to Austen and the Declaration of Independence" (312). Nassrin's folder is an example of this exotic mythologizing of the United States and a troubling reminder of the girls' loss of self, agency, and belonging that occurs in the very process of their liberation as readers. It suggests how the Western literary canon travels via didactic pedagogy to produce repetition rather than agency—precisely Spivak's (2004) concern. Similarly, the two photographs of the women trouble one of the central tropes of the memoir: the room of one's own, where the women turn aside from the Islamic theocracy and nurture the self. Ultimately, the embedded biographical narratives of each of the girls is a reminder one way or another that this separation cannot be sustained and that it is not their destiny to transcend history but rather to live through it. *Reading "Lolita" in Tehran* tells this story, too, if we care to read it.

The prescience of Said's political critique of the uses of exile in narratives of transcendent individualism is a reminder that this humanist and aesthetic tradition has a long history, as well as a currency in the present. Its revival and extraordinary popularity in this century is a further sign of the ongoing seductiveness of the literature of exile and of the integral connection between this literary tradition and the overwhelming fact of ongoing dispossession and displacement of refugees and exiles and denial of human rights. It is from this, to return to Mottahedeh's remarks at the start of this chapter, that we can understand it is not a coincidence that a memoir that frames relations between America and Iran in these terms should achieve such phenomenal commercial success now. The turn to exilic memoir at a time of resurgent nationalism and patriotism in the war on terror demands that we hold literature and history together and that both the allegro and lento registers remain in play to open the reading room onto the bloody streets.

Bookends: AutoGraphics

I often see a look of surprise on people's faces when I say there are comics outside Britain and the United States. . . . The fact is, there are whole continents of
comics to discover.

PAUL GRAVETT, QUOTED IN ROGER SABIN, *ADULT COMICS*

There can be no conclusive ending to this pursuit. The
transits of life narrative remain a breaking story, and controversies continue to erupt (the hoax, and the scandal, for
example), images resurface (such as "the Afghan girl"), cartoon wars rage, and new convergences of life narrative in
words and image emerge. I want to return to the beginning,
to revisit both the question and the autobiographical avatar that set this book in motion. And so: "To what extent
does our theorizing itself need to be made by contemporary practice at these 'rumpled' sites of the experimental?"
(Smith and Watson 2001b, 1). It is no surprise that Salam
Pax, an avatar produced by the new technology of life narrative that begins this book, the weblog, records reading
and loving Marjane Satrapi's autobiographical comic book
Persepolis (2003). Pax recognizes a kindred spirit in Satrapi's
Marji, and so he draws another "rumpled site" of contemporary life narrative to our attention: the comics.[1]

On December 7, 2003, Pax records in his weblog from
Baghdad:

I spent most of the day at home reading *Persepolis* . . . a comic book
written by Marjane Satrapi. It is too scary how much we have in common, Iraqis and Iranians I mean. . . . Some of the things about the
start of the Islamic revolution make me think about what is happening

now in Iraq. It was my third attempt to go thru that "comic book," I tried once right after I bought it but it made me wince, this time I went through it in one single go. It is a beautiful book. I had the urge to start translating it and throwing copies of it on the streets of Baghdad. Why can't we learn from other people's mistakes? (*Where Is Raed?*)

Pax is right: *Persepolis: The Story of a Childhood* is a beautiful book. The hardcover first edition in English translation has fine design: a crimson die-cut dust jacket with stylized Persian motifs featuring a cut-out that lets a drawing of Satrapi's young autobiographical avatar Marji peep through; and the black-and-white artwork of comics is shown to full advantage on the fine quality paper. Satrapi's *Persepolis* turns to an alternative technology of autobiography, the graphic memoir of black-and-white comics, and to irony and satire as modes for telling her story of childhood and subsequent exile from Iran after the revolution of 1979. These janus-faced genres hold onto contradiction and absurdity, and Satrapi uses them to bring the West and Iran into the kind of conflicted and ambiguous relation that is inherently unstable, paradoxical, and complicit. Gods and prophets can, and do, appear in person here!

Satrapi's comics can be read in association with the contemporary formation of Iranian exilic literature discussed in chapter 7; however, the iconic art of cartoon drawing calls some of the stark oppositions that shape exilic writing into question. Satrapi's biographical cartoon figures are elemental; they resemble naive and childish woodcuts in their sharply defined iconic black-and-white shapes, which hearken back to the first simple frames of children's books: Dick Bruna's blocky little figures or Ludwig Bemelmans's *Madeline* series. And yet they are sophisticated, too. We are forced to pause and speculate about the extraordinary connotative force of cartoon drawing, which both amplifies and simplifies: "When we abstract an image through cartooning we're not so much eliminating details as we are focusing on specific details. By stripping down an image to its essential 'meaning' an artist can amplify meaning in a way that realistic art can't" (McCloud 1994, 30). In *Persepolis* figures are sometimes strung together like a frieze, sometimes boxed into frames of varying sizes that contain the balloons and strips of words. Nevertheless, they are at the same time human and expressive and highly individual. Character, nuance, and satire are signaled by the angle of a brow a millimeter long, the precise inflection of lips and chin, and a curve on a face the size of a thumbnail. In the act of reading we are forced to pay close attention to the changing relations between the images and words in comics, and the shifting gutters and frames that mirror and reflect black to white. Most strikingly, in *Persepolis 2: The Story of a Return,* a series of images narrate the violent death of a young man, Farzad, chased across the rooftops by the revolutionary guards in Tehran, and Satrapi withdraws words entirely: there are three pages of drawings in frames without words. In minimalist imagery, Satrapi's comics draws on conventions of Persian and Islamic art (for example, the tulip as an icon) as well as Western and Christian iconography (for example, versions of the Pietà are used to indicate a particularly traumatic memory in both volumes of *Persepolis*). Like *Where Is Raed?* there is a sophisticated process of transculturation at work. Here it incorporates both Eastern and Western cultural forms into the popular genre of comics, a form commonly associated with mass entertainment and the first experiences of childhood reading. Although McCloud's remarks on "essential" meaning are risky, they suggest that the cartoonish drawings of *Persepolis* may function as a humanizing form of representation, with the capacity to evoke reading and recognition despite the intractable cultural difference that can be signified by the veiled figure of the autobiographical avatar.

Satrapi's book both recalls and is shaped by a period of totalitarian control and censorship in Iran: the revolution of 1979 and the Islamist theocracy that followed. The possibilities for testimony to trauma in comics emerge if we focus on how Satrapi approaches that most contentious issue of representation, the veil, in that style of cartoon drawing that both amplifies and simplifies. As I argued in chapter 2, the veil is a vexed issue in cross-cultural dialogues, and I have used Leila Ahmed's idea of a discourse of the veil to capture its radically different significations in place and time (1992, 166). Several chapters of this book return to this issue, and here I want to recall these debates one last time to suggest that the distinctive visual medium of comics and the techniques of cartooning, a grammar of frames and gutters, is a language that makes a distinctive intervention in discourse on the veil. Comics opens some possibilities for different significations in graphic art, contesting the dehumanizing frame of reference that frequently mediates representations of veiled women in Western art and texts. For example, we see this from the very beginning of *Persepolis:* the soulful gaze from the recesses of the hijab and the chapter title announce the veil with high drama, but also with irony, as its significance is presented from the perspective of the preadolescent schoolgirl, the very cartoonish figure of Marji, which features the face as a powerful icon (fig. 10).

For Marji, a schoolgirl at the time of the Islamic revolution in 1979, the imposition of the veil and the segregation of the school into gendered domains are signs of momentous social change. But Satrapi registers this

10 Images from page 1 of *Persepolis: The Story of Childhood* by Marjane Satrapi, translated by Mattias Ripa and Blake Ferris, copyright (c) 2003 by L'Association, Paris, France. Used by permission of Pantheon Books, a division of Random House, Inc.

in the child's view and with the child's irreverent sense of proportion and significance. For example, in the frames following these, satire prevails as we see the playground scene of schoolchildren using their newly acquired veils as toys: to skip and to play hide and seek. In this way, Satrapi uses the child's view to cut things to size and to put the veil into a different frame: it is after all a piece of cloth, and its fetishization by adults can seem strange.

Like the feminist activists of the Revolutionary Association of the Women of Afghanistan, Satrapi contests the contraction of representations of Iranian women to a symbol that carries so much weight in Western eyes. As Naghibi and O'Malley (forthcoming) point out, the visual image of the veiled child on the cover of *Persepolis* can be particularly disturbing from some perspectives: a dissonant combination of the familiar (the universal cartoonish figure of the child) and the strange (the veiled and radical other). This effect of dissonance recurs in Satrapi's cartoons. From the very first frames of the comics, we see that Satrapi will incorporate the veil in cartoons that characterize girls and women as distinctive individual and human agents. This is in sharp contrast to Azar Nafisi's representation of the nondescript veiled women in her memoir *Reading "Lolita" in Tehran*. There, women become fully alive and human only when they cast the veil aside. In *Persepolis*, in contrast, differences of emotion, personality, and physique among veiled Iranian girls and women remain vivid, and this is an important statement of gender politics that is sustained throughout Satrapi's cartoons and their figuration of veiled women.

Cartooning isn't just a way of drawing; it is also a way of seeing: "The cartoon is a vacuum into which our identity and awareness are pulled . . . we don't just observe the cartoon, we become it" (McCloud 1994, 36). In emphasizing the particular force of comics, and the demands they make on readers, Scott McCloud argues that cartoon drawings of the face in particular promote identification and "becoming": the more cartoonish (as opposed to realistic) a face is, the more it becomes an icon that has the capacity to produce recognition and associations in our own image. What does this mean in terms of the discourse of the veil? It suggests that by drawing the figure of the veiled child in cartoons, with emphasis on the face, Satrapi is using an icon that is particularly powerful in triggering a humanizing frame of reference. The figure of young Marji at the beginning of *Persepolis* is highly iconic, a style of cartoon drawing that triggers recognition. The association of the veil and the child in the cartoon, then, has a plenitude of signification that cannot be achieved in other forms of representation, that unique effect of "dissonant combination" that is elicited by the cover art of *Persepolis: The Story of a Childhood*. Here is a distinctive new cross-cultural mediation in the discourse of the veil that has the capacity to constitute recognition without requiring that the veil be stripped away. The veil can only be read in terms of its local meanings, which are generated in its own social space, and a reading from the outside will always tend to impose meanings from the social space of the viewer (Young 1997, 89). There can be no singular association suggested by Satrapi's veiled and childish avatar, and no "becoming it" that transcends difference: "If one is to respond ethically to a human face, there must first be a frame for the human, one that can include any number of variations as ready instances. But given how contested the visual representation of the 'human' is, it would appear that our capacity to respond to a face as a human face is conditioned and mediated by frames of reference that are variably humanizing and dehumanizing" (Butler 2005, 29). Yet this encounter with the cartoonish Marji is an opening, a distinctive mediation of cultural difference, and an interpolation of Western readers into a frame of dissonance, association, and juxtaposition that troubles a sense of self and the norms that frame recognition of self and other.

Although the sharply defined contours of black-and-white cartoons are especially powerful in representing the harsh constraints of fundamentalism imposed by the Iranian Revolution, Satrapi refrains from em-

11 Images from page 5 of *Persepolis: The Story of Childhood* by Marjane Satrapi, translated by
Mattias Ripa and Blake Ferris, copyright (c) 2003 by L'Association, Paris, France. Used by
permission of Pantheon Books, a division of Random House, Inc.

bellishing the drawings of the West to produce a stereotypical contrast
to the Middle East in *Persepolis*. In fact, when Marji leaves Iran she goes
to a convent in Austria where the veiled women and institutional surroundings of Catholicism echo the austere public places of the Islamic
republic in Iran in Marji's adolescent view. Isomorphic representations
of West and East are called into question in black and white and on
the issue of the veil—where we might least expect. Satrapi's cartooning
makes a political point. To reduce the Cultural Revolution to the struggle
over the veil—either for or against—is to simplify and inappropriately
reproduce the errors of fundamentalism, represented by Satrapi in mirror imaging of icons within a single elongated frame (fig. 11).

This iconography of Satrapi's cartoons derives from a tactical response
to censorship and to the particular artistic constraints that followed
from enforced veiling after the Islamic revolution in Iran. She signifies
this, for example, by incorporating her own hand and pencil in the act
of cartooning the Pietà image into an Iranian context in the second
volume. *Persepolis 2* offers an Iranian and Islamic genesis for Satrapi's
distinctive cartooning, for this emerged as a tactical engagement with
the censorship of bodies in the flesh and on the page. In a chapter called
"The Socks," Marji is learning to draw in an anatomy class at the university in Tehran. By Islamic state regulation, the model is completely
covered by the chador: "Not a single part of her body was visible. We
nevertheless learned to draw drapes" (2004, 145). And so it is that even
in frames where women are veiled in the chador, with only face and
hand exposed, or in the *maghnaeh* (the hooded head scarf [e.g., fig. 12]),
Satrapi captures individual subjects eloquently. This challenges stereo-

12 Images from page 156 of *Persepolis: The Story of Childhood* by Marjane Satrapi, translated by Mattias Ripa and Blake Ferris, copyright (c) 2003 by L'Association, Paris, France. Used by permission of Pantheon Books, a division of Random House, Inc.

types of veiled women that reduce them to anonymity, and less than human status, and that deny the way the veils can be changed strategically and used instrumentally.

Naghibi and O'Malley (forthcoming) point out that comics in America and the tradition of the *bandes dessinées* in France lack the cultural capital of more traditional literary forms, and so in fact to classify *Persepolis* as autobiography is to elevate its stature. In the United States in particular, they suggest, there is a strong association of the comic book medium with juvenilia. This association is vital for thinking through the implications of reading comics. One of the key arguments of this book is that hybrid forms that take "autobiography" into various media and discourses are increasingly common, and reading across the textual cultures of contemporary life narrative suggests the ongoing metamorphoses that challenge and reformulate the field now. Life narrative is not disciplined, and in particular it is not contained by the Literary or the literary (to recall distinctions made using Ken Gelder's work [2005] in chap. 4). Given this, any attempt to follow the transits of autobiography must necessarily engage with various cultural and technological forms and languages in an interdisciplinary study. The language of comics is distinctive, as McCloud (1994) and Will Eisner (2004) insist, with a unified vocabulary that transcends writing and drawing and produces a distinctive experience of reading and identification. Other books that consider the various and innovative languages and technologies of life narrative and mediations and engagements within Muslim networks hover on the margins of this one. For example, there is more work to be done on the role of theater in the circulation of testimonial narrative in the wake of the war on terror. I have been reminded of this when working on chapter 3, the testimony of asylum seekers, as I presently live among a flourishing subculture of activism in and through theatrical performances about asylum seekers, in some cases by those recently out of detention. Similarly, Michael Fischer's recent book on Iranian cinema (2004) is a reminder that images from recent films and documentaries, most notably from Iran after the revolution, crowd into this field of work.

Can we reasonably claim that some distinctive "transformations in thought" are happening in comics as it engages with the war on terror because of its distinctive visual and verbal languages and signs? *Persepolis* indicates that comics has a distinctive role to play in the work of representing traumatic memory and may be particularly adept at finding room to maneuver amid spaces of contradiction and extreme states of violent contestation—perhaps because of that capacity to produce amplification and simplification at one and the same time in cartoon drawing, as McCloud (1994) suggests.

In a recent polemical essay Marianne Hirsch argues that these are the times when an engagement with the power of visual representations, and the "collateral damage" they produce, is more necessary than ever: "A sustained discussion of words and images, of reading and looking, seems especially urgent at a moment when trauma is instrumentalized as an alibi for censorship" (2004, 1211). Hirsch discusses the careful control of visual representations of trauma associated with the war on terror in the United States in the recent past. There are, for example, the proscriptions on photographs taken at the site of the 9/11 attacks that prevent images of violent death appearing in the media. Constraints on the reproduction of photographs of U.S. deaths in Iraq and Afghanistan and the attempt to contain the photographs taken at Abu Ghraib prison— images originally taken to intimidate detainees—are further instances of censorship and regulation of images. In a remark that suggests a particular potency of the word-image relation of the cartoon, Hirsch points out that it took Garry Trudeau and his comic strip *Doonesbury* to generate powerful empathy with the wounded in Iraq: "Perhaps Trudeau's character BD, an enthusiastic soldier, had to have his leg amputated because the wounds had until then been made invisible in the news pages of the paper" (1210). These remarks on the "collateral damage" produced by visual representations became prescient in the wake of the "cartoon wars" in 2006, when cartoon images of Muhammad stirred violent responses across the world.

Several things are striking about Hirsch's remarks. First, they indicate that comics supplements other visual artifacts, such as the photograph, which they might under some circumstances (such as censorship) replace. Second, Hirsch suggests that comics might produce the emotional engagement with trauma and the "wounding" effect that are associated with more realist forms of visual representation such as the photograph. Censorship reaffirms the expressive power of visual images: they have an extraordinary capacity to produce affect in the spectator. However, like McCloud, Hirsch is interested in pursuing the particular effects generated by the comics. In times of historical crisis, dissent and censorship comics can engage with proscription. We see this in Satrapi's artful incorporation of the constraints imposed on artistic freedom in the wake of the Iranian Revolution, and we see it more recently in Art Spiegelman's graphic life narrative, which stands as his witness to the ground truth of 9/11 in New York: *In the Shadow of No Towers* (2004). Like Satrapi, Spiegelman uses comics and cartooning to engage autobiographically with traumatic memory. In fact, Satrapi has remarked that it was Speigelman's *Maus* that inspired her to use "images as a way of writing" in the form of the autobiographical graphic novel (n.d.).

The front cover of *No Towers* reproduces the iconic black-on-black "afterimage" of the towers that Spiegelman produced for the first issue of the *New Yorker* published after 9/11. In reverse, also embossed black on black, are figures tumbling through the sky and in complete chaos: the sky is falling, and Spiegelman with it. In this way, comics incorporates and supplements the censored sights of ground zero. In the montages of photographs, computer graphics, and comics inside, Richard Drew's photographs of people falling or jumping from the towers are appropriated as Spiegelman inserts his own image: "He is haunted now by the images he didn't witness . . . images of people tumbling to the streets below . . . especially one man (according to a neighbor) who executed a graceful Olympic dive as his last living act" (Spiegelman 2004, 6). Spiegelman lives and works in the immediate vicinity of ground zero, and the attacks on the World Trade Center on September 11, 2001, haunt him still—specifically the sight of the glowing "bones" of the tower immediately before it fell, a sight that remains "burned into the inside of my eyelids" and is unique to his traumatic memory (no one else recalls this particular sight):

That's when Time stands still at the moment of trauma . . . which strikes me as a totally reasonable response to current events! . . .

I see that awesome tower glowing as it collapses! (2004, 2)

Spiegelman's cartoons, his "slow-motion diary of what I experienced" in the wake of traumatic events (2004, iii), were not in the first instance acceptable in the United States and continue to be regarded by some as an idiosyncratic and self-indulgent performance of life narrative as the traumatized American (see, for example, customer comments at Amazon .com [2004]). Instead, the work was published by *Die Zeit* in Germany and was later taken up in France, Italy, and the Netherlands. Spiegelman suggests that, like *Maus,* all this was produced as a way of "sorting through my grief and putting it into boxes" (2004, iv).

Hirsch identifies comics as "biocular" texts: words, images, and word-images work together. Comics, she suggests, has an extraordinary capacity to complicate clear differentiations between word and image; "asking us to read back and forth between images and words, comics reveals the visuality and thus the materiality of words and the discursivity and narrativity of images" (2004, 1213). This is the distinctive vocabulary and grammar of cartooning and comics that McCloud and Eisner insist on too. As a brilliant example of this biocularity, *In the Shadow of No Towers* demands a complex response from its reader/viewer: reality and fantasy, historical and fictional figures coexist and morph into one another: "Comics highlight both the individual frames and the space between them, calling attention to the compulsion to transcend the frame in the act of seeing. They thus startlingly reveal the limited, obstructed vision that characterizes a historical moment ruled by trauma and censorship (1213)." The distinctive expressivity of word and image in comics operates at various levels. There is the register of eidetic memory that is captured powerfully in Spiegelman's recollections of what he saw (sometimes what he alone saw), what he heard, and what he missed—all now imprinted as traumatic memory that tumbles onto the page in montages of drawings, computer-generated images, photographs, and reproductions of old comics.

Essential to the haunting effects and uncanny art of comics is its association with juvenilia: its unique implication in childhood memory. Spiegelman's book triggers this nostalgic reminiscence and association with the first experiences of reading somatically. *No Towers* is an extraordinary artifact. It is very large and weighty—the pages open out to broadsheet size—and it opens vertically. The pages are thick cardboard, heavy stock that is exactly the weight and texture of the nursery book: those very first pages of our encounters with reading words and seeing images. As one reader remarks: "It feels like the pages of a pre-school book and it's all in gorgeous color" (Amazon.com). This turn to childhood memory and nostalgia is accentuated by the inclusion of ten historical reproductions of American comic strips from the late nineteenth and early twentieth centuries, where Richard Outcault's *Hogan's Alley* and Rudolf Dirk's *Katzenjammer Kids* are recycled by Spiegelman: "The only cultural artifacts that could get past my defenses to flood my eyes and brain with something other than images of burning towers were old comic strips; vital, unpretentious ephemera from the optimistic dawn of the twentieth century. That they were made with so much skill and verve but never intended to last past the day they appeared in the newspaper gave them poignancy; they were just right for an end-of-the-world moment" (2004, "The Comic Supplement," np). What is writ large in the intellectual and physical work of reading (and turning) the thick pages of *No Towers,* and in Spiegelman's autobiography of his development as a comic book artist and reader, is the association between juvenilia and the emotional affects of consuming comics. This is a return to an early experience of reading—in fact the process of becoming a reader in the first place—that is the distinctive resonance available to comics in its signification of ideas, events, and emotions. This adds a further dimension to Hirsch's characterization of the comics as biocular text—the haunting traces of childhood memory and representations of trauma coalesce in the act of reading comics.

This notion of comics as memorabilia is developed further in Edward Said's reading of Joe Sacco's comics, *Palestine,* where he also turns to the association with juvenilia in arguing for the haunting power of cartoon drawing by including an autobiographical story of reading comics as an adolescent. Said was part of a generational and class fragment for whom reading comics was a subversive and decadent activity associated with Americanization in a sphere of British colonial influence. Whereas Spiegelman harkens back to comic strip characters such as Kinder Kids, Krazy Kat, and Little Nemo, Said recalls Superman, Tarzan, Captain Marvel, and Wonder Woman: the icons of illicit comic book reading during his own adolescence in Cairo. What Said reaches out for in his "Homage to Joe Sacco" is the feeling that comics frees him to think and imagine and see differently, as an adolescent and now as an adult. He suggests a distinctive experience of reading comics that may have wider connotations for thinking about the genre and its readers as part of a distinctive contract of life narrative:

Comics provided one with a directness of approach (the attractively and literally overstated combination of pictures and words) that seemed unassailably true on the one hand, and marvelously close, impinging, familiar on the other. In ways that I still find fascinating to decode, comics in their relentless foregrounding—far more, say, than film cartoons or funnies, neither of which mattered much to me—seemed to say what couldn't otherwise be said, perhaps what wasn't permitted to be said or imagined, defying the ordinary processes of thought, which are policed, shaped and re-shaped by all sorts of pedagogical as well as ideological pressures. I knew nothing of this then, but I felt that comics freed me to think and imagine and see differently. (2005, ii)

This recalls Marianne Hirsch's association of comics with forbidden images, and the particular visceral and emotional force of the alternative cognitive structures of visual representations. Said and Spiegelman suggest that the intertextual association of comics and juvenilia is endemic to the emotional charge that comics carries with it, especially in the representation of extreme states (such as the Intifada or the Holocaust or terrorism) that lend themselves to surreal and subjective styles of writing trauma into history. Said's remarks on the strange familiarity of comics, their capacity to free us to think and imagine and see differently, suggests that critical opening evoked by Satrapi in *Persepolis* through the dissonance of the cartoonish veiled avatar.

Reading these sophisticated uses of comics to formulate the self in this way suggests they tap into elemental scenes of reading in childhood and adolescence. The uncanny art of comics and the "marvelous closeness" of cartooning draws on a series of things: the minimalism of the cartoon, and its power to capture character, history and place in an economy of pictures and words; its distinctive simultaneous amplification and simplification; the carving of the page in gutters and frames and the work of closure this requires on the part of the reader. What charges life narrative in comics is the particular tension and dissonance it generates by mixing codes from juvenilia into autobiographical narratives of history and trauma. It doesn't do to simplify and essentialize the communities and circuitries of readers that receive comics—the outrage over cartoon images in 2006 is a lesson in the rapid flow of mass-mediated images and the highly unstable public spheres they traverse across cultures. The image of the veiled child will in some contexts be received as a familiar and beloved icon, for example, rather than a dissonant combination of the strange and the familiar. However, the fascination of comics, its distinctive discursive effects and power to engage with forbidden sights and childhood memories, and its capacity to produce a freedom to "think and imagine and see differently" is affirmed by readers in very different historical, cultural, and personal situations, such as Edward Said and Salam Pax.

A number of things about Pax's enthusiasm for *Persepolis* are indicative of the life narratives that I have characterized as soft weapons.

There is Pax's visceral affirmation of the affective power of the text: he winces, then in a rush, one single go, he consumes it and is urged to translate and disseminate Satrapi's comic book for the people on the streets of Baghdad: "It makes me think." The cultural politics of emotion circulate around and through life narratives to powerful effect and affect, and it gives them force and influence in what I have referred to (following Derek Gregory) as "a colonial present," when dark emotions resurface with renewed force: the distinctive fears and hatreds, passions and trauma that circulate in the war on terror. In Pax's celebration of a "beautiful" book and Satrapi's autobiographical avatar, there is also a gesture to the pleasures of the "rumpled sites": those places where life narrative is brought to an edge to shape cross-cultural engagements. "Edge" can be understood variously here: the intersections of the diary and digital media that is Pax's weblog and Amiry's *Ramallah Diaries,* the extremes of writing on skin in testimony incarnate, the hoax where testimony falls into disrepute, and the comics, where the visual and verbal intersect and make demands on readers. It has become increasingly apparent that various literacies emerge as an issue in following life narrative to these ends. For example, the emotional literacy to feel and respond to narratives of trauma and loss; the cultural literacy to accept life narratives from cultures and histories very different to one's own; the ethical literacy to disengage from the discursive force of propaganda and yet remain passionate and committed readers of life story; and the critical, aesthetic, and technological literacy to engage in new media or, as in this case, the visual art of the comics.

Finally, there is one other feature of Pax's enthusiasm and endorsement for *Persepolis* worthy of remark, for he gestures to a story that is not mine to know or tell: the work of contemporary life narratives as they circulate intraculturally and interculturally into other continents, media, genres, and networks of life narrative. In Pax's enthusiasm he imagines translating Satrapi's book, originally published in French, out of English and into Arabic. The transits of autobiography beyond the West and into Muslim and other networks remains an untold story, and an important one that will emerge in languages other than English and books other than this, which is about the ways of seeing through Western eyes. This is a reminder of the epigraph at the very start of this book, which maps the limits of this conversation in English: "The focus of this book is . . . not on the reality of the Other but on the circumstances of its construction and the 'we' who play and are played by this language game" (Frow 1996, 4).

The moment that began this book, the sight of a massed display of life narratives from Iraq and Afghanistan in a bookstore at Melbourne airport, late in 2003, was a sharp and subjective reminder of life narrative and its readers as commodities in a mass market. The trade in books and books as objects—jacketed in peritext and circulating amid epitext—is one economy that drives and shapes this book. By placing Salam Pax and Marjane Satrapi as bookends, as autobiographical avatars in dialogue one with the other at the beginning and end here, I mean to give the first and last words (or frames) to autobiographical representations that make a frontal assault on the imaginaries produced by the war on terror, using media that are particularly appropriate for the times— and these turn out to be permutations of the book and the text, one way and another. There is no simple closure to be made between these very different and yet related avatars. One of the lessons of the recent past is that life narrative is more implicated in history, politics and the conduct of a war than had seemed possible in previous ways of thinking about autobiography in the world. In its jurisdiction are matters of first importance: our regard for relations between self and other, the regulation of the public sphere to determine who is recognized as a human subject, and the communicative ethics of theorizing interdependency.

This touches on the other economy that emerges in this study: the economy of affect. The question of how life narratives connect to ideas and to emotions in our immediate presence shapes this book. Very different kinds of exchange occur in these two economies. On the one hand, life narratives circulate as exotic commodities with economic exchange value. On the other, they also carry in their economy of exchange emotional value and aesthetic value that shape how we think about others, and ourselves, and how we understand what it means to be human. These economies of "marketing the exotic" and the economy of affect are related, but they have very different currencies, values, exchanges, and outcomes. As I now think back to that moment of being arrested by a block display of life narratives at the airport in Melbourne, I am reminded of how powerfully and simultaneously these two economies flow in and through us as readers and as subjects. The constellation of life narratives circulating now are produced in a time of fear and mourning, a distinctively postmillennial age, which has released a new awareness of our fundamental dependency on anonymous others and the importance of narrating lives: "Our capacity to feel and to apprehend hangs in the balance. But so, too, does the reality of certain lives and deaths" (Butler 2004, xxi).

Autobiography can be a lover or a stranger in this process of feeling and apprehending the self and others at the rumpled sites of autobiographical encounters. It can be seductive and play on our vulnerabilities, passions, and pleasures. It can be deceptive and tell a story false. Or it can be a foreign body, producing a bruising and demanding engagement that alters what we know about others and ourselves. Salam Pax describes *Persepolis* as a book that makes him wince and made emotional demands on him that are hard to bear. Pax is surely right to celebrate the value of a beautiful book that troubled him so. In terrible times, autobiographers are called on to transform the book, the page, and the word and to make radical use of the visual and verbal forms and spaces of life narrative. These lives have the power to pull readers into an aporia of reading and looking: that gap between allegro and lento, when reading and seeing are halted—in a productive pause. Here the wounding implications of image and word in flesh and emotion can make the reader wince, and yet, like Pax, we must continue to read on.

 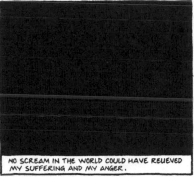

13 Images from page 142 of *Persepolis: The Story of Childhood* by Marjane Satrapi, translated by Mattias Ripa and Blake Ferris, copyright (c) 2003 by L'Association, Paris, France. Used by permission of Pantheon Books, a division of Random House, Inc.

Notes

1. In his discussion of online lives, John Zuern says: "As many critics have pointed out, the 'I' of autobiography and memoir, and even the 'third-person' subject of biography, has never been anything but virtual—an image that coalesces in the space between the welter of lived experience, and the grammars, figures, and narrative conventions of the languages into which that experience is cast, and which it always exceeds" (2003, xi).

2. See, for example, the dialogue between Pax (in italics) and Culpepper in the *Where Is Raed?* blog (http://dear_raed .blogspot.com/):

    > Do they anxiously await us to come and "liberate" them, as our government generally insists they will? [*oh oh . . . did he say "liberate"?*] Raed seems to welcome our prospective liberation [*whaaa? Which part of my rant wasn't clear enough and please don't use that word again it hurts*]—if perhaps with some trepidation. "Ha. Bomb us already. Stop pussyfooting." [*that post was meant to be sarcastic, or do you really believe that resolution will restore international peace and security. . . .*] The site looks believable. Also, however, I WANT to believe. [*here he links to the x-files site—he also thinks I'm from planet K-Pax apparently.*] This alone makes me a little suspicious. They have a somewhat cynical and fatalistic tone that I'd find likely. There are cryptic personal notes. [*These notes are not cryptic. This is Arablish. Because most of the world thinks that communication revolves around the English language we have to adapt our language to these non-arabic enabled systems. Ya3ni to a77*I inglizi to 2aba6il.*] (October 29, 2002)

    Pax translates this Arablish phrase as "You mean I either speak English or nothing at all." This exchange takes up the point that, far from being neutral, technology and the information it produces are always already tied up with the society and culture in which they are produced and/or deployed. Each culture in which a technological device is used places is own signature on the object or system, using it in locally specific ways. See Schirato and Webb (2003, 56).

3. Schirato and Webb (2003) make this point at some length, drawing on the work of Ankie Hoogvelt. Simon Gikandi's discussion of postcoloniality and globalization also emphasizes the connections between images and narratives of global identity, earlier forms of identity, and the material experiences of everyday life and survival: "What are we going to do with those older categories—nation, culture, and English—which function as the absent structure that shapes and yet haunts global culture and the idea of literature itself?" (2001, 633).

4. Regarding life narratives as soft weapons, see, for example, Robert Scholes's remarks in his presidential address, "The Humanities in a Posthumanist World": "The great world is a complicated place. It is a world of weapons, to be sure, but not all the weapons take the form of bombs, guns or other engines of physical destruction. Some of the weapons are rhetorical, taking the form of mythmaking and media domination" (2005, 733).

5. Taylor writes: "By social imaginary I mean something much broader and deeper than the intellectual schemes people may entertain when they think about social reality in a disengaged mode. I am thinking, rather, of the ways people imagine their social existence, how they fit together with others, how things go on between them and their fellows, and the expectations that are normally met, and the deeper normative notions and images that underlie these expectations" (2004, 23). For a discussion of how Charles Taylor's thinking about the self is useful for autobiography study, see David Parker (2002).

6. I am thinking, for example, of Benhabib's sense of the place of narrative in self-making: "We should view human cultures as constant creations, recreations, and negotiations of imaginary boundaries between 'we' and the 'other(s).' The 'other' is always within us and is one of us. A self is a self only because it distinguishes itself from a real, or more often than not imagined, 'other'" (2002, 8).

7. Graham Huggan defines "exoticism" as "an aestheticising process through which the cultural other is translated, relayed back through the familiar." Given this, the identification of Pax as "just like us" is the essence of exoticism at work. A vital component of this definition is the idea that the exotic is not an inherent quality to be found in certain goods, places, or peoples; it is, rather, a particular highly political mode of aesthetic perception. Huggan argues that, in a postcolonial context, "exoticism is effectively repoliticised, redeployed both to unsettle metropolitan expectations of cultural otherness and to effect a grounded critique of differential relations of power" (2001, ix–x). I read this to suggest that tactics of resistance that unsettle this process

of commodification and aestheticization may be effected in postcolonial writing, although this is by no means necessarily so. The case studies in Huggan's book frequently draw attention to what he calls "strategic exoticism": the circulation of cultural goods as exotic and as critiques of exoticism at one and the same time (for example, the ironic self-consciousness of *Midnight's Children* and *A Suitable Boy,* and the staged marginality of *The Satanic Verses* and *The Buddha of Suburbia.*)

8. "Testimony" is defined as first-person accounts of collective trauma, loss, struggle, and survival—a personal story raised to the level of history, which emerges out of a specific political context and rhetorical conditions. "Auto-ethnography" is defined as hybrid text that combines autobiographical and ethnographic writing practices that situate the writer in and through a social milieu that is irreducibly tied to the subject it constructs (see Jolly 2001).

9. This draws on Caren Kaplan's germinal essay on "out-law genres" (1992), which makes connections between geopolitical location and autobiographical genre. Drawing on the work of Barbara and John Beverly, Kaplan turns to life narratives and reading practices (*both* are important) that look beyond the West as a privileged location of autobiographical expression. Most usefully, Kaplan points out that the politics of location determines what instances of narrative production are read as resistance in content or form at specific historical moments.

10. According to the *Oxford English Dictionary,* the term "memoir" precedes "autobiography" by more than a century. "Autobiography" appears in the *OED* in 1809 as "the writing of one's own history". "Memoir" appears in 1659 as a "record of events not purporting to be a complete history but treating of such matters as come within the personal knowledge of the writer." Particularly useful for thinking about the turn to memoir in recent life narrative is the *OED* citation from *Grey's Correspondence* in 1769: "Why then a writer of memoirs is a better thing than an historian."

CHAPTER ONE

All otherwise unattributed dates in chapter 1 are to *Where Is Raed?*

1. For a definition and useful discussion of testimony, see the entry by Bella Brodzki in *The Encyclopedia of Life Writing* (2001).

2. In his discussion of where postcolonialism might begin, Robert J. C. Young makes the following remarks:

Since the early 1980s, postcolonialism has developed a body of writing that attempts to shift the dominant ways that relations between western and non-western people and their worlds are viewed. What does that mean? It means turning the world upside down. It means looking from the other side of the photograph, experiencing how differently things look when you live in Baghdad or Benin rather than Berlin or Boston, and understanding why. It means realizing that when western people look at the non-Western world what they see is often more a mirror image of themselves and their own assumptions than the reality of what is really there, or of how people outside the west actually feel and perceive themselves. (2003, 2)

3.   In a BBC *Newsnight* report transmitted in October 2005, Pax interviewed an Iraqi member of parliament, Adnan al-Janabi, a Sunni moderate who served as vice-chair of the constitutional committee, about the proposed Iraqi constitution and revealed that al-Janabi was his father. Salam also mentioned that his mother was Shia and described his family as being secular in political orientation.

4.   Salam Pax acknowledges this article in his blog on June 3, 2003: "And I was wondering when he will find out and if he will be angry because I didn't tell him. I think he isn't. . . . He uses words like 'chubby' and 'cherubic' to describe me. Ewww. And what is so wrong about saying 'thingy' a lot."

5.   Salam Pax first refers to turningtables (a U.S. soldier blog) on August 7, 2003, and the entry indicates how connections were made through weblogs between civilians and military forces in Iraq:

I have totally forgotten how wonderful it is to have a dinner which lasts forever with friends. . . . I was having such a great time I almost forgot I loaded turningtables on my computer before leaving the office. I am very grateful to the person who sent me an email introducing me to turningtables. I have spent the rest of the night reading the posts. He found Raed:

inside the barracks . . . there are hand prints . . . and names written in bad english . . . tell salam I found raed . . . he wrote his name with his finger next to a really bad self portrait . . .

moja please stay safe.

6.   The company promotes this product as follows: Conflict: Desert Storm II— Back to Baghdad Company Line.

At the height of the 1991 Gulf War. 300 klicks into the heart of Iraq, you must command your squad of Special Forces operatives to strike at Iraq's evil dictator and his fascist regime. Armed with an authentic arsenal of high-tech weapons and vehicles, your squad will face impossible odds in this battle against tyranny. Only strategy and skill will ensure your survival through frantic firefights, gut-wrenching vehicular combat, and gripping stealth operations. "The Mother of All Battles" is coming to your console in Gotham Games' Conflict Desert Storm 2—Back to Baghdad. The troops are in position, so lock and load.

There is much more to be said about the uses of Microsoft's Xbox in military training, and the relations between game designers and the military. See Clive Thompson, "Fingers on the Button" (2004), and also Žižek's suggestion that the war on terror is experienced as a video game in *Welcome to the Desert of the Real* (2002, 37).

7. In May 2003 Salam and Raed travel south as part of the CIVIC (Campaign for Innocent Victims in Conflict), a volunteer organization that sets out to record civilian deaths in Iraq. In recording their journey to Karbala, Najaf, Basra, Samawah, Diwaniya, and Nasiriyah, Pax uploads photographs rather than words: "And look what I saw. . . ."

8. Pax has a link here to an article by an embedded journalist from the *Christian Science Monitor:* "As of the specter of civilian casualties, Private Gritz, like many soldiers have no clear answer. 'The Iraqis strap kids to tanks. What can you do?'"

9. Leigh Gilmore uses "jurisdiction" to discuss autobiographical self-representation as a way of examining how personal accounts can enter the public sphere and make particular claims for the representativeness of experience. In relation to Pax's construction of Baghdad as a domesticated and inhabited space, Gilmore's discussion of the territorial, rhetorical, and discursive dimensions of jurisdiction is useful.

10. Lisa Nakamura discusses the stereotyped performances of race and gender in *Cybertypes* (2002) in an extended critique of the idea that identities are transcended in cyberspace. See, too, Beth Kolko's essay on the whiteness of cyberspace (2000, 213–32).

11. William Gibson is a journalist and science fiction writer, author of the dystopian novel *Neuromancer* (1984), which first used the term "cyberspace."

12. I have in mind here Derek Gregory, and his use of Judith Butler's remarks on performance in *Bodies That Matter:*

Performances create a space in which it is possible for "newness" to enter the world. Judith Butler describes the conditional, creative possibilities of performance as "a relation of being implicated in that which one opposes, [yet] turning power against itself to produce alternative political modalities, to establish a kind of political contestation that is not a "pure opposition" but a difficult labour of forging a future from resources inevitably impure." This space of potential is always conditional, always precarious, but every repertory performance of the colonial present carries within it the twin possibilities of either reaffirming and even radicalizing the hold of the colonial past on the present *or* undoing its enclosures and approaching closer to the horizon of the *post*colonial. (Gregory 2004, 19)

13. I am mindful of Mark Poster's remark that the decentralized structure of the Internet enables non-Western culture to have presence on an equal footing with the West, establishing the grounds for a meeting and exchange of cultures "that is global in scope, albeit favouring the wealthy and the educated everywhere" (2001b, 49). The Internet creates new invisibilities, filters out those who do not have access to online communications and disempowers those who cannot afford start-up fees or who belong to communities that are too poor to distribute these resources: "The Internet is no more universal than print was in eighteenth-century America. Perhaps it is less so" (Poster, 2001b, 126–27).

14. Massive Attack is a pioneering British trip-hop band that influenced much of the dance music produced in the 1990s after the release of their first LP in 1991. See http://www.vh1.com/artists/az/massive_attack/bio.jhtml.

15. Amanda Anderson defines cosmopolitanism as "the capacious inclusion of multiple forms of affiliation, disaffiliation, and reaffiliation, simultaneously insisting on the need for informing principles of self-reflexivity, critique, and common humanity" (1998, 30).

16. Sidonie Smith and Julia Watson refer to "technologies of the self" in autobiography criticism to discuss the ways in which subjects come to self-knowledge in historically specific regimes of truth (2001a, 133).

17. There is a discussion of the politics of naming triggered by representations of New York after the September 11 attacks in Schirato and Webb (2003, 4–7) and Dudziak (2003).

18. The relationship between representations and the material conditions of power, rule, and domination is frequently overstated in postcolonial analysis, as Ania Loomba remarks (2002, 95). Nevertheless, if we accept that the distinctive preoccupation of postcolonialism is the analysis of "the *lived* condition of unequal power sharing globally and the self-authorization of cultural, economic and militaristic hegemony . . . the materialistic critiques of power and how that power or ideology seeks to interpellate subjects within a discourse as subordinate or without agency" (Azfal-Khan and Seshadri-Crooks, 2000, 19), then the commitment to making connections between texts and the historical and material conditions of the moment is fundamental to, and definitive of, postcolonial scholarship.

CHAPTER TWO

1. The book was read aloud in its entirety on the Australian Broadcasting Commission's primetime *Life Matters* radio program in 2003 (Kinsella 2003). A powerful and compelling first-person narrative, it was read by a young Afghan immigrant and in this way it entered hotly contested domestic debates about the incarceration of refugees and asylum seekers in Australia.

2. It is important to note that Mohanty has no intention of constructing a monolithic, singular "Western feminism": "Rather, I am attempting to draw attention to the similar effects of various textual strategies . . . that codify Others as non-Western and hence themselves as specifically Western" (2003, 18).

3. One way of locating articles on the veil is to enter the term "overdetermined signifier" in an Internet search engine. The complex and contradictory associations of the veil as a vehicle for critiques of the situation of women in Islam were tragically apparent following the murder of the filmmaker Theo Van Gogh in Holland in 2004. Van Gogh's film *Submission* presents verses of the Koran written on naked female bodies (an interesting play on testimony incarnate). These images outraged not only Muslim communities who labeled the images as blasphemous, recalling debates over Rushdie's references

to the Koran in *Satanic Verses,* but also feminist activists who found this representation of the female body both undignified and prurient. *Submission* was written by Ayan Hirsi Ali, a former refugee from Somalia and until recently an MP in the Dutch parliament. Useful recent discussions of representations of the veil, which examine its diverse and conflicting associations, include Alvi, Hoodfar, and McDonough (2003), Donnell (1999), Grace (2004), El Guindi (1999), Najmabadi (1993), and Shirazi (2003). For a useful introduction to debates about the veil in France, see Windle (2004).

4. *Voices behind the Veil* (Caner 2003).

5. Daphne Grace points out that Croutier's account of life in a Turkish harem is based on her own family history, and this draws a more complex and diverse picture than the Orientalist paintings that are reproduced in the book (2004, 42). The childhood memoirs by Leila Ahmed (2000) and Fatima Mernissi (1995) offer alternative ways of representing the harem that actively engage with some of these stereotypes. See, too, Lewis (2005) and Yeazell (2000).

6. During the Gulf War, for example, there were a series of racist incidents in Australia where Muslim women had their veils torn off. Ghassan Hage argues that even those who sought to make reparation for these acts of violence demonstrate that tolerance is the prerogative of the dominant, and it is expressed toward something or someone perceived as a passive object (in Gunew). More famously the forced and public stripping of Algerian women to the accompaniment of the Marseillaise in 1958, established veiling as a symbol of nationalism and resistance to French colonialism in Algeria.

7. The tendency of life narrative to bridge differences of culture and religion can be seen, for example the following "Spotlight Reviews of *My Forbidden Face*" from Amazon.com:

Latifa's book is more than just a catalog of Taliban atrocities. For me, three things made her book especially interesting. First Latifa is a devout, modern Muslim. Throughout the book she presents her thesis that the version of Islam espoused by the Taliban had little to do with real religion. The Taliban dictatorship was essentially about men wanting to control and humiliate women. Her reflections about being religious and living in the modern world will interest readers of all faiths who are thinking about these issues. The second feature of her book that I found intersting [*sic*] was how strongly her father supported her and her sisters in wanting to become education [*sic*] and have careers. Also of interest was her account of how the French fashion magazine *Elle* first broke the story. The popular press takes a lot of criticism for being shallow and sensational. *Elle* deserves a lot of credit for taking the leadership in focusing world attention on what was happening to the women of Afghanistan. (Paul A. Spengler from Buffalo, New York)

and:

I read this memoir as an individual project for a Philosophy course. By the end of the book I was absolutely stunned how much I did not know about Islam, Afghanistan and the Taliban. I came to realize through Latifa's explanations and recounts [sic] how absolutely ignorant I was. I assumed that women in Afghanistan had been treated unfairly for centuries, and had no idea how similar life was to American life for most women and men. By the end of the book, I felt utterly guilty for thinking the way I did about Latifa's culture. I am so glad that I read this book, as it was a wonderful eye-opener. I recommend it to all American women so they can understand how precious our freedoms and liberties are. . . . My only complaint is that her recount [sic] is somewhat impersonal. Her memoir is more factual, when I felt she could have put a lot more of her own feelings and emotion into the book. (Ams from Massachusetts, USA)

CHAPTER THREE

1. The United Nations High Commissioner for Refugees (UNHCR) estimates that, in 2003, there were 10.4 million refugees, and the vast majority of these are sheltering in their neighboring countries. Of these, 80 percent of refugees are women and children who are unable to travel long distances without difficulty. It has been estimated that 18 percent of the world's refugees reach Western countries and very few of these give testimony. Robert J. C. Young writes of the Afghan refugee:

    One thing you would be unlikely to do in the Jalozai camp is to read this book, even if you were literate, and it had been translated into Pushto. You would talk a lot, speak to many people about day-to-day problems, sometimes relating longer and harder tales of suffering amid war and famine, trying to make sense of your experiences. If you met any of those from elsewhere working for your support, you would most likely speak to them of your needs—for medicine, for food, shelter. You would not articulate your experiences for the benefit of others you would never meet, you would not translate your life into story or representation for others.(2003, 13)

    In a chapter about the absence of testimony, this is a reminder that silence can be a powerful form of communication in subaltern control. In processes of cross-cultural communication, subaltern life narrative is traded strategically in contexts of unequal exchange. The argument for the importance of understanding testimonial languages in analytic frameworks informed by postcolonial thinking in Bennett and Kennedy's *World Memory* (2003) is relevant here. So, too, is Franklin and Lyons's (2004) insistence that testimony is a political act rather than a gesture of self-expression.

2. One example of a refugee/asylum-seeker monograph is Hala's account of her imprisonment in Wackenhut in *Behind the Burqa* (Swift Yasgur 2002); see, too, *Refugee Boy* (Zephaniah 2001), *Freeing Ali: The Human Face of the Pacific Solution* (Gordon 2005).

3. Examples of edited collections include the PEN-initiated "Another Country" (Scott and Keneally), the gathering of stories of children in *Dark Dreams* (Dechian, Millar, and Sallis 2004), extracts from letters in *From Nothing to*

Zero (Amor and Austin 2003), the collection of testimonies from refugees under temporary protection, *Lives in Limbo* (Leach and Mansouri 2004), and Afghan stories in *Tales from a Suitcase: The Afghan Experience* (Davies and Dal Bosco 2002).

4.　See, for example, "Eye on Wackenhut" at http://www.eyeonwackenhut .com/; the National Coalition of Anti-Deportation Campaigns at http:// www.ncadc.org.uk/; Baxterwatch's former site at http://www.baxterwatch .net/, "Inside Port Hedland" at http://www.porthedland.nomasters.org/, Refugee Media Space, "War on Refugees" (n.d.), and "Who Is Responsible for the Deaths of 353 Asylum-Seekers?" (Suspected Illegal Entry Vessel X, n.d.), one of a series of sites dedicated to the sinking of an asylum-seeker boat (Suspected Illegal Entry Vessel X), with the loss of 353 lives on October 19, 2001.

5.　Derrida makes this very clear in his essay "On Cosmopolitanism": "The interest of the nation-state regulates asylum" (2003, 12). The parallels between global campaigns on behalf of asylum seekers and the antislavery campaigns in the United States and Britain in the nineteenth century are instructive for understanding the critical weaknesses in the current campaigns against detention. In the nineteenth century on both sides of the Atlantic, reform emerged through national infrastructures where public intellectuals in the legislature and judiciary, the Church and the Fourth Estate, were galvanized into public speech against slavery. Now, the global infrastructure of NGOs and the framework of the United Nations that is available to the asylum seekers is weak, lacking purchase in the powerful institutional structures of nation states. The emphasis on transcending national boundaries in human rights discourse may be a superior moral vocabulary (see, for example, Schaffer and Smith [2004a, 8]), but it is a weakness in terms of realpolitik.

6.　I discuss this further in Whitlock 2006.

7.　My thinking about testimony incarnate here follows earlier work on Mary Prince's slave narrative *The History of Mary Prince* ([1831] 1987). Prince, too, requires others, who possess cultural authority, to "read her body" and give witness to the marks of abuse on her back and to testify to their authenticity on her behalf. As in other slave narratives, in the *History* the body is seen to represent truth; although what Mary Prince has to say remains suspect, her flesh cannot lie. See my *The Intimate Empire* (2000) and "Merry Christmas Mary Prince" (2003). Anzaldúa calls this tradition of testimony incarnate "organic writing": "The visceral terms in self-representation used by the most brutally colonized subjects" (Moraga and Anzaldúa 1983, 172). Theo van Gogh's notorious film *Submission* features writing of the Koranic script on the female body and hearkens back metaphorically to this tradition of extreme testimony. For another recent example, see the discussion of Souad's testimony following in chapter 5, where she describes requests from European audiences to see the scars on her body.

8.　The connection to Young's (1997) work here should be clear. As I remarked in the introduction, her communicative ethics is inclined to downplay the usefulness of symmetry and empathic engagement in favor of working toward moral respect through asymmetrical relations, which recognize differences of history, social position, and experience that cannot be transcended. Derek Attridge's writing on creativity, otherness, and the singularity of literature is important here too. Attridge draws substantially on the fiction of J. M. Coetzee, and it follows that he attends to encounters with the other in acts of reading and interpretation of texts. He emphasizes the creativity that follows from the glimpsed apprehension of otherness: "If I succeed in responding adequately to the otherness and singularity of the other, it is the other in its relating to me—always in a specific time and place—to which I am responding, in creatively changing myself and perhaps a little of the world as well" (2004, 33).

CHAPTER FOUR

1. An extensive collection of materials on the docudrama (including a transcript) is archived at PBS (Frontline 2005), including a study of the controversy by Thomas White and Gladys Ganley.

CHAPTER FIVE

1. A record of the statements issued by Random House is archived at http://www.randomhouse.com.au/norma.htm.
2. For Rana Husseini's story, see Abunimah (2004).
3. *Honor Lost* includes some acknowledgments that are not reproduced in the Bantam edition, and *Forbidden Love* includes a page titled "What Can You Do?" that calls on readers to protest against honor crimes. This was the page of links to Jordanian activists that alerted them to Khouri's book, and it is not reproduced in the American edition. In this chapter I have used *Honor Lost* (Khouri 2003b) as a standardized title throughout (including quotations) unless there is a specific reference to the different cover image or subtitle or campaign details included in *Forbidden Love* (Khouri 2003a). All page references are to *Honor Lost.*
4. Quotations in the first paragraph are from Bolt (2004a, 2004b).
5. "Sally Morgan has sold 500,000 copies of *My Place* which . . . tells of whites being mean to her Aboriginal family. For instance, she says a white pastoralist, Howden Drake-Brockman, fathered her grandmother, and then committed incest with her to produce her mother. All false, says Drake-Brockman's daughter Judith—and a slur of a good man. She points out errors in Morgan's chronology and has asked her to take a DNA test to prove her claim. Morgan hasn't replied, and her book still sells" (Bolt 2004b).
6. At the end of 1998, the *New York Times* broke the story that Rigoberta Menchú's autobiography, published in English in 1984 during the civil war in Guatemala, was filled with inaccuracies and misrepresentations. In his book

Rigoberta Menchú and the Story of All Poor Guatemalans (1998), the anthropologist David Stoll concluded the book was not the eyewitness account it claimed to be because Menchú describes a number of experiences as her own that she herself had not had.

7. "A reader," posted at www.amazon.com January 3, 2004; accessed March 3, 2006.

8. At Jean Sasson's official website (as of December 5, 2005), there is a list titled "What I'm Reading Now: September 2002," which includes the following:

> *Honor Lost* by Norma Khouri published by Atria Books (I've been asked to read and then if I like it, to "blurb" this book, which won't be out for a few more months. So I won't say much about it other than I've read it and I predict it will be a best-seller. It's a true story that will make your blood boil yet it will make you determined to do something to stop "honor killings," so common in certain parts of the world. Since I don't want to spoil the suspense, I won't say anymore, but let me tell you, BUY this book when it comes out. You can thank me later!)

9. The dedication at the end of the book reads: "My dear Dalia, in your life you made me laugh and cry. You managed to touch my soul and become part of me forever, and in your death you've become my purpose for living. I write this book in loving memory of you, and I pray that God keeps you safe and happy until we meet again. Till then, *ya gazallae,* I know your spirit strengthens me, and your memory comforts me, and you will always remain a special part of my life" (Khouri 2003b, 211).

10. This is, in part, what distinguishes the Khouri hoax, as Malcolm Knox suggests: "Khouri's hoax will take its place in a long Australian tradition of literary fraud, from Ern Malley to Helen Darville-Demidenko. But no other fraudulent book has had such wide sales or impact, and in Darville's case the deception only involved her persona, not her book. Khouri has misled the world both on the page and in person" (2004a). By January 2006, as controversy raged about the legitimacy of memoirs by James Frey and JT Leroy, Norma Khouri's name was used as a synonym for "hoax": "American publishing was reeling from a double dose of the Khouris yesterday after two high-profile authors were unmasked as apparent frauds" (Waldren 2006).

11. The term "moral grammar" is used by Robert Manne in his discussion of the Demidenko hoax. In *The Culture of Forgetting* (1996), Manne reflects on the "the literary-critical confusion, the historical ignorance and the multicultural sentimentality" that was flushed out by this controversy. See Manne's "Reflections on the Demidenko Affair" in *The Way We Live Now* (1998, 197–205). Kate Legge makes a similar point more explicitly about the Khouri affair: "Fact checkers, editors, hardened sceptics, character judges, gut instincts—all failed to detect any problem and no one who knew enough about this woman's past came forward to challenge her makeover" (2004, 2).

12. Coe and Freedman (1998) suggest a series of questions that are useful lines of

enquiry for this kind of rhetorical study: What sorts of communication does the genre encourage, what sorts does it constrain against? Who can—and who cannot—use this genre? Does it empower some people and silence others? What values and beliefs are instantiated within this set of practices? What are the political and ethical implications of the rhetorical situation constructed, audience invoked and context assumed by a particular genre?

13. "SURGIR is a Swiss foundation that works with women, anywhere in the world, who are subjected to criminal traditions, women who are martyrs in their soul and in their bodies, and with the children of these women. SURGIR fights vigorously against the injustice of the customs that victimize them" (Souad 2004, 211).

14. See, for example, Glazov (2004):

> Thus, a sobering reality stares us in the face: Souad's soul-tearing journey does not exist in a vacuum. It is a chilling and powerful reminder to us of the essence of the War on Terror.
>
> Islamic fundamentalists know—all too well—that the only way their cultures will survive is for one half of the human race to remain caged and enslaved. But the West stands in stark opposition to that pathological and death-seeking quest. And the West's values continue to spread with lightning speed. In the age of globalization, mass communication and the Internet, the reality of Western women's free choice and control over their own identity—and sexuality—is a force that cannot be stopped.

15. Souad suggests she was born into personhood in Europe: "It's a curious thing, the destiny of Arab women—in my village at least. We accept beating as natural. No thought of rebellion occurs to us" (51); "I had almost no sense of myself. I didn't know what I looked like, whether or not I was pretty. I wasn't aware of being human, of thinking, of having feelings. What I had always known was fear, the suffering and humiliation of being tied up like an animal in the stable and beaten so hard I had no feeling in my back" (68). Franklin and Lyons (2004) point out that there is an aporia in public discourse about Palestine, and testimony from the Occupied Territories of the West Bank is especially hard to locate.

CHAPTER SIX

1. These editorial reviews are selected almost at random from a copious collection at Amazon.com, downloaded February 17, 2005.

2. There is now an extensive and useful collection of articles that discuss the ethical implications of Krog's memoir. See, for example, the articles by Bennett (2003), and Grunebaum and Henri (2003), as well as the excellent introduction to issues of memory and trauma in Bennett and Kennedy (2003); Meira Cook (2001); Sarah Ruden (1999); and Whitlock (2004a).

3. Reuters points out that embedded journalists were present at the Crimean

War in 1854 and the Boer War at the turn of the twentieth century. However, the contrast is with the Gulf War of 1991, where journalists were restricted to daily briefings by Central Command. For the generation of reporters covering the Iraq war twelve years later, embedding was new (Reuters 2004, ix).

4. Contrast Wright's response to the embedded Reuters correspondent Matthew Green, for example, who worries about small acts that might transform him from observer into participant and who observes Marines discussing combat as a mark of their difference: "[Their] surprise initiation began to glow inside, flickers of bravado eroding their fear. This was a feeling I would never share. I was writing not fighting. They had crossed a line during the 30-minute firefight, become a different kind of Marine than the one they had been that morning. I was still just a reporter" (Green 2004, 64).

5. See, for example, the reviews at the Amazon.com site, where veterans of both Gulf Wars adopt the memoir as speaking accurately of their combat experience. The reader reviews also reflect the very different ways the book travels and accumulates a varied readership. Some read *Generation Kill* and find their view that this is "the greatest military the earth has ever seen" reinforced (J. L. Harmon, Florida USA), while others attest to the piercing quality of the writing and the feeling that the book makes it difficult to sustain generalizations about who and what Americans are (M. S. Mills, Beijing, China).

CHAPTER SEVEN

1. See, for example, Vick (2004). The memoir has yet to be translated into Persian and few Iranians have read it. Vick's article includes several responses by Tehran residents that describe the book as "brilliant . . . But it has nothing to do with Iran" as they experience it in 2004, although Vick points out that speaking openly in the Islamic Republic can still be a problem. Nafisi herself emphasizes the ideological transformations underway in Iran in an article in the *Middle East Forum* (2003a), where she argues that young Iranians find what modernity has to offer appealing and are drawn to the language of secular liberalism and its architects, de Tocqueville and Arendt. These values are promoted through Nafisi's "The Dialogue Project" (Nafisi, n.d.). Useful discussion of how Nafisi appeals to Western readers appears at the "Donkeys Party Papers" website (Donkeys Party 2004), which draws together a community of Iranian scholars; there is a discussion of Nafisi's appearance for Audi in May 2004. See, too, Mottahedeh (2004).

2. There is some debate about the accuracy of this translation. For example, it has been suggested that Adorno does not speak of this as the highest form of morality and "home" might also be translated as "self" in this instance.

3. Relevant here, too, are Gikandi's remarks on the survival of the idea of consensual Englishness through the new English literature emerging from the global culture of professional émigrés (2001, 654).

1. Scott McCloud's definition of "comics" is useful: a noun plural in form, used
    with a singular verb. "Juxtaposed pictorial and other images in a deliberate
    sequence, intended to convey information and/or to produce an aesthetic
    response in the viewer" (1994, 9). The distinction between cartoons and
    comics is important, too: cartoons are an approach to image making that
    abstracts and simplifies, and cartooning is frequently used in the medium of
    the comics.

References

Abunimah, Ali. 2004. "A Hoax and Honor Lost for Norma Khouri."
   Daily Star (Beirut), August 10. http://dailystar.com.lb/article
   .asp?edition_id=10&categ_id=5&article_id=7113 Accessed
   November 11, 2005.
AcaDemon. n.d. "Term Papers and Essays." http://www.academon
   .com/lib/essay?KEYW=Nafisi/. Accessed June 1, 2005.
Adorno, Theodor. 1984. *Minima Moralia: Reflections from a Damaged
   Life.* London: Verso.
Ahmed, Leila. 1992. *Women and Gender in Islam.* New Haven, CT:
   Yale University Press.
———. 2000. *A Border Passage: From Cairo to America—a Woman's
   Journey.* New York: Penguin Books.
Ahmed, Sara. 2004. *The Cultural Politics of Emotion.* New York:
   Routledge.
Ahmed, Sara, and Jackie Stacey. 2001. *Thinking through the Skin.*
   London: Routledge.
Alavi, Nasrin. 2005. *We Are Iran: The Persian Blogs.* Brooklyn, NY:
   Soft Skull Press.
Allan, Stuart, and Barbie Zelizer, eds. 2004. *Reporting War: Journal-
   ism in Wartime.* London: Routledge.
Alvi, Sajida Sultana, Homa Hoodfar, and Sheila McDonough, eds.
   2003. *The Muslim Veil in North America.* Toronto: Women's
   Press.
Amazon.com. http://www.amazon.com/gp/customer-reviews/.
   Accessed February 17, 2005.
———. 2004. "*In the Shadow of No Towers* (Hardcover): Customer
   Reviews." http://www.amazon.com/exec/obidos/tg/detail/-/
   0375423079/qid=1117511086/sr=8-1/ref=pd_csp_1/104
   -2052991-7711909?v=glanceands=booksandn=507846/.
   Accessed February 25, 2004.

Amiry, Suad. 2005. *Sharon and My Mother-in-Law: Ramallah Diaries.* London: Granta Books.

Amor, Meaghan, and Janet Austin, eds. 2003. *From Nothing to Zero: Letters from Refugees in Australia's Detention Centres.* Footscray, Australia: Lonely Planet.

Anderson, Amanda. 1998. "Cosmopolitanism, Universalism, and the Divided Legacies of Modernity." In *Cosmopolitics: Thinking and Feeling beyond the Nation,* ed. Pheng Chean and Bruce Robbins, 265–89. Minneapolis: University of Minnesota Press.

Anzaldúa, Gloria. 1987. *Borderlands/La Frontera: The New Mestiza.* San Francisco: Spinsters/Aunt Lute.

Appadurai, Arjun. 1996. *Modernity at Large: Cultural Dimensions of Globalization.* Minneapolis: University of Minnesota Press.

Armstrong, Sally. 2002. *Veiled Threat: The Hidden Power of the Women of Afghanistan.* New York: Four Walls Eight Windows.

Asayesh, Gelareh. 1999. *Saffron Sky: A Life between Iran and America.* Boston: Beacon Press.

Attridge, Derek. 2004. *The Singularity of Literature.* London: Routledge.

Attwood, Bain. 2001. "'Learning about the truth': The Stolen Generations." In *Telling Stories: Indigenous History and Memory in Australia and New Zealand,* ed. Bain Attwood and Fiona Magowan, 183–212. Crows Nest, NSW: Allen & Unwin.

Attwood, Bain, and Fiona Magowan, eds. 2001. *Telling Stories: Indigenous History and Memory in Australia and New Zealand.* Crows Nest, NSW: Allen & Unwin.

Ayres, Chris. 2005. *War Reporting for Cowards: Between Iraq and a Hard Place.* London: John Murray.

Azfal-Khan, Fawzia, and Kalpana Seshadri-Crooks, eds. 2000. *The Pre-Occupation of Postcolonial Studies.* Durham, NC: Duke University Press.

Bahrampour, Tara. 2000. *To See and See Again: A Life in Iran and America.* Berkeley: University of California Press.

Bailey, Sally, and Granville Williams, 1997. "Memoirs Are Made of This: Journalists' Memoirs in the United Kingdom, 1945–95." In *A Journalism Reader,* ed. Michael Bromley and Tom O'Malley, 351–77. London: Routledge.

Balfour, Ian, and Eduaardo Cadava, eds. 2004. "And Justice for All? The Claims of Human Rights." Special issue, *South Atlantic Quarterly* 103, nos. 2–3 (Spring/Summer).

Barkan, Elazar. 2001. *The Guilt of Nations: Restitution and Negotiating Historical Injustices.* Baltimore MD: Johns Hopkins University Press.

Bebow, John, 2003. "Charging into Bad-Guy Country with Custer." In *Embedded: The Media at War in Iraq — an Oral History,* ed. Bill Katovsky and Timothy Carlson, 1–10. Guilford, CT: Lyons Press.

Benard, Cheryl. 2002. *Veiled Courage. Inside the Afghan Women's Resistance.* New York: Broadway Books.

Benhabib, Seyla. 2002. *The Claims of Culture: Equality and Diversity in the Global Era.* Princeton, NJ: Princeton University Press.

Bennett, Jill. 2003. "*Tenebrae* after September 11: Art, Empathy, and the Global Politics of Belonging." In *World Memory: Personal Trajectories in Global Time,* ed. Jill Bennett and Rosanne Kennedy, 177–94. Basingstoke: Palgrave Macmillan.

Bennett, Jill, and Rosanne Kennedy. 2003. *World Memory: Personal Trajectories in Global Time.* Basingstoke: Palgrave Macmillan.

Beverley, John. 1999. *Subalternity and Representation: Arguments in Cultural Theory.* Durham, NC: Duke University Press.

Bhabha, Homi. 1994. *The Location of Culture.* London: Routledge.

Bloom, Harold. 1994. *The Western Canon: The Books and School of the Ages.* New York: Harcourt Brace.

Bolt, Andrew. 2004a. "Presumed Guilty Again." *Sunday Mail,* May 23, 57.

———. 2004b. "Why We Love a Hard Luck Story." *Sunday Mail,* August 1, 33.

Boyd-Barrett, Oliver. 2004. "Understanding: The Second Casualty." In *Reporting War: Journalism in Wartime,* ed. Stuart Allan and Barbie Zelizer, 25–42. London: Routledge.

Brennan, Timothy. 1997. *At Home in the World: Cosmopolitanism Now.* Cambridge, MA: Harvard University Press.

———. 2004. "From Development to Globalization: Postcolonial Studies and Globalization Theory." In *The Cambridge Companion to Postcolonial Literary Studies,* ed. Neil Lazarus, 120–38. Cambridge: Cambridge University Press.

Brett, Judith. 2000–2001. "Why John Howard Can't Say Sorry." *Arena Magazine* (December–January), 35–41.

Brodsky, Anne E. 2003. *With All Our Strength: The Revolutionary Association of the Women of Afghanistan.* New York: Routledge.

Brodzki, Bella. 2001. "Testimony." In *The Encyclopedia of Life Writing,* ed. Margaretta Jolly, 870–71. London: Fitzroy Dearborn.

Brooks, Geraldine. 2003. *Nine Parts of Desire: The Hidden World of Islamic Women.* Sydney: Anchor Books.

Buss, Helen. 2001. "Memoirs." In *The Encyclopedia of Life Writing, ed.* Jolly, Margaretta, 595–97. London: Fitzroy Dearborn.

———. 2002. *Repossessing the World: Reading Memoirs by Contemporary Women.* Waterloo: Wilfred Laurier University Press.

Butler, Judith. 2005. *Giving an Account of Oneself.* New York: Fordham University Press.

———. 2004. *Precarious Life: The Powers of Mourning and Violence.* London: Verso.

Caner, Ergun Mehmet, ed. 2003. *Voices behind the Veil: The World of Islam through the Eyes of Women.* Grand Rapids, MI: Kregel.

Caruth, Cathy. 1996. *Unclaimed Experience: Trauma, Narrative and History.* Baltimore, MD: Johns Hopkins University Press.

Castiglia, Christopher. 1996. *Bound and Determined: Captivity, Culture-Crossing and White Womanhood from Mary Rowlandson to Patty Hearst.* Chicago: University of Chicago Press.

Chavis, Melody Ermachild. 2003. *Meena: Heroine of Afghanistan.* New York: St. Martin's Press.

Chean, Pheng, and Bruce Robbins, eds. 1998. *Cosmopolitics: Thinking and Feeling beyond the Nation.* Minneapolis: University of Minnesota Press.

Children Out of Detention. http://www.chilout.org/. Accessed June 1, 2005.

Clifford, James. 1997. *Routes. Travel and Translation in the Late Twentieth Century.* Cambridge MA: Harvard University Press.

Coe, Richard, and A. Freedman, 1998. "Generative Rhetoric." In *Theorizing Composition,* ed. M. Kennedy, 136–47. Westport, CT: Greenwood.

Coetzee, J. M. 1982. *Waiting for the Barbarians.* Harmondsworth: Penguin Books.

Colley, Linda. 2003. *Captives: Britain, Empire and the World, 1600–1850.* London: Pimlico.

Collins, Jim, ed. 2002. *High-Pop: Making Culture into Popular Entertainment.* Malden, MA: Blackwell.

Cook, Meira. 2001. "Metaphors of Suffering: Antje Krog's *Country of My Skull.*" *Mosaic* 34, no. 3 : 73–89.

Cooke, Miriam, and Bruce B. Lawrence, eds. 2005. *Muslim Networks from Hajj to Hip Hop.* Chapel Hill and London: University of North Carolina Press.

Dalziell, Rosamund, ed. 2002. *Selves Crossing Cultures: Autobiography and Globalisation.* Melbourne: Australian Scholarly Publishing.

Davies, Will, and Andrea Dal Bosco. 2002. *Tales from a Suitcase: The Afghan Experience.* South Melbourne: Lothian Books.

De Bellaigue Christopher. 2004. *In the Rose Gardens of the Martyrs: A Memoir of Iran.* New York: HarperCollins.

Dechian, Sonja, Heather Millar, and Eva Sallis, eds. 2004. *Dark Dreams: Australian Refugee Stories by Young Writers, Aged 11–20 Years.* Kent Town: Wakefield Press.

Denby, David. 1997. *Great Books.* New York: Simon & Schuster.

Derrida, Jacques. 1994. *Specters of Marx: The State of the Debt, the Work of Mourning, and New International.* Translated by Peggy Kamf. New York: Routledge.

———. 1998. *Demeure: Maurice Blanchot.* Paris: Galliard.

———. 2003. *On Cosmopolitanism and Forgiveness.* London: Routledge.

Dixon, Robert. 2002. "Citizens and Asylum Seekers. Emotional Literacy, Rhetorical Leadership and Human Rights." *Cultural Studies Review* 8, no. 2 (November): 11–25.

———. 2004. "Cosmopolitan Australians and Colonial Modernity." *Westerly* 49 (November): 122–37.

Donkeys Party. 2004. "Azar Flying." http://www.donkeys-party.com/threads/nafisi_01.html/. Accessed March 16, 2005.

Donnell, Alison, ed. 1999. "The Veil: Postcolonialism and the Politics of Dress." Special issue, *Interventions,* vol. 1, no. 4.

Douglas, Allen, and Fedwa Malti-Douglas. 1994. *Arab Comic Strips: Politics of an Emerging Mass Culture.* Bloomington: Indiana University Press.

Dow Evans, Timothy. 2000. *Light Writing and Life Writing: Photography in Autobiography.* Chapel Hill: University of North Carolina Press.

Dudziak, Mary L., ed. 2003. *September 11 in History: A Watershed Moment?* Durham and London: University of North Carolina Press.

Dumas, Firoozeh. 2004. *Funny in Farsi: A Memoir of Growing Up Iranian in America.* New York: Random House.

Eakin, Paul John. 1992. *Touching the World. Reference in Autobiography.* Princeton, NJ: Princeton University Press.

———. 1999. *How Our Lives Become Stories: Making Selves.* London: Cornell University Press.

Editorial. 2004. "Time for Author to Explain Her Story." *Australian,* July 30.

Egan, Susanna. 2004. "The Company She Keeps: Demidenko and the Problems of Imposture in Autobiography." *Australian Literary Studies* 21, no. 4:14–27.

———. 1999. *Mirror Talk: Genres of Crisis in Contemporary Autobiography.* Chapel Hill: University of North Carolina Press.

Eisner, Will. 2004. *Comics and Sequential Art.* Tamarac, FL: Poorhouse Press.

Farr, Cecilia Konchar. 2005. *Reading Oprah.* Albany: State University of New York Press.

Fischer, Michael M. J. 2004. *Mute Dreams, Blind Owls, and Dispersed Knowledges: Persian Poesis in the Transnational Circuitry.* Durham, NC: Duke University Press.

Fowler, Karen Joy. 2004. *The Jane Austen Book Club.* Camberwell, Australia: Viking.

Franklin, Cynthia, and Laura E. Lyons. 2004. "Bodies of Evidence and the Intricate Machines of Untruth." In "Personal Effects: The Testimonial Uses of Life Writing." Special issue, *Biography* 27, no. 1 (Winter): v–xxii.

Frontline. 2005. "Death of a Princess." *Frontline.* http://www.pbs.org/wgbh/pages/frontline/shows/princess/. Accessed November 20, 2005.

Frow, John. 1996. *Cultural Studies and Cultural Value.* Oxford: Clarendon Press.

Frye, Northrop. 1976. *The Secular Scripture: A Study of the Structure of Romance.* Cambridge, MA: Harvard University Press.

Garrels, Anne. 2003. *Naked in Baghdad.* New York: Farrar, Straus & Giroux.

Geertz, Clifford. 2003. "Which Way to Mecca? Parts 1 and 2." *New York Review of Books,* June 12, 27–30; July 3, 36–39.

Gelder, Ken. 2005. *Popular Fiction: The Logics and Practices of a Literary Field.* London: Routledge, 2005.

Genette, Gerard. 1997. *Paratexts: Thresholds of Interpretation.* Cambridge: Cambridge University Press.

Gikandi, Simon. 2001. "Globalization and the Claims of Postcoloniality." *South Atlantic Quarterly* 100, no. 3 (Summer): 627–58.

Gilmore, Leigh. 2001. *The Limits of Autobiography: Trauma and Testimony.* Ithaca, NY: Cornell University Press.

———. 2002. "Jurisdictions: *I, Rigoberta Menchú, The Kiss,* and Scandalous Self-Representation in the Age of Memoir and Trauma." *Signs: Journal of Women in Culture and Society* 28, no. 2:695–718.

Glazov, Jamie. 2004. "We Are All Souad," June 9. frontpagemag.com/Articles/ReadArticle.asp?ID=13698. Accessed June 9, 2004.

Gómez-Peña, Guillermo. "The Virtual Barrio @ the Other Frontier (or the Chicago Interneta)." In *Reading Digital Culture,* ed. David Trend, 281–86. Malden, Mass.: Blackwell.

Good, Howard. 1998. *Girl Reporter: Gender, Journalism, and the Movies.* Lanham, MD: Scarecrow Press.

Goodwin, Jan. 2003. *Price of Honor: Muslim Women Lift the Veil of Silence on the Islamic World.* Rev ed. New York: Plume.

Gordon, Michael. 2005. *Freeing Ali: The Human Face of the Pacific Solution.* Sydney: UNSW Press.

Grace, Daphne. 2004. *The Woman in the Muslin Mask.* London: Pluto Press.

Green, Matthew. 2004. "So Are We Nearly There?" In *Under Fire: Untold Stories from the Front Line of the Iraq War,* ed. Reuters, 64. Upper Saddle River, NJ: Reuters.

Gregory, Derek. 2004. *The Colonial Present.* Malden, MA: Blackwell.

Grewal, Inderpal. 1996. *Home and Harem. Nation, Gender, Empire, and the Cultures of Travel.* Durham, NC: Duke University Press.

Grunebaum, Heidi, and Yazir Henri. 2003. "Re:membering Bodies, Producing History: Holocaust Survivor Narrative and Truth and Reconciliation Commission Testimony." In *World Memory: Personal Trajectories in Global Time,* ed. Jill Bennett and Rosanne Kennedy, 101–18. Basingstoke: Palgrave Macmillan.

Guillory, John. 2002. "The Sokal Affair and the History of Criticism." *Critical Inquiry* 28, no. 2 (Winter): 470–508.

Guindi, Fadwa El. 1999. *Veil: Modesty, Privacy and Resistance.* Oxford: Berg.

Gunew, Sneja. 2004. *Haunted Nations: The Colonial Dimensions of Multiculturalisms.* London: Routledge.

Gutteridge, Luke. 2003. "E3: Take 2 Return to Baghdad." Review of *Conflict: Desert Storm 2—Back to Baghdad.* May 13. http://www.ferrago.com/story/1566. Accessed November 23, 2004.

Hage, Ghassan. 2003. *Against Paranoid Nationalism: Searching for Hope in a Shrinking Society.* Annandale, New South Wales: Pluto Press.

Hakakian, Roya. 2004. *Journey from the Land of No.* Sydney: Bantam.

Hannerz, Ulf. 2004. *Foreign News: Exploring the World of Foreign Correspondents.* Chicago: University of Chicago Press.

Harlow, Barbara. 1987. *Resistance Literature.* New York: Methuen.

Hayles, Katherine N. 1999. *How We Became Posthuman: Virtual Bodies in Cybernetics, Literature, and Informatics.* Chicago: University of Chicago Press.

Hedges, Chris. 2004. "On War." *New York Review of Books,* December 16, 1–8. http://www.nybooks.com/articles/1730/. Accessed January 2, 2005.

Hersh, Seymour M. 2004. *Chain of Command. The Road from 9/11 to Abu Ghraib.* Camberwell, Australia: Allen Lane.

Hess, Stephen, and Marvin Kalb, Marvin, eds. 2003. *The Media and the War on Terrorism.* Washington, DC: Brookings Institution Press.

Hirsch, E. D. 1987. *Cultural Literacy. What Every American Needs to Know.* Boston: Houghton Mifflin.

Hirsch, Marianne. 2004. "Editor's Column: Collateral Damage." *PMLA* 119, no. 5 (October): 1209–15.

Hogan, Rebecca. 1991. "Engendered Autobiographies: The Diary as a Feminine Form." *Prose Studies* 14 (September): 95–107.

Huggan, Graham. 2001. *The Postcolonial Exotic: Marketing the Margins.* London: Routledge.

Ignatieff, Michael. 2004 "Camera as the Weapon." *Sydney Morning Herald,* November 20.

Jolly, Margaretta, ed. 2001. *The Encyclopedia of Life Writing.* London: Fitzroy Dearborn.

Kadir, Djelal. 2003. "Introduction: America and Its Studies." *PMLA* 118, no. 1 (January): 9–24.

Kaplan, Caren. 1992. "Resisting Autobiography: Out-Law Genres and Transnational Feminist Subjects." In *De/Colonizing the Subject,* ed. Sidonie Smith and Julia Watson, 115–38. Minneapolis: University of Minnesota Press.

———. 1996. *Questions of Travel: Postmodern Discourses of Displacement.* Durham, NC: Duke University Press.

Katovsky, Bill, and Timothy Carlson, eds. 2003. *Embedded: The Media at War in Iraq—an Oral History.* Guilford, CT: Lyons Press.

Katz, Ian. 2003. Introduction to *The Baghdad Blog,* by Salam Pax, ix–xiv. Melbourne: Text.

Keeble, Richard. 2004. "Information Warfare in an Age of Hyper-militarism." In *Reporting War: Journalism in Wartime,* ed. Stuart Allan and Barbie Zelizer, 43–58. London: Routledge.

Keenan, Thomas. 1997. *Fables of Responsibility: Aberrations and Predicaments in Ethics and Politics.* Stanford, CA: Stanford University Press.

———. 2004. "Mobilizing Shame." In "And Justice for All? The Claims of Human Rights," ed. Ian Balfour and Eduaardo Cadava. Special issue, *South Atlantic Quarterly* 103, nos. 2–3 (Spring/Summer): 435–50.

Khouri, Norma. 2003a. *Forbidden Love. A Harrowing True Story of Love and Revenge in Jordan.* Sydney: Transworld Publishers.

———. 2003b. *Honor Lost: Love and Death in Modern-Day Jordan.* New York: Atria.

Kilbey, Jane. 2001. "Carved in Skin: Bearing Witness to Self-Harm." In *Thinking through the Skin,* ed. Sara Ahmed and Jane Stacey, 124–41. London: Routledge.

Kinsella, Christine, producer and director. 2003. "First Person—*My Forbidden Face.*" Part of *Life Matters.* July 21. Australian Broadcasting Corporation Radio National. http://www.abc.net.au/rn/talks/lm/stories/s903100.htm. Accessed December 1, 2005.

Kitzmann, Andreas. 2003. "That Different Place: Documenting the Self within Online Environments." In "Online Lives," ed. John Zuern. Special issue, *Biography* 26, no. 1 (Winter): 48–67.

Knightley, Phillip. 2003. *The First Casualty.* London: Andre Deutsch.

Knox, Malcolm. 2004a. "Her Life as a Fake: Bestseller's Lies Exposed." *Sydney Morning Herald,* July 24, 1.

————.2004b. "We Were Inseparable, Says Hoaxer's Chicago Flatmate." *Sydney Morning Herald,* July 27, 6.

Kolko, Beth E. 2000. "Erasing @race: Going White in the (Inter)Face." In *Race in Cyberspace,* ed. Beth E. Kolko, Lisa Nakamura, and Gilbert B. Rodman, 213–32. London: Routledge.

Kolko, Beth E., Lisa Nakamura, and Gilbert B. Rodman, eds. 2000. *Race in Cyberspace.* London: Routledge.

Kousha, Mahnaz. 2002. *Voices from Iran: The Changing Lives of Iranian Women.* Syracuse, NY: Syracuse University Press.

Kristeva, Julia. 1997. "Powers of Horror: An Essay on Abjection." In *The Portable Kristeva,* ed. Kelly Oliver, 229–64. New York: Columbia University Press.

Krog, Antje. 1998. *Country of My Skull: Guilt and Sorrow and the Limits of Forgiveness in the New South Africa.* Johannesburg: Ruden.

La Capra, Dominick. 2001. *Writing History, Writing Trauma.* Baltimore, MD: Johns Hopkins University Press.

Lamb, Christina. 2002. *The Sewing Circles of Herat.* New York: HarperCollins.

Latifa. 2002. *My Forbidden Face.* London: Virago.

Lazarus, Neil, ed. 2004. *The Cambridge Companion to Postcolonial Literary Studies.* Cambridge: Cambridge University Press.

Leach, Michael, and Faith Mansouri, eds. 2004. *Lives in Limbo: Voices of Refugees under Temporary Protection.* Sydney: UNSW Press.

Legge, Kate. 2004. "Hoaxer So Hard to Read." *Australian,* July 31–August 1, 2.

Leith, Denise. 2004. *Bearing Witness: The Lives of War Correspondents and Photojournalists.* Sydney: Random House.

Lejeune, Phillipe. 1989. *On Autobiography.* Edited by John Paul Eakin. Translated by Katherine Leary. Minneapolis: University of Minnesota Press.

————. 2000. *"Cher écran . . . ": Journal personnel, ordinateur, Internet.* Paris: Éditions du Seuil.

Lewis, Justin, and Rod Brookes, 2004. "How British Television News Represented the Case for the War in Iraq." In *Reporting War: Journalism in Wartime,* ed. Stuart Allan and Barbie Zelizer, 283–300. London: Routledge.

Lewis, Reina. 1996. *Gendering Orientalism: Race, Femininity and Representation.* London: Routledge.

————. 2005. *Rethinking Orientalism: Women, Travel, and the Ottoman Harem.* New York: Rutgers.

Little, Graham. 1999. *The Public Emotions: From Mourning to Hope.* Sydney: ABC Books.

Logan, Harriet. 2002. *Un/veiled: Voices of Women in Afghanistan.* New York: HarperCollins.

Long, Elizabeth. 2003. *Book Clubs: Women and the Uses of Reading in Everyday Life.* Chicago: University of Chicago Press.

Loomba, Ania. 2002. *Colonialism/Postcolonialism.* London: Routledge.

Maass, Peter. 2003. "Salam Pax is Real." June 2. http://slate.msn.com/id/208347/. Accessed November 21, 2004.

MacKenzie, John M. 1995. *Orientalism: History, Theory and the Arts.* Manchester: Manchester University Press.

Mahmoody, Betty, with William Hoffer. 1987. *Not without My Daughter.* London: Bantam.

Makkler, Irris. 2003. *Our Woman in Kabul.* Sydney: Bantam Books.

Mann, Tom. 2003. *Desert Sorrow: Asylum Seekers at Woomera.* Kent Town: Wakefield Press.

Manne, Robert. 1996. *The Culture of Forgetting: Helen Demidenko and the Holocaust.* Melbourne: Text.

——. 1998. *The Way We Live Now: The Controversies of the Nineties.* Melbourne: Text.

Marr, David, and Marian Wilkinson. 2003. *Dark Victory.* Crows Nest, NSW: Allen & Unwin.

Martinkus, John. 2004. *Travels in American Iraq.* Melbourne: Black Inc.

Marx, John. 2004. "Postcolonial Literature and the Western Literary Canon." In *The Cambridge Companion to Postcolonial Literary Studies,* ed. Neil Lazarus, 83–96. Cambridge: Cambridge University Press.

McCalman, Iain. 2004. "The Empty Chador." *International Herald Tribune Online.* August 4. http://www.iht.com/articles/532567.html/.

McCloud, Scott. 1994. *Understanding Comics: The Invisible Art.* New York: HarperCollins.

McMaster, Don. 2002. *Asylum Seekers: Australia's Response to Refugees.* Melbourne: Melbourne University Press.

McNeill, Laurie. 2003. "Teaching an Old Genre New Tricks: The Diary on the Internet." In "Online Lives," ed. John Zuern. Special issue, *Biography* 26, no. 1 (Winter): 24–47.

McRobbie, Angela. 2004. "Feminism and the Socialist Tradition . . . Undone?" *Cultural Studies,* 18, no. 3 (July): 503–22.

Mehta, Sunita, ed. 2002. *Women for Afghan Women.* New York: Palgrave.

Mernissi, Fatima. 1987. *Beyond the Veil: Male-Female Dynamics in Modern Muslim Society.* Bloomington: Indiana University Press.

——. 1995. *Dreams of Trespass: Tales of a Harem Girlhood.* New York: Addison Wesley.

Meyer, Kim Middleton, 2002. "'Tan' talizing Others: Multicultural Anxiety and the New Orientalism." In *High-Pop: Making Culture into Popular Entertainment,* ed . Jim Collins, 90–113. Malden, Mass.: Blackwell.

Milani, Farzaneh. 1992. *Veils and Words: The Emerging of Iranian Women Writers.* Syracuse: Syracuse University Press.

Miller, J. Hillis. 2002. *On Literature.* London: Routledge.

Modjeska, Drusilla. 2002. *Timepieces.* Sydney: Picador.

Moeller, Susan D. 1999. *Compassion Fatigue: How the Media Sell Disease, Famine, War and Death.* New York: Routledge.

———. 2004. "A Moral Imagination: The Media's Response to the War on Terrorism." In *Reporting War: Journalism in Wartime,* ed. Stuart Allan and Barbie Zelizer, 59–76. London: Routledge.

Mohanty, Chandra Talpade. 2003. *Feminism without Borders: Decolonizing Theory, Practicing Solidarity.* Durham, NC: Duke University Press.

Moja. 2004. "10.15.2004." turningtables. http://turningtables.blogspot.com/. Accessed December 5, 2005.

Montagu, Lady Mary Wortley. [1763] 1988. *Embassy to Constantinople: The Travels of Lady Mary Wortley Montagu.* London: Hutchinson.

Moraga, Cherrie, and Gloria Anzalduá, eds., 1983. *This Bridge Called My Back: Writing by Radical Women of Color.* 2d ed. New York: Kitchen Table Women of Color.

Morgan, Sally. 1988. *My Place.* Fremantle: Fremantle Arts Centre Press.

Mottahedeh, Negar. 2004. "Off the Grid: Reading Iranian Memoirs in Our Time of Total War." *Middle East Report.* September. http://www.merip.og/mero/interventions/mottahedeh_interv.html. Accessed March 16, 2005.

Muslim Women's League. 1999. "Position Paper on 'Honor Killings.'" April. http://www.mwlusa.org/publications/positionpapers/hk.html. Accessed November 12, 2005.

Naficy, Hamid. 1993. *The Making of Exilic Cultures.* Minneapolis: University of Minnesota Press.

———. 2001. *An Accented Cinema: Exilic and Diasporic Filmmaking.* Princeton, NJ: Princeton University Press.

Nafisi, Azar. 2003a. *"Reading 'Lolita' in Tehran: A Memoir in Books*—a briefing by Azar Nafisi." *Middle East Forum.* June. http://www.meforum.org/article/539/. Accessed March 16, 2005.

———. 2003b. *Reading "Lolita" in Tehran: A Memoir in Books.* Sydney: Hodder Headline.

———. 2004a. Interview by Nermeen Shaikh. *AsiaSource.* January 20. http://www.asiasource.org/news/special_reports/nafisi.cfm.

———. 2004b. Interview by Robert Birnbaum. February 5. www.identitytheory.com/interviews/birnbaum139.php/. Accessed February 22, 2005.

———. n.d. "The Dialogue Project." http://dialogueproject.sais-jhu.edu/aboutDP.phpAccessed March 16, 2005.

Naghibi, Nima, and Andrew O'Malley. Forthcoming. "Estranging the Familiar: 'East' and 'West' in Satrapi's *Persepolis.*" *English Studies in Canada.*

Najmabadi, Afsaneh. 1993. "Veiled Discourse—Unveiled Bodies." *Feminist Studies* 19, no. 3 (Fall): 487–518.

———, ed. 1990. *Women's Autobiographies in Contemporary Iran.* Cambridge, MA: Harvard University Press.

Nakamura, Lisa. 2002. *Cybertypes. Race, Ethnicity, and Identity on the Internet.* New York: Routledge.

NauruWire.org. http://members.optusnet.com.au/hazara/hungerstrike.htm/. Accessed June 1, 2005.

Newman, Cathy. 2002. "A Life Revealed." *National Geographic* 201, no. 4 (April): 8–14.

Novick, Peter. 1999. *The Holocaust in American Life.* New York: Houghton Mifflin.

Nussbaum, Martha C. 1995. *Poetic Justice: The Literary Imagination and Public Life.* Boston: Beacon Press.

Oufkir, Malika, with Michèle Fitoussi. 2002. *Stolen Lives: Twenty Years in a Desert Jail.* New York: Hyperion.

Parker, David. 2002. "Locating the Self in Moral Space: Globalisation and Auto-biography." In *Selves Crossing Cultures: Autobiography and Globalisation,* ed. Rosamund Dalziell, 3–21. Melbourne: Australian Scholarly Publishing.

Pax, Salam. 2004–. *Shut Up You Fat Whiner!* http://justzipit.blogspot.com. Accessed March 29, 2006.

———. 2002–4. *Where Is Raed?* http://where_is_raed.blogspot.com/. Accessed November 18, 2004; archived at http://dear_raed.blogspot.com.

———. 2003. *The Baghdad Blog.* Melbourne: Text.

Perera, Suvendrini. 2002a. "A Line in the Sea: The Tampa, Boat Stories and the Border." *Cultural Studies Review* 8, no. 1 (May): 11–27.

———. 2002b. "What Is a Camp?" *Borderlands e-journal,* vol. 1, no. 1.

———. Forthcoming. "The Gender of Borderpanic: Women in Circuits of Security, State Globalisation and the New (and Old) Empire." In "Women, Crime and Globalization," ed. Maureen Caine and Andrew Howe. Unpublished Manuscript.

Poster, Mark. 2001a. *The Information Subject.* Amsterdam: G&B Arts International.

———. 2001b. *What's the Matter with the Internet?* Minneapolis: University of Minnesota Press.

Pratt, Mary Louise. 1992. *Imperial Eyes: Travel Writing and Transculturation.* London: Routledge.

Prince, Mary. [1831] 1987. *The History of Mary Prince, a West Indian Slave.* Edited by Moira Ferguson. London: Pandora Press.

Probyn, Elspeth. 2002. "Shame Travels Strangely: Transcultural Emotion." Paper presented at the symposium "Transculturalisms Canada: Cultural Mingling Between, Among, Within Cultures." University of British Columbia, February 21–24. http://www.webct.ubc.ca/SCRIPT/Transculturalisms/scripts/serve_home/. Accessed April 19, 2004.

———. 2005. *Blush: Faces of Shame.* Minneapolis: University of Minnesota Press.

Pugliese, Joseph. 2002. "Penal Asylum: Refugees, Ethics, Hospitality." *Borderlands e-journal,* vol. 1, no. 1.

———. 2004. "Subcutaneous Law: Embodying the Migration Amendment Act 1992." *Australian Feminist Law Journal* 21:23–34.

Quinby, Lee. 1992. "The Subject of Memoirs: *The Woman Warrior's* Technology of Idiographic Selfhood." In *De/Colonizing the Subject,* ed. Sidonie Smith and Julia Watson, 297–320. Minneapolis: University of Minnesota Press.

Radway, Janice. 1987. *Reading the Romance: Women, Patriarchy, and Popular Literature.* London: Verso.

Rayburn, Rosalie. 2004. "Iraqi Prison Abuse Allegations Put "Mayada" in New Light." *ABQJournal.com.* June 24. http://www.abqjournal.com/venue/books/191102books06-27-04.htm/. Accessed December 5, 2005.

Refugee Action Committee. n.d. "Refugee Stories." http://www.refugeeaction.org/stories/refugee_stories.htm Accessed June 1, 2005.

———. 2003. "How Australia Treats Innocent People: Some Detainees' Accounts." http://www.refugeeaction.org/inside/innocent.htm. Accessed June 1, 2005.

Refugee Media Space. n.d. "War on Refugees." http://refugee.autonomous.org/ Accessed November 20, 2005.

Reuters, ed. 2004. *Under Fire: Untold Stories from the Front Line of the Iraq War.* Upper Saddle River, NJ: Reuters.

Richardson, Laurel. 2000. "Evaluating Ethnography." *Qualitative Inquiry,* 6, no. 2: 253–55.

Riverbend. 2005. *Baghdad Burning: Girl Blog from Iraq.* London: Marion Boyars.

Robins, Kevin, and Frank Webster. 2001. *Times of the Technoculture: From the Information Society to the Virtual Life.* London and New York: Routledge.

Rose, Gillian. 2002. *Visual Methodologies.* London: Sage.

Roy, Arundhati. 2004. *The Ordinary Person's Guide to Empire.* London: Flamingo.

Ruden, Sarah. 1999. *"Country of My Skull:* Guilt and Sorrow and the Limits of Forgiveness in the New South Africa." *Ariel* 30, no. 1: 165–79.

Sabin, Roger. 1993. *Adult Comics: An Introduction.* London: Routledge.

Sacco, Joe. 2005. *Palestine.* Seattle: Fantagraphics Books.

SAID. 2004. *Landscapes of a Distant Mother.* Chicago: University of Chicago Press.

Said, Edward. 1995. *Orientalism.* London: Penguin.

———. 2002. *Reflections on Exile and Other Essays.* Cambridge, MA: Harvard University Press.

———. 2005. "Homage to Joe Sacco." In *Palestine,* by Joe Sacco. Seattle: Fantagraphics Books.

Salamon, Julie. 2004. "Author Finds That with Fame Comes Image Management." *New York Times* June 8. Reprinted at Notesonline, http://www.socialdemocrats.org/Notesonline6-04.html/. Accessed December 5, 2005.

Sanders, Mark 2002. *Complicities: The Intellectual and Apartheid.* Durham, NC: Duke University Press.

Sasson, Jean. 2003. *Mayada: Daughter of Iraq.* London: Doubleday.

———. [1994] 2004. *Daughters of Arabia.* London: Bantam Books.

———. [1999] 2004. *Desert Royal.* London: Bantam Books.

———. [1992] 2004. *Princess.* London: Bantam Books.

———. n.d.-a. "Letter from Mayada." http://www.jeansasson.com/Letter_from_mayada.htm/. Accessed August 19, 2004.

———. n.d.-b. "Princess Trilogy." http://www.jeansasson.com/princess_trilogy.htm/. Accessed December 5, 2005.

———. n.d.-c. "What I'm Reading Now." http://www.jeansasson.com/what_im_reading_now.htm/. Accessed December 5, 2005.

Satrapi, Marjane. 2003. *Persepolis: The Story of a Childhood.* London: Jonathan Cape.

———. 2004. *Persepolis 2: The Story of a Return.* New York: Pantheon.

———. n.d. "On Writing *Persepolis.*" As told to Pantheon staff. http://www
.randomhouse.com/pantheon/graphicnovels/satrapi2.html

Schaffer, Kay, and Sidonie Smith. 2004a. "Conjunctions: Life Narratives in the
Field of Human Rights." *Biography* 27, no. 1 (Winter): 1–24.

———. 2004b. *Human Rights and Narrated Lives: The Ethics of Recognition.* New York:
Palgrave Macmillan.

Schirato, Tony, and Jen Webb. 2003. *Understanding Globalization.* London: Sage.

Scholes, Robert. 2005. "The Humanities in a Posthumanist World." *PMLA* 120,
no. 3 (May): 724–733.

Schudson, Michael. 2002. "What's Unusual about Covering Politics as Usual."
In *Journalism after September 11,* ed. Barbie Zelizer and Stuart Allan, 36–68.
London: Routledge.

Scott, Rosie, and Thomas Keneally, eds. 2004. "Another Country." Special issue,
Southerly, vol. 64, no. 1.

Seaton, Jean. 2003. "Understanding not Empathy." In *War and the Media,* ed. Daya
Kishan Thussu and Des Freedman, 45–54. London: Sage.

Shah, Saira. 2003. *The Storyteller's Daughter.* New York: Alfred A. Knopf.

Shawn. 2003. Review of "Conflict: Desert Storm II Back to Baghdad." *Electronic
Gaming Monthly* (December).

Shirazi, Faegheh. 2003. *The Veil Unveiled: The Hijab in Modern Culture.* Gainesville:
University Press of Florida.

Silberstein, Sandra. 2004. *War of Words: Language, Politics and 9/11.* London:
Routledge.

Singh, Mala. 1994. "South Africa and the Reconstructive Agenda." In *Social
Construction of the Past,* ed. George C. Bod and Angela Gilliam. London:
Routledge.

Smith, Andrew. 2004. "Migrancy, Hybridity and Postcolonial Literary Studies."
In *The Cambridge Companion to Postcolonial Literary Studies,* ed. Neil Lazarus,
241–61. Cambridge: Cambridge University Press.

Smith, Sidonie, and Julia Watson. 2001a. *Reading Autobiography: A Guide for Interpreting Life Narratives.* Minneapolis: University of Minnesota Press.

———. 2001b. "The Rumpled Bed of Autobiography: Extravagant Lives, Extravagant Questions." *Biography* 24, no. 1 (Winter): 1–14.

Sommer, Doris. 1988. "Not Just a Personal Story: Women's Testimonies and the
Plural Self." In *Life/Lines: Theorizing Women's Autobiography,* ed. Bella Brodzki
and Celeste Schenck, 107–30. Ithaca, NY: Cornell University Press.

Sontag, Susan. 2003. *Regarding the Pain of Others.* New York: Picador.

Sorapure, Madeleine, 2003. "Screening Moments, Scrolling Lives: Diary Writing
on the Web." In "Online Lives," ed. John Zuern. Special issue, *Biography* 26,
no. 1 (Winter): 1–23.

Souad. 2004. *Burned Alive.* London: Bantam Press.

Spiegelman, Art. 1996. *The Complete Maus.* New York: Pantheon Books.

———. 2004. *In the Shadow of No Towers.* New York: Pantheon.

Spivak, Gayatri Chakravorty. 1999. *A Critique of Postcolonial Reason: Toward a History of the Vanishing Present.* London: Harvard University Press.

———. 2004. "Righting Wrongs." *South Atlantic Quarterly* 103, nos. 2–3 (Spring–Summer): 523–82.

Steger, Manfred B. 2004. *Globalization: A Very Short Introduction.* Oxford: Oxford University Press.

Stoll, David. 1998. *Rigoberta Menchú and the Story of All Poor Guatemalans.* Boulder, CO: Westview Press.

Suspected Illegal Entry Vessel X. n.d. "Who Is Responsible for the Deaths of 353 Asylum-Seekers?" http://www.sievx.com/. Accessed December 5, 2005.

Swift Yasgur, Batya. 2002. *Behind the Burqa—Our Life in Afghanistan and How We Escaped to Freedom.* Hoboken, NJ: John Wiley & Sons.

Tama, Mario. n.d. "Afghanistan." http://www.mariotama.com. Accessed January 5, 2006.

Taylor, Charles. 2004. *Modern Social Imaginaries.* Durham, NC: Duke University Press.

Thompson, Clive. 2004. "Fingers on the Button." *Sydney Morning Herald,* Good Weekend, December 4, 28–32

Thussu, Daya Kishan, and Des Freedman, eds. 2003. *War and the Media.* London: Sage.

Tully, Annie. 2004. "An Interview with Marjane Satrapi." *Bookslut,* October. http://www.bookslut.com/features/2004_10_0030261.php. Accessed March 31, 2006.

Tumber, Howard. 2004. "Prisoners of News Values? Journalists, Professionalism, and Identification in Times of War." In *Reporting War: Journalism in Wartime,* ed. Stuart Allan and Barbie Zelizer, 190–205. London: Routledge.

Tyler, Heather. 2003. *Asylum: Voices behind the Razor Wire.* South Melbourne: Lothian Books.

van Toorn, Penny. 1999. "Tactical History Business: The Ambivalent Politics of Commodifying the Stolen Generations." *Southerly* 59, nos. 3–4 (Spring–Summer): 225–66.

Vick, Karl. 2004. "Sorry, Wrong Chador: In Tehran 'Reading *Lolita*' Translates as Ancient History." Washington Post, July 19. http://www.washingtonpost.com/wp-dyn/articles/A60490-2004 Jul18.html/. Accessed March 16, 2005.

Waldren, Murray. 2006. "Authors' Front Falling to Pieces." *Australian,* January 11.

Ween, Lori. 2003. "This Is Your Book: Marketing America to Itself." *PMLA* 118, no. 1 (January): 90–102.

Whitlock, Gillian. 2000. *The Intimate Empire.* London: Continuum.

———. 2003. "Merry Christmas, Mary Prince." *Biography* 26, no. 3 (Summer): 440–42.

———. 2004a. "Consuming Passions." *Tulsa Studies in Women's Literature* 23, no. 1 (Spring): 13–28.

———. 2004b, "Tainted Testimony: The Khouri Affair." *Australian Literary Studies* 21, no. 4: 165–77.

———. 2005. "The Skin of the Burqa: Recent Life Narratives from Afghanistan." *Biography* 28, no. 1 (Winter): 54–76.

———. 2006. "Acts of Remembrance." In *The Invention of History: Past and Present in Settler Societies,* ed. Annie Coombes, 82–101. Manchester: Manchester University Press.

Windle, Joel. 2004. "Schooling, Symbolism and Social Power: The Hijab in Republican France." *Australian Educational Researcher* 31, no. 1 (April): 95–112. Available at http://www.aare.edu.au/aer/online/40010g.pdf/ as of December 2004.

Wright, Evan. 2004. *Generation Kill: Devil Dogs, Iceman, Captain America and the New Face of American War.* New York: G. P. Putnam's Sons.

———. 2005. "Into Iraq with 'Generation Kill': An Interview with Evan Wright." By Angelo Matera. January 5. http://www.godspy.com/reviews/. Accessed February 14, 2005.

Yeazell, Ruth Bernard. 2000. *Harems of the Mind: Passages of Western Art and Literature.* New Haven, CT: Yale University Press.

Young, Iris Marion. 1997. *Intersecting Voices: Dilemmas of Gender, Political Philosophy and Policy.* Princeton, NJ: Princeton University Press.

———. 2000. *Inclusion and Democracy.* Oxford: Oxford University Press.

Young, Robert J. C. 2003. *Postcolonialism: A Very Short Introduction.* Oxford: Oxford University Press.

Yousefi, Mary. 2004. "Mary's Story." In "Another Country," edited by Rosie Scott and Thomas Keneally. Special issue, *Southerly,* vol. 64, no. 1.

Zelizer, Barbie. 2004. *Taking Journalism Seriously: News and the Academy.* Thousand Oaks, CA: Sage.

Zelizer, Barbie, and Stuart Allan, eds. 2002. *Journalism after September 11.* London: Routledge.

Žižek, Slavoj. 2002. *Welcome to the Desert of the Real! Five Essays on September 11 and Related Dates.* London: Verso.

Zoya, with John Follain and Rita Cristofari. 2002. *Zoya's Story: An Afghan Woman's Struggle for Freedom.* New York: HarperCollins.

Zucchino, David. 2004. *Thunder Run.* New York: Grove Press.

Zuern, John, ed. 2003. "Online Lives." Special issue, *Biography* 26, no. 1 (Winter): v–xxv.

Index

Note: Italicized page numbers indicate figures. Names with "al-" are alphabetized by last segment of name (e.g., al-Jazeera is alphabetized under Jazeera, al-).

abject: "death infecting life" landscapes of, 160; definition of, 131, 141–42
About Woomera (film), 84
Abu Ghraib prison scandal: abstractions unraveled in, 31; attempt to contain, 194; dehumanization in, 81; image reproduction in, 32; Iraqi testimony on, 138; posters of, in Iran, 163; reading *Mayada* after, 98
Adorno, Theodor, 173, 178, 183–84
Adu, Freddy, 21, 22, 166
Afghan Girls Fund, 71
Afghanistan: asylum seekers and refugees from, 74–75, 84–85, 210n1; history of, 47; ignored by world, 55; Soviet and U.S. invasions of, 7–8, 69–72, 73; West's codification of, 72–73. *See also* Taliban
Afghan women: empathic engagement with vs. as objects of hate, 81; *National Geographic* photograph of, 69–72, 73, 86; as rationale for violence, 70, 102; scopic regime in representations of, 61; terms of speaking set by, 62; as volatile subjects, 63–65. *See also* women activists, Afghan
Afghan women's autoethnographies: boundaries of, 67–68;

circulation of, 17–18; collective focus of, 65–66; contradictions in, 56–57; covers of, *46*, 58–61, 63–65; customer reviews of, 61–62; ethical response to, 68; explosion of, 51–52; peritexts of, 57–58; transcultural process and, 48–49. *See also My Forbidden Face* (Latifa)
Agamben, Giorgio, 82
agency: autobiography as double, 22–23; expectations of, 62; idioms of, 56, 67–68; technologies of the self and, 18–19; testimony as occasion for, 126–27
Ahmed, Leila, 50, 189
Ahmed, Sara: on emotions and bodies, 77–78, 85, 142; on hated objects, 80–81
Ali, Ayan Hirsi, 208–9n3
Allan, Stuart, 140
Amanpour, Christiane, 146
Amazon.com: books linked on, 51–52; *Honor Lost* on, 106; response to criticism of *Mayada* on, 98–99; reviews on, 61–62, 196, 209–10n7, 215n5
Amiry, Suad, 129–30, 199
Amnesty International, 75, 81
Anderson, Amanda, 34, 35, 208n15
anthropology, journalism compared with, 147–49, 151–53